LORE and VERSE

SUNY series in Chinese Philosophy and Culture
Roger T. Ames, editor

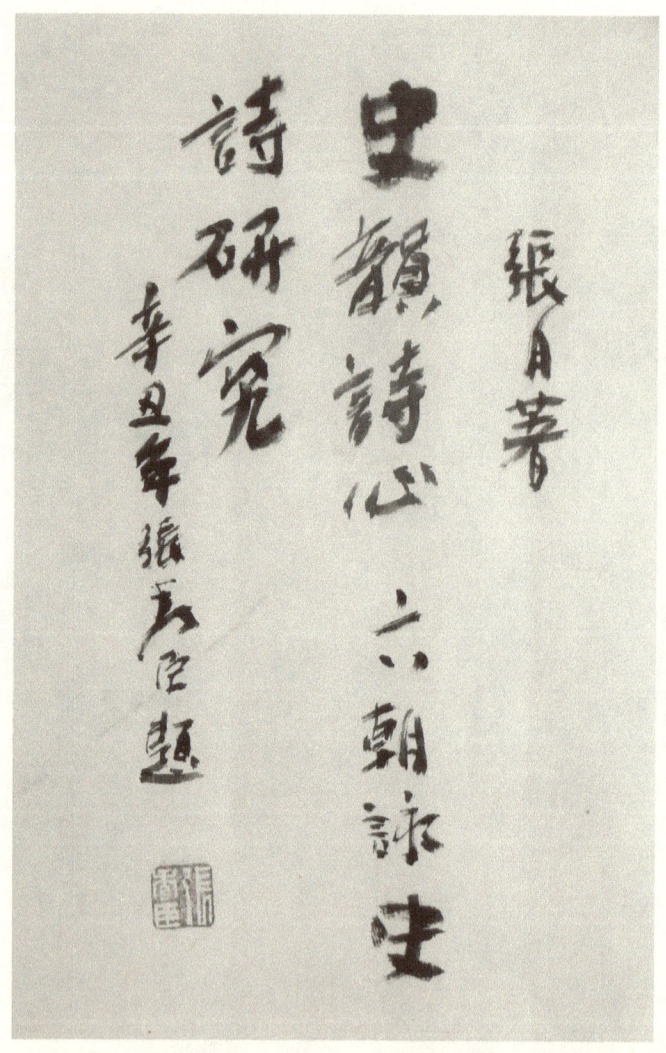

LORE and VERSE

POEMS ON HISTORY
IN EARLY MEDIEVAL CHINA

Yue Zhang

Cover: *Gaoyi tujuan* 高逸圖卷, Sun Wei 孫位 (fl. 881). Shanghai Museum.

Published by State University of New York Press, Albany

© 2022 State University of New York

All rights reserved

Printed in the United States of America

No part of this book may be used or reproduced in any manner whatsoever without written permission. No part of this book may be stored in a retrieval system or transmitted in any form or by any means including electronic, electrostatic, magnetic tape, mechanical, photocopying, recording, or otherwise without the prior permission in writing of the publisher.

For information, contact State University of New York Press, Albany, NY
www.sunypress.edu

Library of Congress Cataloging-in-Publication Data

Name: Zhang, Yue, (Professor of Chinese literature) author.
Title: Lore and verse : poems on history in early medieval China / Yue Zhang.
Description: Albany : State University of New York Press, 2022. | Series: SUNY series in Chinese philosophy and culture | Includes bibliographical references and index.
Identifiers: LCCN 2021040865 (print) | LCCN 2021040866 (ebook) | ISBN 9781438486918 (hardcover : alk. paper) | ISBN 9781438486932 (ebook) | ISBN 9781438486925 (pbk. : alk. paper)
Subjects: LCSH: Chinese poetry—221 B.C.–960 A.D.—History and critcism. | History in literature. | Literature and history—China.
Classification: LCC PL2313 .Z485 2022 (print) | LCC PL2313 (ebook) | DDC 895.11/050902—dc23/eng/20211018
LC record available at https://lccn.loc.gov/2021040865
LC ebook record available at https://lccn.loc.gov/2021040866

10 9 8 7 6 5 4 3 2 1

To my family

Contents

Terms and Conventions	ix
The Chronology of Chinese Dynasties	xi
Acknowledgments	xiii
Introduction	1
Chapter 1 What Are Poems on History in Early Medieval China?	13
Chapter 2 Retrospective Memory and Zuo Si's "Poems on History"	29
Chapter 3 Prospective Memory and the Reception of Zuo Si's "Yongshi" in Early Medieval China	55
Chapter 4 Tao Yuanming's Perspectives on Life as Reflected in His Poems on History	73
Chapter 5 Cultural Memory and Xie Zhan's Poem on Zhang Liang	97
Chapter 6 Approaches to Lore in the "Yongshi" Section of the *Wen xuan*	121
Conclusion	153
Notes	159
Bibliography	201
Index	215

Terms and Conventions

This book uses traditional Chinese characters and the Pinyin system of transliteration to keep consistent with current usage in North America. When sources that originally used the Wade-Giles system of transliteration are cited, the Wade-Giles transliterations are converted into Pinyin except for the titles of the publications and the author's name. Endnotes and bibliography largely follow *The Chicago Manual of Style* (17th edition), but they also take into account the conventions of premodern Chinese literary and cultural studies. An official or standard history is often a collective project and not written, compiled, or edited by one scholar, so this book cites its title instead of the author, compiler, or editor appearing on the front cover of the history. This book cites a multiple-volume Chinese primary source, such as a standard history, literary collection, or book of philosophy, by its *juan* number and page number in the format "x.y." *Juan* is a unit of division of a traditional Chinese manuscript which can be translated as "fascicle" or "chapter." The *juan* number of these texts is often more useful for the purposes of citation than the volume number. With respect to the translated, annotated, or commented edition of a primary source, as these commentaries and translations are a substantial work of scholarship, this book often cites the translator, annotator, or commentator rather than the original author, compiler, or editor. The use of another scholar's translation of a primary source is indicated by an endnote; all other translations and annotations are my own.

This book uses the BCE and CE calendar era designations instead of B.C. and A.D. The English translations of Chinese titles such as official and document titles generally follow Charles O. Hucker, *A Dictionary of Official Titles in Imperial China* (Stanford, CA: Stanford University Press, 1985), and David R. Knechtges and Taiping Chang, eds., *Ancient and Early*

Medieval Chinese Literature: A Reference Guide, 4 vols. (Leiden: Brill, 2010, 2014). For explaining the meaning of certain characters, I largely provide the definitions given by Paul W. Kroll in *A Student's Dictionary of Classical and Medieval Chinese* (Leiden: Brill, 2017).

The Chronology of Chinese Dynasties

This chronology largely follows Endymion Wilkinson, *Chinese History: A Manual*, 2nd ed. (Cambridge, MA: Harvard University Asia Center, 2000), 10–12.

Xia 夏	ca. 21st–ca. 16th centuries BCE
Shang 商	ca. 1600–1045 BCE
Zhou 周	1045–256 BCE
Western Zhou 西周	1045–771 BCE
Eastern Zhou 東周	770–256 BCE
Spring and Autumn 春秋	770–476 BCE
Warring States 戰國	475–221 BCE
Qin 秦	221–206 BCE
Han 漢	202 BCE–220 CE
Western Han 西漢	202 BCE–8 CE
Xin 新	9–23 CE
Eastern Han 東漢	25–220
Three Kingdoms 三國	220–280
Wei 魏	220–265
Shu 蜀	221–263
Wu 吳	222–280
Jin 晉	265–420
Western Jin 西晉	265–316
Eastern Jin 東晉	317–420

Northern and Southern Dynasties 南北朝	420–589
Southern Dynasties 南朝	420–589
Liu Song 劉宋	420–479
Qi 齊	479–502
Liang 梁	502–557
Chen 陳	557–589
Northern Dynasties 北朝	386–581
Northern Wei 北魏	386–534
Eastern Wei 東魏	534–550
Western Wei 西魏	535–556
Northern Qi 北齊	550–577
Northern Zhou 北周	557–581
Sui 隋	581–618
Tang 唐	618–907
The Five Dynasties and Ten Kingdoms 五代十國	902–979
Five Dynasties 五代	907–960
Ten Kingdoms 十國	902–979
Song 宋	960–1279
Northern Song 北宋	960–1127
Southern Song 南宋	1127–1279
Liao 遼	916–1125
Jin 金	1115–1234
Yuan 元	1279–1368
Ming 明	1368–1644
Qing 清	1644–1912

Acknowledgments

In the process of writing this book, I have obtained feedback from a myriad of friends and scholars in Canada, the US, and China, especially Graham Sanders, J. Michael Farmer, and David Chai. I deeply appreciate their advice, generosity, timely responses, and tremendous help. Graham Sanders, Dylan Suher, and Brian Khul proofread my writing at different stages. Their cooperation and hard work ensured the readability of this book, though I am responsible for any deficiencies that remain. I will continue working on this topic and publishing my new findings in the future.

I have presented different parts of this book at various gatherings, including the Association for Asian Studies annual conferences and its regional (Midwest, Southwest, and New England) conferences, the American Oriental Society annual conferences and its Western Branch conferences, and the Southeast Early China Roundtable, as well as other events organized by universities in the US, Canada, and China, such as Harvard University, Columbia University, the University of Toronto, Beijing University, and the University of Hong Kong. I am grateful to the conference organizers and discussants, such as Peter K. Bol, Wendy Swartz, Atsuko Sakaki, Fu Gang 傅剛, Keith Knapp, Andrew Chittick, Hao Ji 郝稷, and Hu Qiulei 胡秋蕾, who provided me with opportunities to present my research and to obtain useful feedback and suggestions.

Parts of this book have been published in prior forms in academic journals, such as the *Journal of Oriental Studies*, copublished by the School of Chinese at the University of Hong Kong and Center for Chinese Language and Cultural Studies at Stanford University; *Frontiers of Literary Studies in China*, published by China's Higher Education Press; the *Journal of Chinese Humanities*, published by Brill; and *China Review International*, published by University of Hawai'i Press. The publication information can be found in the bibliography section. I am grateful to the editors of these journals, such as Isaac Yue 余文章, Weng Limeng 翁立萌, Benjamin K. Hammer, and Roger T. Ames, for publishing my articles, and to the journals for permitting me to include material from these articles in this book. My appreciation also goes to the anonymous reviewers, who presented detailed critical and constructive comments.

This book has been supported by several research grants, notably a five-year PhD fellowship from the University of Toronto, a Chiang Ching-kuo Foundation Doctoral Fellowship, a Start-up Research Grant (SRG2019-00197-FAH) and a Multiple-Year Research Grant (MYRG2020-00018-FAH) from the University of Macau, a Friends of the Princeton University Library Research Grant, and a Florence Tan Moeson Fellowship from the Library of Congress. In addition to these research grants, the Young Scholars Visiting Scheme, sponsored by the CUHK-CCK Foundation Asia-Pacific Center for Chinese Studies at the Chinese University of Hong Kong, and the Fudan University Visiting Fellowship, sponsored by the International Center for Studies of Chinese Civilization, provided me with both intellectual and financial resources to work on this book. I thank Lai Chi Tim 黎志添 of the Chinese University of Hong Kong for accepting my application and offering an effective and fruitful research environment. I sincerely appreciate the mentorship and friendship from Dai Yan 戴燕 and Chen Yinchi 陳引馳 of Fudan University. Other funds were also very helpful for making this book possible, including various internal grants from the University of Toronto, Valparaiso University, and the University of Macau, such as the Julia Ching Memorial Fellowship, the Ting Fang Chung Scholarship, the Kwok Sau Po Scholarship, summer fellowships, research travel grants, and conference grants, as well as external grants from several libraries of major research universities, such as Harvard University, Stanford University, the University of Chicago, and the University of Michigan at Ann Arbor.

During the final stage of my manuscript revision, I joined the Department of Chinese Language and Literature at the University of Macau, and I am also affiliated with its Institute of Advanced Studies in Humanities and Social Sciences. Both the department and institute have provided me with an encouraging, warm, interdisciplinary atmosphere to discuss and improve my work. Many thanks go to my colleagues, particularly Xu Jie 徐杰, Zhu Shoutong 朱壽桐, and Tang Chon Chit 鄧駿捷.

I am grateful to the State University of New York Press, particularly associate director and editor in chief James Peltz, series editor Roger T. Ames, senior production editor Ryan Morris, senior marketing manager Michael

Campochiaro, and former senior acquisitions editor Christopher Ahn, who were very generous in providing their expertise and guidance throughout the long process of bringing this work to fruition.

Finally, I would like to express my deepest thanks to my family members in China and the US. They have unstintingly given me their strong support, patience, and understanding. They shouldered many of my family responsibilities to provide me with the time and care necessary for me to engage in scholarly activities. With my highest respects and gratitude, this book is dedicated to them.

Introduction

China has a long history and, accordingly, a rich tradition of commemorating that history in both ritual and writing. Chinese intellectuals have honored their forebears and significant historical figures through allusions in poetry, the establishment of temples and cults, the construction of monuments, and the composition and carving of inscriptions, to name only the most common of such practices. Cultural memory plays an important role in shaping the Chinese literary and historical tradition, and the subgenre of Chinese verse known as poems on history (*yongshi shi* 詠史詩) has been a major vehicle for producing and transmitting cultural memory. Chinese poets have long cited historical events and quoted the figures featuring in them, on topics such as political administration, literary refinement, and diplomatic negotiation, as a means to shape Chinese cultural memory and identity.[1] This introduction discusses the methodological framework of cultural memory and outlines the book structure.

Lore and Verse provides a detailed analysis of *yongshi shi* in early medieval China (220–589) from the perspective of cultural memory.[2] Lore refers to a body of knowledge transmitted orally and eventually written down, and verse refers to poetry. Written Chinese history was passed down as part of a larger body of lore that is no longer fully extant. Stories that were passed down orally were at a particularly acute risk of being lost as channels of transmission were disrupted. Poets in early medieval China likely had access to a larger swath of lore than is available to us today. While it is impossible for us to reconstruct this lost lore and difficult to determine which accounts of lore poets may have been aware of, one can nevertheless read and search as broadly as possible through sources such as standard histories (to which this book gives preference if the content is the same as or similar to other sources), pseudo-histories, anecdotes, regional histories, literary collections, and writings of philosophy, a process expedited through the use of databases and computer-assisted searches.[3]

This book treats *yongshi shi* as a prime example of the operation of cultural memory in the reception and transmission of Chinese history and literature. Through the study of *yongshi shi* and cultural memory, I will answer a series of key questions: What kinds of historical events are remembered by poets? What approaches do they adopt to deal with cultural memory? Aside from praising historical people and articulating their emotions, what other purposes do poets aim to achieve? As poets capture the essence of historical moments and employ them in a short-form literary genre such as *yongshi shi*, they must necessarily abbreviate the historical accounts on which they draw. Given that constraint, why do they choose to retain certain details and omit others? Which historical moments inspire poets to compose these poems? Posing these questions allows us to investigate the political, historical, and social contexts shaping *yongshi shi* and cultural memory. The answers to these specific questions are useful for broader research into the development and transformation of early medieval Chinese culture and, thinking beyond this particular period, crucial to grasping how poets use their writing to both convey and shape their understanding of cultural memory.

A recent volume on memory studies in Chinese literature divides the scholarship on memory in early and medieval China into five categories, saying,

> The most fertile topic has been how the dead or departed are remembered. . . . The historiography of events, dynasties, time periods, customs, regions, and places as both shaping and shaped by social memory, and social memory as shaped by standard narrative tropes and cultural patterns, have drawn increasing scholarly attention. . . . Reception studies have highlighted a third aspect of memory in medieval China. . . . mnemonic techniques used by individuals, and the value placed on memorization of texts, are aspects of memory in medieval China that have received relatively little study to this point. . . . A final aspect of memory to be discussed here concerns the many ways in which the new was justified by grounding it in a purported, remembered old.[4]

Considering the above-listed works, the present book aims to contribute to the existing scholarship surveyed above by applying a cultural memory framework to premodern Chinese literature and focusing on *yongshi shi* in early medieval China. Cultural memory is a concept and methodology pioneered by Jan and Aleida Assmann.[5] According to Jan Assmann, cultural memory

> has become a central concern, not only for archaeology and comparative literature, the two disciplines in the context of which we started, but also within all branches of cultural studies as well as history, arts, and even politics.[6]

Jan Assmann believes that cultural memory, as distinct from the psychological and scientific concepts of memory, constitutes "the exterior dimensions of the human memory."[7] He divides this external aspect of memory into four categories: mimetic memory, memory of things, communicative memory, and cultural memory.[8] Mimetic memory refers to the memory generated from imitating a behavior or following an instruction, as in memorizing instructions for machine or tool usage.[9] Memory of things refers to memory based on the items associated with one's own identity, such as the memory of personal clothing and food preferences.[10]

Cultural memory and communicative memory are two forms of collective memory, a concept introduced and developed for the study of psychology by Maurice Halbwachs (1877–1945). Assmann extends the theory into the realm of culture. He defines communicative memory as "memories related to the recent past. . . . These are what the individual shares with his contemporaries. A typical instance would be generational memory that accrues within the group, originating and disappearing with time or, to be more precise, with its carriers."[11] By way of contrast, cultural memory encompasses such social mechanisms for remembering the more distant past as rituals and ceremonies, oral transmission, written accounts, and such physical objects as monuments, museums, and stelae.[12] The influence of cultural memory endures longer than generations of communicative memory. Assmann explains that the difference between communicative and cultural memory is "the difference between the everyday and the festive, the profane and the sacred, the ephemeral and the lasting, the particular and the general. It can perhaps best be grasped in terms of the fluid as opposed to the fixed, but care must be taken not to equate this contrast with the difference between the oral and the written."[13] My book will focus on the spaces created by early medieval Chinese literati for fostering and celebrating the cultural memory of historical figures and events.

With respect to the commemoration of past historical figures, Assmann, following the scholarship of Karl Schmid, Otto G. Oexle, Joachim

Wollasch, and K. E. Müller, divides memories of the deceased into two categories: retrospective memory and prospective memory. He defines retrospective memory as "the more universal, original, and natural form . . . the one through which a group goes on living with its dead, keeping them present, and thereby building up an image of its own unity and wholeness, of which the dead naturally form a part."[14] Retrospective memory focuses on the "presentification" of historical figures, bringing them into contemporary dialogues in order to shape an identity and origin for them similar to that of those still living. In employing retrospective memory, the living often place themselves alongside their role models in the stream of the tradition. Whereas retrospective memory legitimates and rationalizes the words and actions of the living by situating them among past exemplary figures, the second category, that of prospective memory, "consists in 'achievement' and 'fame'—the manner in which the dead have rendered themselves unforgettable."[15] Prospective memory focuses on how the reputation of historical figures is transmitted.[16] The concept of retrospective memory aids us in examining how historical figures were received in poems, while the concept of prospective memory aids us in understanding how poets fashioned their works to be remembered by later literati. Positive reception, culminating in canonization, conveys one's reputation to future generations.

Cultural memory and reception studies form the macro perspective that guides my research,[17] while intertextuality provides the micro perspective necessary to establish textual connections and cultural continuities between historical sources and individual poems. As Jan Assmann points out, "Textual continuity entails a framework of references that cancel out the break inherent in writing—a framework within which the texts may remain present, effective, and accessible even over thousands of years."[18] New writing that borrows diction and style from previous sources renews the cultural lineage, drawing on the strength of these rich intertextual links while at the same time popularizing and securing the status of the older sources.

The concept and methodology of cultural memory is crucial for analyzing *yongshi shi*. In writing *yongshi shi*, Chinese literati and poets often retrospectively crafted the same (or at least a similar) identity as the historical figures they celebrated, and they prospectively created a continuous lineage for transmitting their values and reputation to future generations. This continuous tradition of cultural memory informs a poet's reception of historical figures, which then in turn shapes that tradition through further intertextual connections. When poets compose poems about historical figures and their stories, they do not simply reiterate longer historical accounts, but rather select which parts of the stories they wish to lyricize, a choice which speaks to their own agendas and/or the contemporary reception of historical figures and events.

This monograph is the first English-language book dedicated entirely to studying *yongshi shi*. Prior to this book, Hans Frankel devoted an entire chapter of his book on Chinese poetry to poems on historical themes, in which he offers close readings of a selection of poems from the Western Jin (265–316) to Northern Song (960–1127) dynasties, focusing on explaining allusions, elucidating moral lessons and values, and analyzing literary techniques, particularly the contrasts drawn between ephemeral human history and the eternity of nature.[19] This book integrates Frankel's close reading, an appropriate and useful method in analyzing history-oriented poems that are often loaded with allusions and symbols, with insights drawn from cultural memory in interpreting *yongshi shi*.

This book also builds on the discussion of nostalgia and the past in Stephen Owen's *Remembrances*, which analyzes classical Chinese texts drawn from a wide range of genres: poems, rhapsodies, lyrics, anecdotes, and fiction.[20] He points out the use of synecdoche in discussing literati experiences. The fragments and incomplete parts become the media through which literati thought of and imagined past events and composed literary pieces to express feelings of melancholy and nostalgia. Owen's book has inspired me to continue an investigation into the relationship between memory and Chinese literature, focusing on the specific problem of cultural memory and *yongshi shi*.

With respect to Chinese-language scholarship, Zhao Wangqin 趙望秦 and Zhang Huanling 張煥玲 point out that there is scant research on *yongshi shi* in the early medieval period compared with the substantial work done on *yongshi shi* in the Tang and Song dynasties, and especially *yongshi shi* from the Mid- and Late Tang. The bulk of modern Chinese scholarship puts forward a grand, progressive, linear literary-historical narrative for the development of *yongshi shi* over time, providing a broad overview of the genre and of major and minor figures who wrote *yongshi shi*.[21] However, these works do not typically provide much analysis based on a close reading of the poetry itself, nor do they explore newer, nontraditional critical approaches. Rather than seeking to cover every example of *yongshi shi* in early medieval China, or to narrate its development over multiple periods, the present work instead focuses on analyzing a selection of representative poems that show how cultural memory is demonstrated and negotiated in the *yongshi shi*.

The first chapter lays the foundation for the core discussion, defining the term *yongshi shi* in early medieval China via an exploration of previous scholarship on its connotations. Robert Joe Cutter identifies the poems composed by Cao Zhi 曹植 (192–232), Wang Can 王粲 (177–217), and Ruan Yu 阮瑀 (ca. 165–212) on the "three good men" 三良 as "poems on visits to famous sites" (*denglin shi* 登臨詩), a subgenre closely related to "poems meditating on the past" (*huaigu shi* 懷古詩). Cutter argues that the three poets probably visited the tomb of the "three good men," though these poems were titled "Yongshi."[22] Cutter's observation raises important questions that merit further investigation: What were *yongshi shi* in early medieval China? What is the relationship between *yongshi shi* and *huaigu shi* in this period? As these questions are key to the larger concerns of the book, this opening chapter addresses them by investigating the definition and scope of *yongshi shi* in early medieval China, the necessity of rectifying our understanding of the term, and its current (sometimes problematic) usage by modern scholars. In contrast to previous scholarship that has taken a broadly retrospective approach, this chapter explores the definition and scope of the term *yongshi shi* within the confines of a specific time period, early medieval China. This chapter also examines the usage of the words *yong* 詠 and *shi* 史 in classical Chinese materials, focusing on the "Bibliographical Treatise" ("Jingji zhi" 經籍志) of the *History of the Sui Dynasty* (*Suishu* 隋書) and the "Yongshi" section of the *Selections of Refined Literature* (*Wen xuan* 文選). Through this analysis, this chapter delves into the deeper connotations of *yongshi shi*. The final part of the chapter explains why poems with titles that include the term *yongshi* might not belong to the *yongshi* category. The fluidity of manuscript culture meant that titles were highly mutable and might be given to the poem by anthologists, editors, literary critics, or the poets themselves. In summary, this chapter examines the importance in early medieval China of historiography, literary culture, allusion, social dislocation, and "pure conversation" (*qingtan* 清談)—all of which enabled writers to make full use of cultural memory and to compose *yongshi shi* that articulated their emotions through historical allusions.

After the first chapter delineates the scope and definition of *yongshi shi* within the context of the early medieval period, the second chapter explores the relationship between retrospective memory and *yongshi shi*, focusing on the Western Jin (265–316) poet Zuo Si's 左思 (ca. 250–ca. 305) "[Poems] on History" ("Yongshi" 詠史) series, which has often been regarded as a milestone in the development of the poetic subgenre *yongshi shi*. Michael Farmer interpreted these poems as a way to "ruminate on historical themes in order to criticize contemporary affairs and reflect Zuo's frustration at his inability to advance politically or socially in Luoyang."[23] Farmer rightly points out the sociopolitical implications and significance of these poems. This chapter builds on this insight, but moves in another direction, highlighting how Zuo used retrospective memory to actively place himself alongside exemplary figures from the past and bring those figures into contemporary debates. Through this application of retrospective memory, Zuo consoles his emotions, legitimates his pursuits, and makes sense of his frustration. In this vein, this chapter investigates the purpose behind his use of historical figures within his poetry. Zuo actively pursues an affinity with the historical figures in his poems: what happens to him in the present also happened to these figures in the past. This chapter argues that Zuo used historical figures not only to express his emotions but also to skillfully place himself into the larger context and lineages of exemplary historical figures. Zuo is thus telling later generations that they should remember him with the same reverence—he is invoking history as a force for self-idealization and promotion. Viewing this from the perspective of retrospective memory reveals the complexity of Zuo's appropriation of earlier historical sources, and it deepens and complicates our understanding not only of the purpose of Zuo's "Yongshi" series but also of how and why history was disseminated through poetry in early medieval China.

While the second chapter focuses on Zuo's "Yongshi" from the perspective of retrospective memory, the third chapter traces the prospective memory and reception of Zuo Si's "Yongshi" in early medieval China—that is, how the poet's reflections on historical figures influenced later understanding of the personalities, historical themes, and even the poems associated with those figures. Scholars such as Kōzen Hiroshi 興膳宏 and Xu Chuanwu 徐傳武 have recognized Zuo's "Yongshi" as representing an alternative to the poetic style of ornamental amplification popular in his time. Zuo's poems break from the norms of the *yongshi* subgenre, which usually mimic historical narration, and conclude with a conventional moral assessment.[24] How did this style, which was somewhat unconventional during his time, come to be largely accepted later in the early medieval period? How did the reception of the style and content of Zuo's "Yongshi" influence his prospective memory? To better understand how this prospective memory was formed, this chapter examines three levels of reception for these poems. First, it discusses the poetic practice of establishing intertextual links between Zuo Si's poems and other literary works, followed by an analysis of the earliest literary criticism of Zuo Si's poems. It then analyzes an anecdote about the

Northern Wei official Xue Cheng 薛憕 (fl. 520), which illuminates how these poems were employed in educated elite discourse. Finally, the chapter explores the literary and cultural factors that influenced the decision of the editors of the *Wen xuan* to include these poems in the "Yongshi" section of the anthology. The choices made by the editors stand as both a powerful indicator of the aesthetics of poetry in that historical moment and as a significant influence on later poetic reception. Investigating these stages of reception allows us to understand how poets, critics, and readers imitated, commented on, and used these *yongshi shi*. Furthermore, reception studies can help to uncover similarities and discrepancies in literary borrowing (of diction, imagery, figure of speech, etc.) in the processes of poetic composition and transmission. The retrospective self-idealization and promotion and the process of prospective reception of Zuo's poems illustrate how the memory of the literary past is shaped and mediated by the intellectual and cultural zeitgeist of this period.

Both retrospective and prospective memory are vehicles for commemorating historical figures. Early medieval Chinese poets adopted, adapted, and negotiated with cultural memory to place themselves retrospectively in a long lineage of exemplary figures, and to prospectively convey their reputation to the future by highlighting, identifying with, following, and praising the virtues of these figures from the past. Cultural memory influenced which figures they chose and how they represented those figures, but poets also negotiated with cultural memory in order to make sense of the past and articulate their own emotions and views. The next chapter, chapter 4, shifts focus to the Eastern Jin period (317–420) and explores how Tao Yuanming 陶淵明 (ca. 365–427), one of the best-known and most-studied Chinese poets from before the Tang dynasty (618–907), communicated his personal sense of history. Over the years, Tao's pastoral-style poetry, his biography, and his reclusive lifestyle have received much attention from scholars using both traditional text-centered approaches and new approaches informed by manuscript culture, reception studies, and research into reading practices.[25] This chapter diversifies recent research by focusing on Tao's *yongshi shi*, which constitute roughly one-fourth of Tao's extant oeuvre.[26] It discusses Tao's perspective on life reflected in these poems.[27] Tao was fascinated by history and developed an idiosyncratic but relatively stable perspective, which encompassed three main issues: the concern for the appreciation of scholars (or lack thereof), the possibility and means of following the Dao in poverty, and the relationship between engaging in versus retreating from politics. Tao engaged in critically evaluating historical figures and events according to his own idiosyncratic principles, which led him to sometimes even reject the verdicts rendered by conventional history. This chapter also integrates the various aspects of Tao's perspective on life with his cultural memory of historical figures, delineating the intricate relationship between the two in order to better understand Tao's thought and his literary works. Tao internalizes and is aware of these different issues, adding his own individual memory, logic, and aesthetic touches, which distinguish him from his predecessors.

Yongshi shi not only reflected the relationship between poetry, cultural memory, and reputation construction but also demonstrated the relationship between politics, power legitimation, and memory, which are investigated in chapter 5. It moves chronologically to the transition between the Eastern Jin and Liu Song dynasties, examining how poetic composition, ritual, and ceremony continued the cultural memory of Han dynasty general Zhang Liang 張良 (ca. 250–186 BCE), forming a tradition that had profound political implications. This chapter primarily focuses on a less-studied figure from the well-known Xie clan, Xie Zhan 謝瞻 (385–421), and his long poem on Zhang Liang, which was composed during Liu Yu's 劉裕 (363–422; r. 420–422) northern expedition. This chapter places Xie's poem in the context of other poems, composed during the same expedition, on visiting the temples dedicated to Zhang Liang and Liu Bang. Andrew Chittick, citing the opinions of early medieval Chinese historians, describes Liu Yu's northern expedition as "the most ambitious and successful ever undertaken by any Jiankang military leader."[28] Chittick argues that although Liu's concrete objectives were somewhat murky, he was not aiming, as is often the popular perception, at reunifying China. Instead, Chittick believes that Liu sought, first, to strengthen the Yellow River as a protective screen against invasion and, second, to obtain valuable documents, materials, and scholars from the Later Qin (384–417) court and aristocratic families.[29] The analysis of the poems in this chapter facilitates our understanding of Liu's objectives and concerns in his expedition, and offers new insight into the sociopolitical significance of the *yongshi shi* as a manifestation of cultural memory. In an article that focuses on the Xie family, Cynthia L. Chennault stresses the changes in the status of the Xie family during the Southern Dynasties period (420–589).[30] Looking at Xie Zhan, Xie Zhuang 謝莊 (421–466), and Xie Tiao's 謝朓 (464–499) response to these changes, she concludes that the "common thread through the case studies is the instability at court that posed dangers to the lives of high officials."[31] Chennault's research focuses on the influence of dynastic changes exerted on the eminent Xie family, particularly their response to the family's declining influence in the political and military arena. Departing from her research, this chapter attaches more importance to the other side of the story: the rising power of the lower social class, represented by Liu Yu, in obtaining power from the aristocratic families. In order to do this, this chapter contains a full English translation and close reading of Xie Zhan's poem on Zhang Liang. It then explores how Xie Zhan, Zheng Xianzhi 鄭鮮之 (364–427), and Fan Tai 范泰 (355–428) paid tribute to Liu Yu, their ruler and first emperor of the Liu Song dynasty, by commemorating Zhang Liang and Liu Bang. Liu Yu employed this cultural memory of Han figures as political propaganda to legitimate his rulership and promote his governance abilities and virtues. While these poems served a political function, they also reveal the idiosyncrasies of the writers and their complex psychological states during a period of social transition and transformation.

Finally, chapter 6 addresses the importance of the literary anthology *Wen xuan*, which was compiled and edited at the end of the early medieval period. This chapter highlights the different ways poets connected cultural memory to poetry and, by focusing on poets' approaches to lore, it demonstrates the sophistication of *yongshi shi* in early medieval China. Stephen Owen has examined poems on visiting historical sites in the Late Tang (827–860). He focuses on how natural images, historical figures, and diction used in one poem influenced other poems on the same topic, as well as how later poems expanded the connotations of those elements. Therefore, through intertextuality, a family of formulas and patterns for poems on certain historical sites and figures is formed.[32] In another book on the characteristics of early classical Chinese poetry (dating from roughly the first to third century CE), Owen cautions us that poetry in this period often had "its recurrent themes, its relatively stable passages and line patterns, and its procedures."[33] Poets adopted shared templates, shared topics, and a common language to compose poems. Our perception of these poems has been largely shaped by Qi–Liang literati at the end of the early medieval period. His arguments have challenged the established narrative of literary history, instead suggesting that writing poetry was a shared cultural practice and was less creative and innovative than we previously thought. This chapter treats all the materials related with historical figures and events as a collective lore to which a poem refers. Although it is impossible to trace all the oral and written sources that an early medieval writer could access, this chapter lays out the stable and fluid aspects of the relationship between lore and poetry with the aid of databases of ancient classical Chinese texts. It examines how lore of historical figures and events is circulated and distributed into poems. Specifically, this chapter looks at the relationship between the *yongshi shi* poems collected in the "Yongshi" section of the *Wen xuan* and the accounts of lore to which they correspond. The assumption is that the historical elements in *yongshi shi* are an amalgam of historical, unofficial, and anecdotal texts combined in a way that creates a new meaning in poetry. The relationship between a *yongshi shi* and the accounts of its associated historical figures or events is complex, less a dichotomy than a spectrum, with completely personal expression at one end and neutral historical accounts at the other. The approaches of poets to lore can be roughly divided into three major categories, based on the relationship between a poet's own emotions and the lore: close citation of lore, the use of such accounts as supporting commentary, and the contextualization of lore in the form of allusions. Analysis of the direct links between the poems and these accounts reveals some similar words and phrases, suggesting that poets may have read these sources, or at the very least, that the sources available today drew upon the same body of lore that the poets drew upon.

In early medieval China, cultural memory was conveyed through a variety of media and forms: through writing, such as historical accounts, collections of anecdotes, and literary works; through physical monuments, such as temples or stelae; and through visual arts, such as painting and calligraphy. *Yongshi shi* were a particularly important tool for commemorating historical figures and shaping cultural identity. As a document of how historical figures and events have become part of the poetic tradition, *yongshi shi* illustrate the issues surrounding history, cultural memory, and the commemoration of absence.

Chapter 1

What Are Poems on History in Early Medieval China?

When Confucius was asked what he would do first if given a state to govern, he replied, "If I had to state my first action, it would be to rectify names. If names are not rectified, then speech will not function properly, and if speech does not function properly, then undertakings will not succeed."[1] 必也正名乎! 名不正, 則言不順; 言不順, 則事不成.[2] Confucius felt that the act of ensuring that words are understood correctly was essential to governing a country; certainly, when it comes to conducting literary research, this process of "rectifying names" is no less important. Before one examines the literary subgenre of *yongshi shi*, it is essential to first refine its definition in order to comprehend all of the nuanced meanings encompassed by the term.

This chapter discusses the definition of *yongshi shi* in early medieval China.[3] Unlike previous scholarship, which has analyzed *yongshi shi* diachronically and summarized its meaning retrospectively, this chapter focuses on *yongshi shi* within a specific time period: early medieval China. In so doing, it explores the definition and scope of this term within a more limited historical context. The crux of this analysis is centered on the concept of *shi* 史 and its use in the *yongshi shi* 詠史詩 of early medieval China. In addition, this chapter encourages closer scrutiny of the genre of poems explicitly titled "Yongshi" 詠史. The fluidity of manuscript culture meant that titles were often mutable and came to the poems by various means: the poets themselves, but also anthologists, editors, and literary critics.

Current Definition and Scope of *Yongshi shi*

Yongshi shi, translated as "poems on history," and *huaigu shi* 懷古詩, often translated as "poems meditating on the past" or "poems yearning for antiquity," are two major subgenres of Chinese poetry that deal with historical figures and events.[4] Scholars frequently define *yongshi shi* in contrast with *huaigu shi*. However, it is notoriously difficult to make an explicit distinction between the two.

There have been numerous attempts to define these subgenres in relation to one another. Two contemporary scholars have provided useful overviews on these various definitions, along with their own insights into *yongshi shi*. First, Zhang Runjing 張潤靜 summarizes the differences between these two closely related subgenres:

> Theoretically speaking, we can point out many differences between the two subgenres of poetry: *yongshi shi* are often the reflections prompted by the reading of historical accounts, while *huaigu shi* are often the expression of the feelings evoked when visiting historical heritage sites; the former usually adopts narration and argument, while the latter frequently expresses the poets' feelings and describes natural scenes, accompanied with arguments; *yongshi shi* are often about specific historical events or figures, emphasizing certain ideologies or moral evaluations, while *huaigu shi*...often focus on expressing sentiments, attitudes and philosophical reflections on the general "past," etc.
>
> 理論上講，我們可以指出二者的許多區別：詠史詩常表現為讀史有感，懷古詩常表現為觸景興詠；前者在表達方式上多用敘述、議論，後者則多為抒情、寫景，兼有議論；詠史詩往往是就具體的歷史事件或人物來寫作，注重表達一種思想觀念或道德評價，而懷古詩通常……集中於表達對於籠統的"過去"的某種情感態度和哲理思考，等等。[5]

Zhang holds that *yongshi shi* are more intellectually engaging, as they emerge out of reading historical accounts and meditating on historical events and people, whereas *huaigu shi* emphasize poets' reflections upon visiting historical places of interest.

Another representative modern voice is Wei Chunxi 韋春喜. His book, *The History of Pre-Song Poems on History* (*Song qian yongshi shi shi* 宋前詠史詩史), is the first to systematically lay out the literary history of this subgenre from the pre-Qin period all the way to the Song dynasty. In his introduction, Wei defines *yongshi shi* as chanting verse and composing reflections based on historical figures, events, and relics in order to articulate the emotions of the poet, advance arguments or present insights from history, or to use history for entertainment, admonition, remonstration, or education.

以歷史人物、事件、古跡等為題材或感觸點，對之進行吟詠、思索，藉以抒發思想感情，表達議論見解、歷史感悟或借詠史以娛樂、諷諫、教育等的一種詩歌類型。[6]

Wei argues in favor of a broad definition of *yongshi shi* which includes all possible retrospective poetry topics. Building upon this foundation, Wei then sets out three main criteria for defining *yongshi shi*: the topic, the emotions of the poet, and the arguments or views contained within the poem.[7]

Zhang and Wei are only two representative voices from among the numerous scholars who have sought to define *yongshi shi*. Two standard sets of criteria, based on degree of mediation and style, respectively, have been widely accepted by academics. According to the first, *yongshi shi* results from a poet's reflective contemplation on historical figures and events as mediated by historical lore (oral or written), while *huaigu shi* emerges from the stream of thoughts and feelings evoked by viewing actual historical relics, ruins, and sites.[8] With respect to style, the writers of *yongshi shi* typically employ rational, analytical attitudes towards historical events and people, whereas *huaigu shi* writers tend to openly express their personal feelings and nostalgia.[9]

Modern scholars have developed these definitions of *yongshi shi* by first examining numerous poems across multiple centuries to draw generalized characteristics of the subgenre, and then applying that definition uniformly across each dynastic period. While this method has its benefits, it also suggests that the term was static over centuries in premodern China. On the contrary, its connotations have shifted over the centuries depending on the hermeneutical practices and tastes of different literary, historical, and social reading cultures.

The following discussion places *yongshi shi* in the early medieval Chinese cultural context to illuminate its connotations during this period. It examines the usage of the term in poems from the period, in literary anthologies such as *Selections of Refined Literature* (*Wen xuan* 文選) and *The Finest Literary Writings of the Tang Dynasty* (*Tang wencui* 唐文粹), and in "The Bibliographical Treatise" ("Jingji zhi" 經籍志) in *The History of the Sui* (*Suishu* 隋書).

The Concept of *Yong* and *Shi* in Early Medieval China

Before examining the *yongshi shi* subgenre, we must first understand *yong* 詠 and *shi* 史. The traditional form of the character for *yong* consists of two parts: a speech radical (*yan* 言) and a character that means "enduring" (*yong* 永). *Yong* 詠 is the act of chanting and singing, often according to a theme, as in *yongshi shi* and in "poems on things" (*yongwu shi* 詠物詩). Stephen Owen translates it as "intoning" and explains that "through the patterning of song, a text becomes fixed and repeatable."[10] This explanation for the term *yong* has a long history. It appears in the *Book of Documents* (*Shangshu* 尚書), which states, "The poem (*shi*) articulates what is on the mind intently (*zhi*); song makes language (*yan*) last."[11] 詩言志, 歌詠言.[12] Thus, in *yongshi shi*, through the action of "intoning" (*yong* 詠) the words, the legends and lessons represented by historical figures are widely circulated and transmitted over a prolonged (*yong* 永) period of time.

The meaning of *yong* 詠 has not remained static over the centuries, however. According to Fan Ziye 范子燁, in early medieval China *yong* was associated with "pure conversation" (*qingtan* 清談).[13] Fan offers several examples from early medieval texts, such as the following:

> Someone asked Wang Yifu (256–311): "What was Shan Tao like as far as his meanings and principles were concerned? In which category did he belong?"
>
> Wang replied, "This man had never been willing to cast himself as a conversationalist. However, without even reading the *Laozi* or the *Zhuangzi*, from time to time he heard them recited, and frequently agreed with their ideas."[14]
>
> 人問王夷甫: "山巨源義理何如? 是誰輩?" 王曰: "此人初不肯以談自居, 然不讀《老》、《莊》, 時聞其詠, 往往與其旨合."[15]

In the final sentence, Wang Yan 王衍 (courtesy name Yifu 夷甫) discusses the oral transmission and reception of *Laozi* and *Zhuangzi*. The word *tan* (談), translated above as "conversation," is paralleled with *yong* (詠), indicating that *yong* should be interpreted as a practice within *qingtan*—that is, demonstrating one's character through debates and conversations.[16] *Qingtan* developed out of "pure discussion" (*qingyi* 清議) in the Eastern Han dynasty (25–220), a discourse of commenting on a person's appearance and abilities. Officials at all levels evaluated the character of individuals according to social opinions about them, and selected exemplary people to become part of the official class. This system was largely associated with Confucian ethics; people who were locally renowned for obeying the rules of social etiquette were felt to possess a better moral character and thus were promoted. Officials hoped that, ideally, this system would teach people to behave appropriately and ethically, and that this would eventually lead to proper governance. In practice, it enabled certain groups of literati to become powerful authorities on moral worth. If these groups described someone positively, that person could be promoted quickly, whereas a negative commentary could ruin a career before it even began.[17]

In early medieval China, many literary and historical works were dedicated to evaluating the abilities, performance, and moral character of potential officials. Works such as *Evaluations of Historical Personages* (*Renwu zhi* 人物志) and *Miscellaneous Records of the Western Capital* (*Xijing zaji* 西京雜記) were ready source material for composing poems on historical figures and events. A myriad of *yongshi shi* provide portraits of human figures, such as Yan Yanzhi's 顏延之 (384–456) "Poems on the Five Lords" ("Wujun yong" 五君詠), which comments on five of the Seven Sages of the Bamboo Grove (*Zhulin qixian* 竹林七賢), a group of virtuous men during the transition between the Three Kingdoms and the Western Jin. Literary criticism of this period also evaluated writers according to a ranking system similar to that for officials; for example, Zhong Rong's 鍾嶸 (ca. 468–ca. 518) *Gradation of Poets* (*Shipin* 詩品) ranks poets and offers commentary on their works. As a practice employed in *qingtan* conversations, *yong* served a variety of literary, social, and political functions in the early medieval period.

Shi 史, as with *yong*, has a complex meaning that has shifted over the ages. Scholars have already done substantial research into the duties and obligations of a *shi*. According to Sheldon Hsiao-peng Lu, a *shi*'s responsibilities are

> to record events and speeches, reserve archives and documents, draft state papers and edicts, read and announce governmental decisions, attend religious ceremonies and state rituals, and oversee astronomical matters such as making calendars and observing and recording natural phenomena.[18]

This succinct summary includes all the possible roles that a *shi* played retrospectively. From a diachronic perspective, the emphasis on the different responsibilities of the *shi* has changed over time. In discussing the various understandings of the position presented by Xu Shen 許慎 (ca. 58–ca. 147), Wang Guowei 王國維 (1877–1927), and Xu Fuguan 徐復觀 (1903–1982), Wai-yee Li argues that

> [t]he Han rationalization of the meaning of the word *shi* thus marks the transition from the magical authority of the historian as shaman-astrologer to the moral authority of the historian as inquirer into the causes and consequences of human action in time.[19]

Thus, Li emphasizes the evolution of the *shi* role as it transitioned from focusing on heavenly matters to focusing on human affairs. This shift led to the metonymic usage of the term to refer to the "writings of a historian."[20] Furthermore, On-cho Ng and Q. Edward Wang point out that *shi* and historical writings are connected in their aims of teaching the past, prefiguring the future, cultivating morality, guiding statecraft, spreading propaganda, legitimizing political pursuits, and shaping cultural belonging.[21]

To better grasp how *shi* was understood in the writing culture of early medieval China, it is useful to examine the scope and connotations of the term according to the "Jingji zhi" in the *Suishu*. The *Suishu* was compiled by Wei Zheng 魏徵 (580–643) in the Tang dynasty (618–907). After the founding of the new dynasty, Tang rulers set out to glean lessons from the past. The second emperor of the dynasty, Taizong (Li Shimin 李世民 [598–649; r. 626–649]) summoned officials and scholars to compile eight historical accounts of the short-lived dynasties that preceded the Tang, including the Sui. The "Jingji zhi" of the *Suishu* is a catalog of the written works which were circulated or known in that dynasty, arranged according to the categories of "classical canons" (*jing* 經), "historical accounts" (*shi* 史), "master works" (*zi* 子), and "individual collections" (*ji* 集). In comparing the *Suishu* to the historiography of the Han dynasty, Albert E. Dien points out that "[a] Han dynasty bibliography lists only eleven works of history, totaling some 45 *juan* as a subcategory of the classics. The *Suishu* [History of the Sui], coming at the end of the period, has 874 works of history in 16,558 *juan* in a class of its own."[22] Early medieval China was a period in which the genre of historical writing developed substantially.

The *shi* section of the *Suishu* includes standard or official histories (*zhengshi* 正史), as well as various annotated editions ranging from the *Shiji* to the *History of Chen* (*Chenshu* 陳書).[23] In early medieval China, many historical accounts were presented in well-organized compilations, which provided an abundance of materials for writers. This made it relatively convenient, compared to prior ages, for scholars to access historical writings and commentaries.[24] Based on the many annotated editions listed in the "Jingji zhi," the *Shiji* and *Hanshu* were quite popular during this period. These editions include the twelve-*juan Pronunciation and Meaning of the Shiji* (*Shiji yinyi* 史記音義), the three-*juan Pronunciation of the Shiji* (*Shiji yin* 史記音), the two-*juan Pronunciation of the Hanshu* (*Hanshu yin* 漢書音), the one-*juan Annotations of the Hanshu* (*Hanshu zhu* 漢書注), and the three-*juan Continuing Hermeneutics of the Hanshu* (*Hanshu xu xun* 漢書續訓).[25]

Along with the *zhengshi*, the *shi* section of the "Jingji zhi" also includes accounts labeled "ancient history" (*gushi* 古史), such as the *Annals of the Jin Dynasty* (*Jinji* 晉紀) and the *Documents of Liang* (*Liangdian* 梁典).[26] The creators of these works, modeling themselves on the Han historians Ban Gu 班固 (32–92) and Sima Qian 司馬遷 (ca. 145–86 BCE), composed histories of the recent past of their own societies, using the style and structure of the ancient work *Annals of Spring and Autumn* (*Chunqiu* 春秋). The *shi* section also contains "unofficial histories" (*yeshi* 野史), such as *Stories of Emperor Wu of the Han* (*Han Wu gushi* 漢武故事) and *Stories of the Ages and Recent Anecdotes* (*Shishuo xinyu* 世說新語).[27]

In his analysis of "Jingji zhi," Dien states that "more than half of the categories in this class are usually not considered to be histories in the usual sense of the word."[28] This observation is appropriate for the books and documents included in the *yeshi* section. For instance, seemingly fantastic works such as Gan Bao's 干寶 (ca. 282–351) *In Search of the Supernatural* (*Soushen ji* 搜神記) and the *Classic of Mountains and Seas* (*Shanhai jing* 山海經) were included in the *yeshi* category, suggesting that what modern readers may view as ghost stories, folklore, or legends were treated as history at that time. This hypothesis is supported by the preface to *Soushen ji*, in which Gan Bao states,

> Even though we examine ancient fragments in the written documents and collect bits and pieces which have come to the present time, these things are not what has been heard or seen by one person's own ears and eyes. How could one dare say there are no inaccuracies? . . . From this evidence we can see that problems in the witnessing of events have existed since ancient times. . . . Nevertheless, the state does not eliminate the office charged with writing commentaries on historical documents, and scholars do not cease in their recitations of the texts. Is this not

because what is lost is inconsequential and what is preserved is vital? . . . Coming now to what these records contain, it is enough to make clear that the spirit world is not a lie. . . . I will count myself fortunate if in the future curious scholars come along, note the basis of these stories, and find things within them to enlighten their hearts and fill their eyes. And I will be fortunate as well to escape reproach for this book.[29]

雖考先志於載籍，收遺逸於當時，蓋非一耳一目之所親聞睹也，又安敢謂無失實者哉……從此觀之，聞見之難，由來尚矣……然而國家不廢注記之官，學士不絕誦覽之業，豈不以其所失者小，所存者大乎？……及其著述，亦足以發明神道之不誣也……幸將來好事之士錄其根體，有以游心寓目而無尤焉。[30]

Thus, Gan Bao maintains that his purpose for compiling these stories was to preserve proof for the existence of the apparently supernatural found in historical accounts not included in the standard histories.[31] He argues that it is difficult to record such supernatural phenomena based on first-hand observations because some of them took place ages ago, and even if several people witness the same event, they will inevitably have different perspectives on it. As Gan points out, it is rare to achieve complete consensus across multiple sources or even within one's own interpretation. Rather than pursuing the impossible ideal of total historical accuracy, Gan instead presents discrepancies in the narrations of and judgments on historical figures and events, and records a variety of different historical accounts. His record of the supernatural was meant to overcome the doubts of his contemporaries by showing that the accounts of these phenomena rested on a solid historical foundation. Interestingly, as a court historian under Emperor Yuan of the Jin dynasty 晉元帝 (276–323; r. 318–23), Gan Bao also compiled the *Jinji*. The fact that he served in this capacity suggests that the problems of writing history and historical records were of serious concern for him.

Another example of how broad the concept of *shi* was in early medieval China is the critical discourse around the *Shanhai jing* during the period. Although the *Suishu* acknowledges that the choice is controversial, it places *Shanhai jing* in the *shi* section. Richard E. Strassberg, the English translator of *Shanhai jing*, argues that this classification "reflected a growing recognition of [*Shanhai jing*] as the *locus classicus* of such later genres as the local gazetteer, which presented information about the geography, history, folklore and customs of individual counties."³² Strassberg then points out that Sima Zhen 司马贞 (679–732) would often use *Shanhai jing* as evidence for his comments on the *Shiji*.³³ Thus, the concept of *shi* in this period includes both official histories and supernatural stories about spirits. In writing *yongshi shi*, literati could and did draw upon both types of sources.

Despite this broader understanding of *shi* in early medieval China, the distinctions between different types of historical records were not lost on the compiler of the *shi* section of the "Jingji zhi," who notes that not all the listed items are faithful records of past events. The compiler notes that the third subsection of the "Jingji zhi," containing "miscellaneous histories" (*zashi* 雜史) and "miscellaneous biographies" (*zazhuan* 雜傳)—a group that includes the *Annals of Wu and Yue States* (*Wuyue Chunqiu* 吳越春秋) and the *Book of the Extinct State of Yue* (*Yue jue ji* 越絕記)³⁴—contains arbitrarily organized, often haphazard accounts written to enable scholars to remember a period of past chaos. The compiler acknowledges that these works are very different from faithful historical works such as the *Chunqiu*, *Shiji*, or *Hanshu* and that some of the stories in the *zashi* are bizarre, strange, or ironic.³⁵ The kind of information collected under the *shi* label, even within works we would recognize as historical, is in fact highly diverse.³⁶

The numerous interpretations of *shi* and the various types of records located in the *shi* section of the *Suishu* indicate how the concept of *shi* evolved over centuries—from a government office for conducting astrological rituals and recording people and events to a wide range of material (not all aimed at accuracy) associated with events of the past. This section has sought to define the concepts of *yong* and *shi* and explore their roles in early medieval China. The next section will seek to capture how literati conceived of, categorized, and delineated the concept of *yongshi shi* by looking at the first extant *yongshi shi* and the "Yongshi" section of the *Wen xuan*.

The Concept of *Yongshi shi* in Early Medieval China

The first extant poem on history referred to by the title "Yongshi" by an identifiable author was written by Ban Gu 班固 (32–92). It is unclear what the title of this first *yongshi shi* actually is. The *Shipin* mentions Ban's *yongshi* twice, but it is difficult to know whether Zhong Rong was referring to the title or topic of the poem. The earliest extant source of this poem appears in Li Shan's 李善 (630–689) annotated version of the *Wen xuan*. Modern editions often treat "Yongshi" as the title of this poem.³⁷ A translation of the poem follows:

	三王德彌薄.	The three kings' virtue grew increasingly thin,
	惟後用肉刑.	only then were flesh-cutting punishments used.
	太蒼令有罪.	The Director of Granaries was charged with a crime
4	就逮長安城.	and was arrested in Chang'an.
	自恨身無子.	He was bitter that he had no sons of his own,
	困急獨煢煢.	in his urgent distress he felt helpless and alone.
	小女痛父言.	His youngest daughter was pained by her father's words,
8	死者不可生.	those who die cannot be brought back to life.
	上書詣闕下.	She went to the palace gates to present a letter to the throne,
	思古歌雞鳴.	thinking of antiquity, she sang "Cockcrow."
	憂心摧折裂.	Her anxious heart was breaking,
12	晨風揚激聲.	and she raised the stirring sounds of the "Dawnwind Hawk."
	聖漢孝文帝.	Emperor Wen of the Sagely Han felt pity,
	惻然感至情.	stirred by her intense feeling.
	百男何憒憒.	A hundred male children would be in such a muddle,
16	不如一緹縈.	no match for a single Tiying.[38]

In this poem, Ban employs the *Shiji* style to narrate Tiying's 緹縈 (fl. 177 BCE) attempt to rescue her father. The poet's own voice appears at the end, in a concluding couplet, which approvingly compares Ti's behavior with her male counterparts. This format—first narrating a biography and then concluding with a comment on the subject's deeds at the end—is employed by Ban Gu throughout the *Hanshu* itself. Some scholars have criticized Ban's "Yongshi" as simply another vehicle for presenting official history, as the poem focuses on narrating the history rather than examining his own life in relation to historical figures. Others have had a more positive assessment of Ban Gu's "Yongshi" style, emphasizing that his method ultimately became one of the dominant approaches in the Chinese literary tradition to writing *yongshi shi*.[39]

After Ban Gu, poets were frequently drawn to write about historical figures and events due to several factors. First, historical writing and commentaries on historical accounts developed substantially during the early medieval period, which in turn provided writers with increased access to historical accounts and divergent interpretations. This enabled them to critically engage with these materials by composing poetry. Scholarly commentaries on historical writings glossed obscure words or used evidential research to cast doubt on certain passages. Abridged versions of historical accounts were circulated widely.[40] Second, many poets were displaced by the social chaos and military conflict of the early medieval period. Fleeing chaos or forced into exile, they passed historic sites, which inspired their poems on historical figures and events. Third, employing allusions was a way to avoid the dangers brought on by stating sociopolitical issues too directly. The political instability of the period was such that many scholars and poets lived through two or three short dynasties during their lifespans. Naturally, they were often concerned about their own safety and did not want to become the targets of political jealousy or pawns in the political struggles of warring clans. Historical allusions provided a roundabout way to express one's frustrations while maintaining plausible deniability. Fourth, alluding to the past was a way to demonstrate poetic talent and attract the attention of powerful figures who could employ them as officials. As Tian Xiaofei notes, the trend toward an ornate literary writing style replete with historical allusions was so pronounced that encyclopedias that catered to the needs of literati employing historical allusions began to be compiled: "In the early years of the Liang it was fashionable to employ a large number of recondite allusions in one's poetry. The compilation of encyclopedias in this period was therefore very much a response to practical needs."[41] It should be noted, however, that not all contemporary literati were pleased with this phenomenon. In his *Shipin*, Zhong Rong strongly criticizes this trend, instead emphasizing the importance of describing images directly rather than through allusions. Lastly, the development of papermaking in the Eastern Han period also influenced how ideas were recorded and circulated, as it was now easier to write down thoughts. Although paper was still relatively expensive in early medieval China, copying preferred words, passages, or occasionally an entire text onto paper was a simple way to transmit history in whole or in part.

In the early medieval period, the majority of the pieces titled "Yongshi" are based on readings of historical records. Examples include Zhang Xie's 張協 (d. ca. 307) poem on Shu Guang 疏廣 (d. 45 BCE) and Shu Shou 疏受 (d. 48 BCE), and Lu Chen's 盧諶 (ca. 285–ca. 351) poem on Lin Xiangru 藺相如 (ca. 329–ca. 259 BCE).[42] The increasing popularity, accessibility, and speed of transmission of historical writings, particularly the *Shiji* and *Hanshu*, prompted new compositions.[43] In the preface to his series "Nine Poems after Reading the *Shiji*" ("Du *Shi* shu jiuzhang" 讀史述九章), Tao

Yuanming 陶淵明 (ca. 365–427) writes, "I read the *Shiji* and was stirred by the reading experience, so I wrote down my thoughts" 余讀《史記》有所感而述之.⁴⁴ It is not certain whether he read the entire *Shiji* or just a section of it, because we have no information about where he might have obtained the *Shiji*. Nevertheless, the title clearly shows that the *Shiji* was popular among and accessible to Eastern Jin intellectuals. As the number of historical works increased, *yongshi shi* became a more prominent poetic subgenre. Yu Xi's 虞羲 (fl. 510) "Poem on General Huo's Northern Expedition" ("Yong Huo jiangjun beifa shi" 詠霍將軍北伐詩) is another example of a poet expressing emotions stirred by reading accounts of historical figures. By writing these poems, these poets could assure themselves their experiences were not *sui generis*, and console themselves by adding their own names to the lineage of great historical and cultural figures.

In addition to poems inspired by reading historical accounts, the *yongshi shi* genre also includes poems about visiting historical relics. This can readily be seen in the "Yongshi" section of the *Wen xuan*, compiled by Xiao Tong 蕭統 (501–531) and his editorial team, which includes twenty-one poems written by nine poets between 196 and 479 CE.⁴⁵ The poems included in this section reflect both the idiosyncratic tastes of Xiao and his editorial team and the intellectual atmosphere of the Southern Dynasties (420–589). Of the twenty-one poems in the "Yongshi" section of the *Wen xuan*, several are most likely based on poets' visits to historical sites. Two poems—one composed by Wang Can and one by Cao Zhi—seem to reflect the experience of visiting the tomb of the "three good men." The poems share a similar structure: they first comment on Lord Mu's behavior, then narrate the story of the three good men, and eventually cite the "Huangniao" poem. However, the two poems emphasize different aspects of the story.⁴⁶ This type of poem has since been reclassified by modern scholars as *huaigu shi*, so it is significant to note that the *Wen xuan* classified it as *yongshi shi* initially. This particular style of poem was in fact far from uncommon; in early medieval China, many poems were written about visits to historical relics and heritage sites. Examples include Zheng Xianzhi's "Passing by the Zhang Zifang Temple" ("Xingjing Zhang Zifang miao" 行經張子房廟), Fan Tai's "Going through the Temple of Emperor Gao of the Han" ("Jing Han Gao miao" 經漢高廟), and He Xun's 何遜 (d. 518) "Passing by Sun Quan's Tomb" ("Xingjing Sunshi ling" 行經孫氏陵).⁴⁷ It is only in later periods that this type of poem was reclassified as *huaigu shi*. The poetry section of the *Tang wencui*, for example, includes two separate categories for poems about historical figures and places: *yongshi*, with 15 *juan*, and *huaigu*, with

18 *juan*.⁴⁸ However, Xiao Tong and the editorial team of the *Wen xuan* did not distinguish between poems inspired by a poet's reading of a historical account and those that emerged from a poet's visit to a historical site.

Another subgenre of poetry that includes examples of *yongshi shi* is "Music Bureau Poetry" (*yuefu shi* 樂府詩). The extant poems of this subgenre were compiled in the *Collection of Music Bureau Poetry* (*Yuefu shiji* 樂府詩集) by Guo Maoqian 郭茂倩 (1041–1099) during the Northern Song dynasty (960–1127). Although *yuefu shi* sometimes have titles that refer to historical figures or events, the content may not have any explicit relation to them. These are typically poems in which new lyrics are set to an old tune, such as Cao Cao's 曹操 (155–220) and Cao Pi's 曹丕 (187–226) "Poems on Qiu Hu" ("Qiu Hu shi" 秋胡詩), which are not *yongshi shi*. Yan Yanzhi's 顏延之 (384–456) "Qiu Hu shi," by way of contrast, is explicitly based on the historical lore of Qiu Hu and thus belongs to this category. Generally speaking, *yongshi shi* in early medieval China include both poems based on a poet's reflection on reading historical accounts and poems based on the poet's contemplation of the past after visiting historical relics. The next section will examine the intriguing phenomenon of early medieval Chinese poems that explicitly adopt "Yongshi" as their title.

"Yongshi" as Title

Although poem titles are not always reliable in early medieval China, what was labeled as *yongshi* at the very least informs us about what types of poems were considered *yongshi shi* during the attributor's time period. Many *yongshi shi* in early medieval China possess the same title as the subgenre. For example, the poets Wang Can, Zhang Xie, Zuo Si, Yuan Hong 袁宏 (ca. 328–ca. 376), and Bao Zhao 鮑照 (ca. 414–466) all have poems on various specific topics entitled "Yongshi." It has been debated whether these poems were originally given the title "Yongshi" or if this title was a generic label applied to them later. Robert Joe Cutter maintains that there is no certainty that "Yongshi" was used as their original titles:

> A few *yongshi* exist from Jian'an times. While it is sometimes difficult to know just when Jian'an poems acquired the titles they have today, it does not appear that the "Yongshi shi" (Poem on History) title attached to Ban Gu's old piece was common then. Ruan Yu and Wang Can each have a piece by that name about

the three courtiers who went to the grave with Duke Mu of Qin about 620 B.C.E., but it is more usual for poems dealing with historical events to bear other kinds of titles, and Cao Zhi's poem on the Duke Mu incident is entitled "San liang" (Three Good Men).[49]

Cutter's observation is further corroborated by recent studies on Chinese manuscript culture by Stephen Owen, Tian Xiaofei, and Christopher Nugent, which bring into question the idea that any poems from this period would have a fixed title.[50] For example, Tian argues that

> [p]oems, particularly from before the age of print culture, often seem to pick up titles and authors along the way and are made to fall into place where they "belong." In any case, we should keep in mind that our subsequent reading of this series of poems must be put in the context of the textual fluidity of manuscript culture.[51]

Thus, while the poem title is a useful indicator of the poem's genre, it is not always reliable in the early medieval period.

Conclusion

This chapter examines the early medieval concept of *yongshi shi* as presented in sources from the period or slightly after it. It compares the current definition of *yongshi shi* with that of *huaigu shi*. The problem with the current understanding of *yongshi shi* is that scholars tend to treat it as a fixed concept, generalizing from *yongshi shi* across dynasties and retrospectively applying the concept derived from this generalization to *yongshi shi* in a particular period. However, the scope and connotation of *yongshi shi* have changed over time. In order to unfold its definition in the early medieval period, this chapter traces the complex meanings of *yong* and *shi*. *Yong* often refers to the behavior of singing and chanting on a given theme or topic. In early medieval China, it was used in connection with *qingtan* to comment on and evaluate contemporary or historical figures. This type of *yong* thus both expressed the emotions of a given literatus and served multiple literary, historical, and political functions. Like *yong*, *shi* also has a rich meaning, and scholars have long investigated its development, functions, and scope. It originally referred to a government official who acted as both a ritualist, responsible for observing astrological rites, and as a historian, responsible for keeping court records. Later, it referred to historical writing or a historical account.

Historical writing itself was a diverse category in early medieval China, as indicated by the breadth of the *shi* section in the "Jingji zhi." The works considered *shi* by the "Jingji zhi" include but are not limited to standard or official history, ancient history, unofficial history, and other miscellaneous histories or biographies. *Yongshi shi* was no less diverse a category. Several factors contributed to the proliferation of *yongshi shi* in early modern China: an increase in the number of historical accounts, both original accounts and commentaries on those accounts; literati who traveled more widely than in earlier periods; the popular trend of using allusions; and the availability of paper as a medium for writing, to name only a few. The section of the *Wen xuan* anthology dedicated to "Yongshi" contains both poems dedicated to reading historical accounts and poems about visiting historical relics. Other poems included within the category in early medieval China were inspired by historical themes explored in the *yuefu* style of poetry, or simply had "Yongshi" or "Surveying the Ancient" ("Langu" 覽古) as the title. Although the titles of many early medieval Chinese poems contain the term *yongshi*, it is imperative that we consider the historical context of how these poems might have been categorized. Due to the fluidity of manuscript culture in early medieval China, it is possible that the editors of anthologies and compendia, or even later literary critics, gave these poems the title "Yongshi" for multiple reasons that may have changed over time. All we can reliably conclude about poems that bear the title "Yongshi" is that these poems were considered *yongshi shi* at the time when this label was attributed to them.

Chapter 2

Retrospective Memory and Zuo Si's "Poems on History"

The first chapter set the stage by discussing the meanings and use of *yongshi shi* in early medieval China. This chapter will build on that discussion of the relationship between the genre and cultural memory by investigating the specific case of how Zuo Si 左思 (ca. 253–ca. 305) adopted retrospective memory in his writings.[1] Zuo Si, whose given name was also styled Taichong 太沖 (alternatively written 泰沖), was a native of Linzi 臨淄 (modern-day Zibo 淄博, Shandong) and a famous literary figure of the Western Jin dynasty (266–316).[2] A relatively substantial amount of Zuo's writing survived into the early medieval Chinese period (222–589)—the "Bibliographical Treatise" of *The History of the Sui Dynasty* (*Suishu* 隋書) records a five-*juan* edition of his collected works.[3] However, of that, only three rhapsodies (*fu* 賦) and fourteen poems are still extant. The best known of these surviving works are his "Rhapsody on the Three Capitals" ("Sandu fu" 三都賦) and "[Poems] on History" ("Yongshi" 詠史).

This chapter addresses how Zuo's poems, in their use of retrospective memory, related and contributed to the *yongshi* subgenre, as well as how they reflected the broader context of Western Jin society. In these poems, Zuo compares himself favorably to historical figures and references lessons from their lives when discussing different stages of his own. Zuo uses the experience of these historical exemplars to demonstrate his lofty ideals, discuss the collapse of his ambitions, and explore alternatives for unappreciated scholars such as himself. Moreover, because Zuo was not politically successful, these poems became an alternative path to becoming part of posterity.

Three main theories have been proposed on when Zuo's "Yongshi" were composed. The first, based on lines in the first poem, is that they were written when he was young, before the Western Jin unified the country.[4] The second holds that these poems could not have been composed when Zuo was young because the divergent styles, moods, and spirit in them reflect different periods in the poet's life, and draw on a variety of life experiences.[5] The third theory points to the coherence of the "Yongshi" as a set—the first poem serves as a preface, and the next seven use miscellaneous historical and literary allusions to expand on the themes established in the first to articulate the poet's feelings—as evidence that the poems were composed as a set relatively late in Zuo's life.[6] I find the third theory the most compelling. Not only do the poems form a coherent set, but their reflective tone, their autobiographical style, and the summary they provide of his life all signify that Zuo was thinking about the impression he wished to leave for posterity. Zuo's "Yongshi" cover a wide range of life experiences, and include a number of historical allusions and archetypes: the ambitious youth, the unappreciated man of talent, the scholar eager for fame and reputation, and the recluse withdrawing from court to enjoy studying ancient documents. Zuo places himself in "conversation" with each of these stages of life, in an effort to find a suitable position for himself in the past, present, and future, and thus to transcend the limits of time and space.

Demonstrating Lofty Ideals and Vision

Zuo Si was far from the first Chinese writer to seek to capture his own image in poetry. That ideal has been entrenched in the Chinese literary tradition at least since the *Shangshu* stated that "the poem articulates what is intently on the mind." 詩言志[7] The "Great Preface" to the *Classic of Poetry* (*Shijing* 詩經) subtly adjusts this relationship between poetry and intent: "The poem is that to which what is intently on the mind goes. In the mind it is 'being intent'; coming out in language, it is a poem." 詩者. 志之所之也. 在心爲志. 發言爲詩.[8] Here poetry becomes a medium, the external verbal manifestation of internal intent. The "Great Preface" goes on to stress that poetry should be a spontaneous, involuntary, and therefore genuine expression of one's feelings. One recurring complication to the poetics of genuine spontaneity in the "Great Preface" is the self-conscious attempts at literary immortality through poetry. During the Three Kingdoms (220–280), in his "Discourse on Literature" ("Lunwen" 論文), Cao Pi 曹丕 (187–226) argues that literary writing is the surest route for achieving eternal fame: "I would say that literary works are the supreme achievement in the business of state, a splendor that does not decay. A time will come when a person's life ends; glory and pleasure go no further than this body. To carry both to eternity, there is nothing to compare with the unending permanence of the literary work." 蓋文章經國之大業. 不朽之盛事. 年壽有時而盡. 榮樂止乎其身. 二者必至之常期. 未若文章之無窮.[9] These words were especially appealing to the poets who lived in the chaotic and turbulent era of early medieval China, when it was difficult for educated men to achieve their dreams of political power. These men, frustrated in their ambitions, turned to poetry. They used historical lore and allusions to create an ideal self, and to ensure a place for themselves in literary history.[10]

Zuo Si carefully crafts the image he presents in his poems. To assure later readers that his actions stem from virtuous motives, he affects an indifference toward material comforts and a lack of desire for fame or power. By composing poetry through stitching together pieces of historical lore, Zuo was able to make his own sense of the past and shape his own self-image. Zuo's first "Yongshi" is transparently about the poet's own image. Zuo describes that, from a young age, he not only was a skillful writer but also had high personal standards and sought role models among the great historical figures. David Knechtges describes the first poem as "not on a historical theme at all, but . . . a brief 'autobiography.' "[11] A translation of the poem follows:

詠史八首　　Eight Poems on History, I[12]

	弱冠弄柔翰,	At twenty, I skillfully played with a soft writing brush.[13]
	卓犖觀羣書.	Outstanding and talented, I read every kind of book.[14]
	著論准過秦,	When making arguments, I took "The Faults of Qin"[15] as my model.
4	作賦擬子虛.	When writing rhapsodies, I imitated the style of "Sir Vacuous."[16]
	邊城苦鳴鏑,	The border cities bitterly suffered from whistling arrows,
	羽檄飛京都.	Feathered dispatches rapidly flew to the capital.[17]
	雖非甲冑士,	I was not a soldier equipped with a helmet and armor,
8	疇昔覽穰苴.	But I had learned all of Rangju's[18] military strategies.
	長嘯激清風,	My long whistle stirred up sublime moral values.[19]
	志若無東吳.	In my mind, it was as if the Eastern Wu were no longer.[20]
	鉛刀貴一割,	Only the initial cut of a lead knife[21] is valued.

12	夢想騁良圖.	I dreamed my ambitions would be of good use.
	左眄澄江湘,	Looking to the left, I would pacify the region of the Yangtze and Xiang Rivers.²²
	右盼定羌胡.	Glaring to the right, I would subdue the Qiang and Xiongnu.
	功成不受爵,	After attaining such achievements, I would not accept any rank of nobility.
16	長揖歸田廬.	Hands clasped, I would bow deeply and return to my cottage.

According to *The History of the Jin Dynasty* (*Jinshu* 晉書), Zuo was a slow learner when he was young. Zuo Si's father often expressed to his friends the concerns over the young Zuo Si's lack of abilities: "When young, Zuo Si tried to learn Zhong and Hu style calligraphy and play the zither, but was not successful. His father, Zuo Yong, told his friends, 'Zuo Si's comprehension and understanding do not compare to mine when I was young.'" 思小學鍾、胡書及鼓琴, 並不成. 雍謂友人曰: 思所曉解, 不及我少時.²³ Zuo Yong's assessment is corroborated in an unofficial history: "Since his mother died while he was very young, his father was over-indulgent and his early education was slighted."²⁴ 思蚤喪母, 雍憐之, 不甚教其書學.²⁵ Where the standard history suggests that Zuo Si lacked natural talent, the unofficial history sees a problem of nurture, not nature, blaming Zuo's late blooming on his father's neglect.

In this poem, Zuo Si recalls his early life experience to demonstrate his literary endeavor and achievements, military aspirations, and overall humility. He begins by stressing his literary abilities, claiming that from a young age he was not only skillful at reading and writing, but also had high personal standards and sought role models among great historical figures, such as Jia Yi 賈誼 (200–168 BCE) and Sima Xiangru 司馬相如 (ca. 179–117 BCE). During Zuo's youth, a series of major military engagements took place on the Jin frontier. Although Zuo was not trained as a soldier, he states that he had studied Rangju's 穰苴 famous military strategies and wanted to contribute his talents to the process of unifying the country. In the sixth couplet (l. 11–12), Zuo describes himself by using Ban Chao's famous analogy of a "lead knife," indicating that he wanted to try his best to serve the court during a time of military crisis. Thus, by demonstrating his intentions and ideals as a young man, he attempts to persuade his readers of his dedication to literary and military achievements. After listing his ambitions, he maintains that what differentiated him from other politicians of the period was that he was not focused on fame or reputation but only wanted to use his talents to serve the country. In this first poem, Zuo works consciously and consistently toward building a poetic self for later readers to appreciate and respect.

The third poem in the series makes these autobiographical ambitions even more explicit. In this poem, Zuo explicitly appears via the word "I" (*wu* 吾), a first person pronoun rarely used in classical Chinese poetry, forcefully informing the audience who he is, what ideals he embraces, and with which historical figures he would prefer to be associated:

III[26]

	吾希段干木，	I think highly of Duangan Mu:[27]
	偃息藩魏君．	He brought peace by hedging against Wei's ruler.[28]
	吾慕魯仲連，	I admire Lu Zhonglian:
4	談笑卻秦軍．	He held back the Qin army by talking and laughing.[29]
	當世貴不羈，	Their contemporaries valued their unrestrained behavior.
	遭難能解紛．	When states encountered difficulties, they were capable of solving them.
	功成不受賞，	When they accomplished these deeds, they did not accept rewards.
8	高節卓不羣．	With their lofty principles, they stood above the crowd.
	臨組不肯緤，	When presented with the silk sashes of officialdom, they were unwilling to tie them.[30]
	對珪不肯分．	When awarded the jade tablets of nobility, they were unwilling to allot them.[31]
	連璽爚前庭，	A series of official seals shone before the court,
12	比之猶浮雲．	They likened them to drifting clouds.[32]

This poem echoes the first poem thematically, reaffirming Zuo's ideal of making great contributions without asking for rewards. To celebrate this ideal, Zuo praises two historical figures of the Warring States period (475–221 BCE) for their extraordinary ability to solve thorny political issues: Duangan Mu 段干木 (ca. 475–396 BCE) and Lu Zhonglian 魯仲連 (ca. 305–245 BCE). Duangan Mu was a principled, erudite recluse who was admired tremendously and treated with great dignity by the ruler of Wei, Marquis Wen 魏文侯 (472–396 BCE). Due in part to Duangan's harmonious relationship with Marquis Wen, the Qin army did not dare to attack Wei 魏國 (403–225 BCE), as they believed a state that knew how to respect talent was well governed enough to resist their attack. As for Lu Zhonglian, his adroit diplomatic negotiations and eloquent speech secured the safety of the state of Zhao and the state of Yan. Both men refused to accept awards or titles. For example, Lu Zhonglian considered it venal to accept an official position right after he helped the state of Zhao.[33] The *Shiji* records his rationale in detail:

> [After Lu Zhonglian helped defeat the Qin army] the Lord of Pingyuan wanted to enfeoff Lu Lian. Lu Lian refused three times and in the end remained unwilling to accept. The Lord of Pingyuan laid out wine; after he was in his cups, he rose and stepped forward, presenting one thousand *jin* of gold as a gift to Lu Lian. Lu Lian smiled: "What I value in the knights of the world is how they avert troubles, resolve dilemmas, and cut tangled knots for others without ever receiving anything for it. If they received something for it, that would be a transaction of shopkeepers and traveling peddlers; I could not bear to do so." He then bid farewell to the Lord of Pingyuan, departed, and never sought audience again.[34]

> 平原君欲封魯連, 魯連辭讓 (使) 者三, 終不肯受. 平原君乃置酒, 酒酣起前, 以千金爲魯連壽. 魯連笑曰: "所貴於天下之士者, 爲人排患釋難解紛亂而無取也. 即有取者, 是商賈之事也, 而連不忍爲也." 遂辭平原君而去, 終身不復見.[35]

Zuo's emphasis here on altruistic efforts resembles how he framed his youthful political endeavors. Zuo participated in an intense debate over whether the Jin house had inherited power from the Han (202 BCE–220 CE) or the Wei (213–265) dynasty. Zuo's contribution was the "Sandu fu," a work of more than ten thousand characters (indeed, one of the longest extant rhapsodies), which he spent ten years writing and which informed readers that the Jin replacing the Wei to unify the country represented the legitimate transfer of the Mandate of Heaven. In "Sandu fu," Zuo Si consciously imitates the capital-style rhapsodies of Zhang Heng and Ban Gu of the Han dynasty, an imitation meant to suggest that the Jin dynasty was the legitimate successor to the Han. The style of this work suggests that the Jin dynasty would restore the Han tradition and build another great empire, but he also wanted to place himself in that tradition, alongside Zhang Heng and Ban Gu. This work therefore not only demonstrates Zuo's literary talent but also validates the mandate of the newly established Western Jin dynasty. It is also evidence of Zuo's efforts to seek favor from the court. This long rhapsody, ten years in the making, was thus both a political and literary act.

Zuo had high expectations for the reception of "Sandu fu." According to his biography in the *Jinshu*, "Zuo Si himself thought his writing was not inferior to Ban (Gu) and Zhang (Heng)." 思自以其作不謝班張.[36] However, his writing was initially unappreciated by his peers and Zuo Si, seeking to salvage his reputation, actively sought out several important literati to ask for advice and support. One such figure was Zhang Hua 張華 (232–300),[37] who eulogized "Sandu fu" and gave Zuo a suggestion on how to promote it: "Since your writings have not yet found recognition in the world, you should have them introduced by some gentleman of eminent reputation." 然君文未重於世, 宜以經高名之士.[38] Zuo therefore visited the well-known scholar Huangfu Mi 皇甫謐 (215–282), who spoke highly of Zuo's "Sandu fu" and wrote a preface for it.[39]

After Zhang Hua's and Huangfu Mi's endorsements, the reception of "Sandu fu" turned more positive, even among those who had previously scorned his writing. This critical volte-face led Zhang Zai 張載 (fl. third century) to write a commentary to the "Wei Capital Rhapsody" (*Weidu fu* 魏都賦) section, and Liu Kui 劉逵 (fl. third century) to compose both a preface and commentary to the Wu and Shu portions of the piece. Zhang Hua's and Huangfu Mi's comments, along with Zhang Zai's and Liu Kui's commentaries, greatly increased the circulation of the work. As legend had it, so many people bought paper to copy his rhapsodies that it caused an increase in the price of paper in Luoyang 洛陽.[40] Zuo hoped that the success of his writings would demonstrate his talent and allow him to achieve his political ambitions. However, while the eventual popularity of the "Sandu fu" allowed him to enter Zhang Hua's and Jia Mi's 賈謐 (d. 300) inner circles, it only won him some minor positions in court, such as palace library assistant (*mishulang* 秘書郎) and libationer (*jijiu* 祭酒). Thus, his youthful visions of meaningfully serving the state ultimately went unfulfilled.

Discussing the Collapse of His Ambitions

Whereas Zuo Si's first and third "Yongshi" focus on his ideals and ambitions, the second, sixth, and seventh poems express his disillusionment and disappointment. He expresses these feelings by commenting on exemplary historical figures, demonstrating that his unfulfilled potential had ample precedent in Chinese history. The second "Yongshi," for example, alludes to a historical figure named Feng Tang 馮唐 (fl. 157 BCE):

II[41]

	鬱鬱澗底松,	Luxuriant pines at the bottom of a ravine.[42]
	離離山上苗.	Lush sprouts on the top of a mountain.[43]
	以彼徑寸莖,	With their one-inch-diameter stems,
4	蔭此百尺條.	They overshadow those hundred-foot-long pine branches.
	世冑躡高位,	The descendants of nobility ascend to high positions,
	英俊沈下僚.	While the talented sink to lower offices.
	地勢使之然,	The differing terrain[44] made it so;
8	由來非一朝.	Not the result of a single day.
	金張籍舊業,	The Jin and Zhang[45] relied on the legacy of their ancestors.
	七葉珥漢貂.	Seven generations wore the sables of Han.
	馮公豈不偉?	How could Sir Feng[46] not be great?
	白首不見招.	Even in old age, he was not summoned by the emperor.[47]

This poem points out the importance of family background in deciding one's political career by comparing the fates of Jin and Zhang clan members with Feng Tang. The first four lines establish a contrast between young shoots on the top of the mountain and tall pine trees at the bottom of the ravine. Aside from serving as a poetic contrast, this appearance of a natural image at the beginning of a poem is an important classical literary device in Chinese poetic composition, an "affective image" (*xing* 興), adopted from poetic devices used in the *Shijing*. These natural images are meant to evoke feelings that resonate with the human affairs described in the poem. In this case, the natural disparity between the high-placed sprouts overshadowing the low-lying pines are akin to the Jin and Zhang aristocrats, whose family members could effortlessly obtain high positions, in contrast to the talented and worthy men without family connections who must toil away in lowly positions. Zuo Si was not satisfied with simply employing images of nature as metaphors. He also strengthened his arguments by explicitly contrasting the talented poor, embodied by Feng Tang, with the noble families of Jin and Zhang, whom he transformed from historical figures into icons. Zuo Si directly contrasts people who had real talent and strove hard, yet struggled in their careers, with people who inherited status and easily attained political power. This is the key theme of Zuo Si's "Yongshi": "The descendants of nobility ascend to high positions, / while the talented sink to lower offices." 世冑躡高位. 英俊沉下僚.

However, Zuo's depiction of Feng Tang is highly selective compared to the descriptions of Feng in historical accounts. The *Shiji* states that when the emperor spotted Feng Tang in a crowd, he approached Feng, and the two discussed state concerns. Because of the wise strategies he presented to the emperor, Feng was subsequently promoted to a high position.[48] Thus, although Feng was not discovered in his youth, he was eventually sought out and promoted by Emperor Wen 漢文帝 (r. 180–157 BCE). The *Shiji* records this event:

> He (the emperor) appointed (Feng Tang) as chief commandant of chariots and cavalry with authority over the palace guards. Emperor Jing ascended the throne in 157 BCE and made (Feng) Tang chancellor of Chu, then he was dismissed. But when Emperor Wu was enthroned, he sought out worthy and capable men, and he promoted Feng Tang. However, (Feng) Tang was over ninety years old at the time and was not able to become an official again, whereupon (the emperor) appointed Tang's son, Feng Sui, as gentleman.[49]
>
> 拜唐爲車騎都尉, 主中尉及郡國車士⋯⋯七年, 景帝立, 以唐爲楚相, 免. 武帝立, 求賢良, 舉馮唐. 唐時年九十餘, 不能復爲官.[50]

The contrast between this story and the picture that Zuo Si paints of Feng Tang is clear. Zuo was surely familiar with the history of the Western Han (202 BCE–8 CE), as he taught it to Jia Mi, so he seems to have deliberately altered the image of Feng he presents in his poem. In so doing, Zuo is intentionally prioritizing the purposes of his narrative over the veracity of his account. Eventually, Zuo's depiction of Feng became more influential among later scholars and poets, and successfully supplanted the one found in the historical record.[51] Furthermore, Zuo's lamentation over the discrepancies between ability and status became an oft-quoted phrase, used to describe political inequities.

While Zuo's second "Poem on History" focuses on the unfair advantages conferred by family status, his seventh poem addresses the importance of opportunity. In this poem, Zuo explores four additional frustrated scholars who were eventually able to carve out roles for themselves in court and become well-known historical figures in history. These four great figures were eventually immortalized for posterity despite their initial difficulties, and Zuo hoped that history (or at least his future readers) would vindicate him as well:

VII[52]

	主父宦不達,	Zhufu was not successful in his quest to serve;
	骨肉還相薄.	His kin turned on him in disdain.[53]
	買臣困采樵,	Maichen was reduced to cutting timber;
4	伉儷不安宅.	His wife refused to live with him any longer.[54]
	陳平無產業,	Chen Ping did not have any property,
	歸來翳負郭.	He came home to shelter under the city walls.[55]
	長卿還成都,	Changqing went back to Chengdu;[56]
8	壁立何寥廓.	Nothing in the house but the bare walls.[57]
	四賢豈不偉?	How could these four virtuous men not be great?
	遺烈光篇籍.	Their legacy shines in the historical records.
	當其未遇時,	Before their day arrived,
12	憂在填溝壑.	They worried about being left in the ditch.[58]
	英雄有屯邅,	Heroes have difficulties and frustrations,
	由來自古昔.	It has been this way since ancient times.[59]
	何世無奇才?	Which generation does not have great talents?
16	遺之在草澤.	They are abandoned in fields of wild grass.

In this seventh poem, Zuo Si transplants these historical figures into a literary realm and transforms them into timeless cultural icons through which he could express his own views and emotions. Zuo Si mentions four historical figures from the Western Han dynasty: Zhufu Yan 主父偃 (fl. 127 BCE), Zhu Maichen 朱買臣 (fl. 115 BCE), Chen Ping 陳平 (fl. 178 BCE), and Sima Xiangru. Zuo does not provide a detailed biography of these figures, but instead highlights a few significant moments in their lives, distilling them into icons. In this poem, Zuo selected men who, like himself, were underappreciated scholars and officials whose lives were exceedingly difficult prior to the opportunities that changed their place in history. For instance, the first couplet refers to Zhufu Yan. Zhufu was well versed in military strategy, philosophy, and history, but he was continually pushed aside by rival scholars and so could not secure a political position in his own state:

He (Zhufu Yan) studied the diplomatic and military theories of the Warring States period, and in his later years he studied the *Book of Changes* (*Yijing* 易經), the *Spring and Autumn Annals* (*Chunqiu* 春秋), and the works of various philosophers. He traveled about among the scholars of Qi, but could find none who would treat him with any liberality. On the contrary, they refused to have anything to do with him, so that he could get nowhere in [his native] state of Qi.[60]

學長短縱橫之術, 晚乃學《易》、《春秋》、百家言. 游齊諸生間, 莫能厚遇也. 齊諸儒生相與排擯, 不容於齊.[61]

What was significant for Zuo Si was that each of these four great figures was able to overcome the obstacle of his obscure origins and develop his intellect, persevering until he was able to contribute greatly to society. As Sima Qian writes of another subject of Zuo's poem, Chen Ping:

He devised many ingenious plans to overcome difficulties and to save the state from danger. In the time of Empress Lü, although numerous troubles beset him, he not only succeeded in extricating himself, but secured the dynasty, so he died a dignitary and was known to posterity as an able minister. Truly, "a good beginning makes a good ending!"[62]

常出奇計, 救紛糾之難, 振國家之患. 及呂后時, 事多故矣, 然平竟自脫, 定宗廟, 以榮名終, 稱賢相, 豈不善始善終哉![63]

The moral of Sima Qian's story is that Chen Ping, in his wisdom, triumphed over his tribulations and ultimately gained the recognition he deserved. By contrast, Zuo Si does not emphasize these happy endings; rather, he stresses the troubles that they encountered before they were appreciated. The stories he tells of these four figures reflect his own life; though he had great talent, he felt both unappreciated and abandoned by the state, but he holds out hope that, through his poetry, he would eventually receive the recognition he felt he deserved. According to Gong Kechang 龔克昌, Zuo's situation was typical of his era: "The large families themselves distributed offices according to reputation and power. The Nine-Rank Gradation of the Six Dynasties period was based on this practice. Under the rule of these families, scholars of the lower class felt that it was even more difficult to obtain office."[64]

The last couplet poses a stinging final rhetorical question to imply that he, too, is one of those talented but unappreciated scholars. The four figures Zuo writes about were eventually offered the opportunity to shine; Zuo, however, is left to trudge along in obscurity, never fully realizing his visions of political influence or social affluence. In this way, Zuo's poetic persona becomes a fifth figure, joining the quartet of historical figures that are the subject of his poem.

Zuo Si explains in the second and seventh poems of his "Yongshi" that family background and opportunity were equally essential to a successful political career. Lacking both, however, he ultimately abandons the idealistic aspirations of his youth. In the sixth poem of the series, he vents his rage at the aristocratic and hierarchical social system of his time by commenting on the famous assassin Jing Ke 荊軻 (fl. 227 BCE):

VI[65]

	荊軻飲燕市,	Jing Ke drank in the Yan market,
	酒酣氣益振.	Intoxicated, his vigor was stirred even more.
	哀歌和漸離,	He sang sadly to accompany Jianli's playing,
4	謂若傍無人.	As if there were no one else around.
	雖無壯士節,	Though he was no principled hero,
	與世亦殊倫.	He was different from others in his time.
	高眄邈四海,	He surveyed the world haughtily from on high:
8	豪右何足陳?	Who deserved to be called noble?
	貴者雖自貴,	Though nobles thought highly of themselves,
	視之若埃塵.	He saw them as dust and dirt.
	賤者雖自賤,	Though inferiors saw themselves as inferior,
12	重之若千鈞.	He prized them as the most weighty.[66]

The three best-known accounts of Jing Ke's story are in *Strategies of the Warring States* (*Zhanguo ce* 戰國策), the *Shiji*, and *Master Dan of Yan* (*Yan Danzi* 燕丹子). The basic outline of the story is as follows. Jing Ke, a native of the state of Wei in the Warring States period, travels to the state of Yan. In the Yan marketplace, he demonstrates his unrestrained spirit to his musician friend Gao Jianli 高漸離 (fl. 226 BCE) and to a dog butcher. At that time, Yan was being threatened by the expanding Qin state, and the prince of Yan, hearing of Jing Ke's daring, recruits him to assassinate the Qin ruler. Jing Ke requests three gifts from the prince of Yan, which he could present to the king of Qin to prove his sincerity, allowing him to obtain a personal audience with the king. First, he asks for the head of General Fan Wuqi 樊於期 (d. 227 BCE), a traitor to Qin. Next, he requests a map of part of the territory of Yan—to present such a map to the king of Qin would signify the cession of that territory to Qin. Finally, he requests a poisonous dagger. With the first two gifts, he obtains a private audience with the king. In their private meeting, Jing unrolls the map, in which he has concealed the dagger, grabs the dagger, and tries to capture the king alive. He fails, is overcome, and in the end is executed.

Jing Ke's encounters with Gao Jianli and other friends in the Yan market are only narrated in the *Shiji*, not *Zhanguo ce* or *Yan Danzi*, so the *Shiji* is probably the primary inspiration for Zuo Si's poem. Zuo Si's characterization of Jing Ke in the first two couplets largely follows the *Shiji* account:

> Having reached Yan, Jing Ke became fond of a dog butcher and a skilled dulcimer player, Gao Jianli. Jing Ke was fond of wine, and every day he drank with the dog butcher and Gao Jianli in the marketplace of Yan. After they were well into their cups, Gao Jianli would strike his dulcimer and Jing Ke would sing in harmony in the middle of the marketplace. They would enjoy themselves, then after a while they would weep together, as if there was no one else around.[67]

> 荊軻既至燕，愛燕之狗屠及善擊筑者高漸離。荊軻嗜酒，日與狗屠及高漸離飲於燕市，酒酣以往，高漸離擊筑，荊軻和而歌於市中，相樂也，已而相泣，旁若無人者。[68]

The initial two couplets in this poem reiterate the words and images of the *Shiji*: "Jing Ke drank in the Yan market," "intoxicated," "as if there were no people around." However, the poet does not describe who Jing Ke and Gao Jianli are, or why Jing Ke travels to the Yan state, focusing on Jing Ke's drunkenness in the market to illustrate his unconventional disposition.

The rest of the poem expresses Zuo Si's emotions by commenting on Jing Ke's temperament. Zuo Si's understanding of Jing Ke's character is rooted in the evaluation provided by the *Shiji*:

> Although Jing Ke associated with drinkers, he was by nature recondite and fond of reading. In the [states of] the feudal lords to which he traveled, he established ties to all the worthy, powerful and respected men. When he went to Yan, Venerable

Tian Guang, a retired knight of Yan, treated him very well. [Tian] knew that he was not an average fellow.[69]

荊軻雖游於酒人乎, 然其爲人沈深好書; 其所游諸侯, 盡與其賢豪長者相結.其之燕, 燕之處士田光先生亦善待之, 知其非庸人也.[70]

Zuo Si concurs with Tian Guang's assessment—that Jing Ke was more than he appeared to be. The next three couplets expand on this theme. The fourth couplet is more general. It cites no specific events or details, but simply asserts Jing Ke's contempt for nobles and his heroic decorum. Zuo Si likely expected that the reader's prior knowledge of the Jing Ke story, and Jing Ke's exceptional courage and principle, would compensate for the poem's lack of specificity. Furthermore, by remaining somewhat vague, Zuo Si's poem encourages readers to reflect on the significance of the figure of Jing Ke for themselves, based on their own knowledge of him.

Zuo Si's praise for Jing Ke reaches a zenith in the last two couplets, which use a parallel structure to present Jing's contrasting attitudes for the noble and the poor. In the poem's telling, Jing Ke was neither intimidated by social elites, nor contemptuous of the poor and lowly. The *Shiji* notes that Jing Ke's companion, Qin Wuyang, trembled in the Qin court, while Jing Ke maintained his composure.[71] Jing Ke placed great value on the unyielding loyalty of the poor, as demonstrated by his admiration of lowly Gao Jianli in the Yan market. Jing Ke's admiration of Gao was warranted—after Jing Ke's death, Gao himself tried to assassinate the first emperor of the Qin in his honor, but also failed and was killed.[72] The readers' preconceptions of the famous Jing Ke lore, particularly the version conveyed by the *Shiji*, fill in the gaps left by Zuo Si's general praise. Zuo Si's confidence in the knowledge of his audience allows him to shift rapidly from narrative details to evaluative comments, from particular cases to universal characteristics.[73]

Zuo Si also makes the intriguing choice to highlight the moment when Jing Ke enjoyed his time with his friends in the Yan market, rather than the actual assassination attempt. As in previous poems, Zuo alters the biography of a historical figure to suit his purposes. The moment Zuo chooses vividly demonstrates Jing Ke's maverick behavior in challenging the status quo by associating himself with people at the bottom of the social hierarchy. Zuo does not explain why Jing Ke was so unconventional in his choice of friends, but readers can infer Zuo's subtext by reexamining the biography of Jing Ke: Gao Jianli's assassination attempt proved that Jing's faith in Gao's loyalty was indeed wise. Zuo therefore highlights the moral dimension of Jing Ke's preference for the lowly over the noble.[74] Through commenting on Jing Ke, Zuo Si launches an implicit criticism against the hereditary system in place during his own time, centuries later. Although Zuo lauds and mirrors Jing Ke's attitudes, consistently championing the talented poor and opposing the mainstream hierarchical culture of his time in his poetry, during his life he frequently partnered with and worked for the very aristocratic families he vehemently criticizes. When he was young, the ambitious Zuo sought patronage by joining Zhang Hua's circle. He later became a member of Jia Mi's "Twenty-Four Friends." Both groups were not only literary communities but also elite political alliances. Zuo likely joined Jia's circle to further his own political career.

How can readers reconcile this seeming contradiction? Zuo Si's life was deeply affected by politics and court intrigue. Because of Emperor Hui's 惠帝 (r. 291–306) inability to manage the court, his wife, Empress Jia 賈后 (257–300), took control, purging her opponents. Members of her clan became increasingly powerful, especially her nephew Jia Mi. As Michael Farmer observes,

> The empress's nephew, Jia Mi, was given free rein at court, and officials personally loyal to the empress were placed in charge of governmental affairs. Later historians view the nine years of the empress's control of the Jin court as a virtual reign of terror, describing her with terms such as "jealous, vindictive, cruel, and murderous."[75]

This was the environment in which Zuo sought to succeed and survive. To this end, he developed a deep personal relationship with Jia Mi. The *Jinshu* notes that "Jia Mi appointed Zuo Si to lecture on the *Hanshu*."[76] 祕書監賈謐請講漢書.[77] It would be advantageous for Zuo's career to develop relationships with the elite scholars of his day, but he became profoundly disillusioned by the ostentatious luxury and complicated political struggles of Jia Mi's circle. Zuo's eight "Yongshi" poems place him firmly in the camp of the talented poor, in opposition to the corrupt aristocracy.[78]

Paths Forward for Unappreciated Scholars

With the collapse of his political endeavors, Zuo explored ways in which an unappreciated scholar such as himself could at least achieve literary immortality. In the fourth poem of his "Yongshi," Zuo models himself after the Han dynasty figure Yang Xiong 揚雄 (53 BCE–18 CE):

IV[79]

	濟濟京城內,	How dense and magnificent it is inside the capital,[80]
	赫赫王侯居.	Impressive princes and marquises dwell within.[81]
	冠蓋蔭四術,	Carriage canopies shade the roads in all directions,[82]
4	朱輪竟長衢.	Vermilion wheels fill the long thoroughfares.
	朝集金張館,	At dawn they gather in the Jin and Zhang mansions.
	暮宿許史廬.	At dusk they sleep in the Xu and Shi[83] villas.
	南鄰擊鐘磬,	In the southern district, they beat chimes and bells.
8	北里吹笙竽.	In the northern alley, they blow reeds and wooden pipes.[84]
	寂寂楊子宅,	How quiet and silent Master Yang's residence was!
	門無卿相輿.	No high officials' carriages stopped at his home.[85]
	寥寥空宇中,	Isolated and lonely, he remained in his empty house.[86]
12	所講在玄虛.	What he taught was shrouded in *Mystery*.[87]
	言論準宣尼,	In his speech, he regarded Confucius as the standard.[88]
	辭賦擬相如.	In his rhapsodies, he imitated Sima Xiangru.[89]
	悠悠百世後,	Even after a hundred generations have passed by,
16	英名擅八區.	His illustrious fame occupies the whole world.

Based on the content of the poem, it is possible that it was composed after Zuo Si moved to the capital and saw how the elites lived. The first two couplets provide a general panorama of the bustling atmosphere and magnificent mansions of the capital, while the third and fourth couplets zoom in and focus on the luxurious lifestyles of the wealthy city-dwellers, which entailed extensive politicking and impressive musical performances in sprawling villas. This hustle and bustle in the city acts as a foil to Yang Xiong's situation in the following couplets. In contrast to the homes of the wealthy, Yang's home is seldom visited. Yet this does not mean he was isolated; in fact, he had plenty of disciples, but they were not drawn from the ranks of the elite. Furthermore, Zuo highlights that Yang saw Confucius and Sima Xiangru as his role models, implying that a good scholar and writer not only should hold high moral values (i.e., Confucius) but also possess outstanding literary skills (i.e., Sima Xiangru), often exemplified in ancient paragons. Although Yang was not "successful" in his lifetime in terms of his worldly possessions, his fame as a scholar grew and lasted long after his death, as evidenced by Zuo Si's poem, which was written centuries later. By contrast, many of those nobles who obtained wealth, power, and fame in their lifetime have long since been forgotten.

Naturally, as someone who had failed to gain respect in his lifetime, Zuo Si chose to employ allusions to Yang Xiong in his poem in the hope that future readers would remember his virtue and talent, just as other great historical figures, such as Yang, were posthumously revered (who himself revered paragons of the past).[90] Zuo also attempts to persuade his readers of his own worthiness by demonstrating his long-held ideals through devotion to these historical figures. When Zuo "sings" (*yong* 詠) Yang's praises, he is also simultaneously comforting and praising himself. The two figures shared many similarities in terms of disposition and values. Yang, for his part, was not involved in much court intrigue as far as we know. He participated in politics, but in his later years preferred solitude, and retired to focus on cultivating his morality and literary talent. Although Yang was poor in his lifetime, his philosophical and literary writings have been passed down for generations. Yang's works transcend time and space, whereas the actions of fame-obsessed officials are ephemeral; words have been preserved and transmitted, whereas the memory of deeds has eroded. In a similar fashion, although Zuo sought to serve the country as a young man, after years of political struggle, he felt underappreciated and eventually abandoned his ideals due to the toxic political environment. Like Yang, Zuo escaped the political rat race in his later years and focused on reading ancient documents and writing down his thoughts.

In addition to having a similar worldview and similar life pursuits, Zuo Si and Yang Xiong had high standards in their writing. Both sought to imitate Sima Xiangru's rhapsodies, wrote rhapsodies on the subject of capitals, and composed rhapsodies that became well known. Zuo was, of course, aware of Yang's famous "Rhapsody on the Shu Capital" ("Shudu fu" 蜀都賦). Recent scholars have acknowledged Yang's contribution to this literary genre. According to David Knechtges, "Yang Xiong was the first to move from description of the imperial hunting party to description of a particular place. He wrote the first piece in Chinese literary history on a regional capital—the 'Shu Capital.' Ban Gu, Zhang Heng, and Zuo Si all were inspired by this rhapsody."[91] Zuo so admired Yang that he quoted Yang's comments on poetic principles and the origins of the *fu* (rhapsody) genre in his preface to "Sandu fu."[92] Zuo was following Yang's example in writing a rhapsody on the Shu capital.

The two men shared not only similar life values and approaches to literary creation but physical traits as well. Both Yang and Zuo were homely and stuttered, defects of which they were acutely aware. In a society that emphasized comportment and speech in its educated men, Yang and Zuo both knew that they were likely to be unappreciated in their own time, so they sought to cultivate their talent as writers. It seemed that Zuo saw his literary talent as compensation for his physical shortcomings and as a way to achieve success—if not in the short term in the political arena, at least for the long term in the literary canon. For this reason, Yang was an ideal model, and became a potent emblem of the power and endurance of a literary reputation. The image of Yang Xiong shaped by Zuo Si—talented, dedicated, destined for future greatness, but poor and unappreciated in his own time—also influenced later writings. Zhang Zhengjian 張正見 (ca. 528–ca. 576) imitated Zuo's fourth "Yongshi" in writing a poem in praise of Yang Xiong, "On [Zuo Si's] Poem on the Frustrated Scholar in the Poor Alleyways" ("Fu de luoluo qiongxiang shi shi" 賦得落落窮巷士詩).[93]

Zuo Si positioned Yang Xiong as a figure who was not recognized by his contemporaries but became famous posthumously. And by comparing himself to Yang, Zuo tacitly implies that his own talents are on par with those of Yang and should be appreciated by future readers. Also following in the footsteps of Yang, Zuo realized that he did not belong in the social environment in the capital and made the important decision to leave. In his fifth poem, he contrasts himself with the noble families he left behind:

V[94]

	皓天舒白日，	The bright sky unfurls the white sun,
	靈景耀神州。	The sunlight shines on the divine state.
	列宅紫宮裏，	An array of residences in the Purple Palace,[95]
4	飛宇若雲浮。	Flying eaves are like floating clouds.
	峨峨高門內，	Tall and high, behind the imposing gates,
	藹藹皆王侯。	Numerous and vast, all belong to nobility.
	自非攀龍客，	I am not a dragon-mounted guest.[96]
8	何爲欻來遊？	Why have I suddenly come here to travel?
	被褐出閶闔，	Clothed as a commoner, I go out the palace gate,[97]
	高步追許由。	With long strides, I pursue Xu You.[98]
	振衣千仞崗，	I shake out my clothes on the steep cliff edge.[99]
12	濯足萬里流。	I bathe my feet in the long flowing river.[100]

Whereas the previous poem emphasizes literary creation as a route toward achieving posthumous fame, this poem advocates one's moral value, exploring the possibility of living the life of a recluse. The first three couplets are stylistically similar to the poem on Yang Xiong, offering a broad view of the city to depict its stunning grandeur. The poem then describes the palaces, mansions, and residences of high-ranking officials as a way to convey the luxurious lifestyle in the capital. This glorious and glamorous scene creates an enormous contrast to Zuo Si's conditions.

In the fourth couplet (l. 7–8), Zuo enters the poem, this time by employing the self-reflexive *zi* 自 (I myself). Here, he openly questions his original intentions and expresses regret over his past behavior—perhaps including his attempts to seek patronage. This couplet is a kind of confession. Zuo admits that he no longer fits in with the culture in the capital. Eventually, his attempts at gaining entry to court politics thwarted, he decides to leave.

In the last two couplets, Zuo Si expresses his desire to follow in the footsteps of the recluse Xu You 許由, a paragon of principle in the Chinese cultural imagination by the time of the Western Jin. Zuo claims that he no longer desires to pursue fame or power, as the seemingly glamorous contemporary world is merely an unremitting scramble for success. Qu Yuan 屈原 (ca. 340–278 BCE) purportedly once said of his own departure that it was "[b]ecause all the world is muddy and I alone am clear, and because all men are drunk and I alone am sober."[101] 舉世皆濁我獨清, 眾人皆醉我獨醒.[102] After living in the chaotic, hurly-burly capital city, Zuo was similarly disillusioned with official life and sought tranquility. This decision was inspired in part by Daoism, which advocates withdrawing from the struggles of the political world to embrace a harmonious relationship with nature. He uses the allusion to Xu You, a figure who straddles the indistinct line between myth and history, to create his own living legend.

Zuo had come close to achieving the high ambitions he expressed in his first "Yongshi," when his sister Zuo Fen 左棻 (ca. 253–300) was chosen to become Emperor Wu of Jin's 晉武帝 (r. 265–290) concubine and his whole family moved to the capital.[103] Unfortunately for Zuo Si, his sister was not summoned for her beauty but for her literary talents, and once installed in the rear palace, the homely Zuo Fen was unable to win the emperor's favor and provide Zuo Si with any substantial assistance. After encountering difficulties and frustrations, he eventually abandoned his political aspirations: "I am not a dragon-mounted guest, / Why have I suddenly come here to travel?" 自非攀龍客. 何爲欻來遊?[104] While the first poem describes the ambitions of his youth, the fifth poem allows him to confess in his old age—before it is too late—that he is not cut out for political life. Whether Zuo Si wrote the poems periodically as he aged or all at once as he looked back on his life (or perhaps some combination thereof), poetry served as a way for him to work out the tensions between life's practicalities and his own exacting ideals. Zuo found solace in the stories of these historical figures after he failed to succeed in the political arena.

After stepping outside the capital and expressing his own frustration by writing about various historical figures, Zuo Si, in the final poem of the series, reiterates his belief that unappreciated scholars can build themselves a legacy by living a reclusive life. To this end, he investigates one of life's ironies: those who openly seek fame and power often die prematurely attempting to obtain them, while those who seek to transcend fame and greed are eternally remembered for their virtues by later generations and achieve lasting glory. It is this sort of fame, Zuo Si asserts, that true scholars pursue:

VIII[105]

	習習籠中鳥，	Fluttering, flapping, a bird within a cage,
	舉翮觸四隅。	Beats its wings and touches the four corners.
	落落窮巷士，	The frustrated scholar in the poor alley,
4	抱影守空廬。	Embraces his shadow and guards an empty hut.
	出門無通路，	He goes outside but finds no way forward,
	枳棘塞中塗。	Thorny trees block his road.[106]
	計策棄不收，	His plans and strategies are rejected.
8	塊若枯池魚。	His lonely appearance, like a fish in a dried-up pool.
	外望無寸祿，	Gazing outside, there is not the slightest income,
	內顧無斗儲。	Looking back, there is not even a peck of rice.
	親戚還相蔑，	Relatives turn their backs in disdain,
12	朋友日夜疏。	Friends become more distant each passing day.
	蘇秦北遊說，	Su Qin traveled north to spread his teachings,[107]
	李斯西上書。	Li Si submitted his memorial in the west.[108]
	俛仰生榮華，	A nod of their heads produced honor and glory,
16	咄嗟復彫枯。	Yet within a breath, they withered and died.
	飲河期滿腹，	In drinking from a river, expect only to fill your belly,[109]
	貴足不願餘。	Cherish sufficiency, and do not long for more.
	巢林棲一枝，	Make a nest in the woods to roost on a single tree branch:
20	可爲達士模。	This can be a model for all enlightened scholars.

In this poem, Zuo highlights the importance of achieving contentment. At the beginning of the poem, he discusses the physical and spiritual difficulties that scholars who cannot find political (and therefore financial) success encounter: challenging living conditions, the contempt or indifference of their relatives. This vivid picture echoes his seventh poem on the four worthies. In this poem, Zuo offers Su Qin 蘇秦 (d. 284 BCE) and Li Si 李斯 (284–208 BCE), historical figures who rapidly ascended to powerful positions but just as quickly met their demise, as a contrast to those talented men who were blocked from success. The account of Li Si in the *Shiji* illustrates this point well:

> Beginning in a simple hamlet, Li Si traveled among the feudal lords, then came to serve Qin. "Seizing flaws and faults" was how he assisted the First Emperor in completing His imperial enterprise, and thus became one of his "Three Dukes." He can be said to have been put to an exalted use indeed. . . . In the seventh month of the second year of the Second Emperor (208 BCE), it was proclaimed that [Li] Si should be sentenced to the five punishments and cut in half at the waist in the marketplace of Xianyang. . . . His clan was exterminated to the third degree [of relationship].[110]
>
> 李斯以閭閻歷諸侯, 入事秦, 因以瑕釁, 以輔始皇, 卒成帝業, 斯爲三公, 可謂尊用矣……二世二年七月, 具斯五刑, 論腰斬咸陽市……而夷三族。[111]

Zuo Si uses Li Si's life to make an insightful comment: life, as a rule, is volatile and often violent. Not only is Li Si's life a useful embodiment of the moral lesson Zuo wishes to impart, but alluding to Su Qin and Li Si allowed Zuo Si to protect himself politically. Zuo Si knew all too well that princes in different parts of the empire were jockeying for power and that these power struggles could turn deadly—many of his friends and superiors had died as a result of political coups. Zuo did not want to become one of them. To avoid offending powerful people, he chose to express his resentment towards his own society and life by commenting on historical events and historical personages. He tempered his passionate response to the world around him with these ancient allusions.

In this last poem, Zuo offers an alternative to the desperate struggle for worldly power, suggesting that enlightened scholars should not eagerly seek fame and reputation because these are states subject to sudden, even violent, change. Rather than emulate "successful" politicians such as Su Qin and Li Si, Zuo argues that one should instead behave like the mole and the wren, as depicted in the *Zhuangzi* 莊子, because they only value self-sufficiency and do not yearn for more than they need. Thus, the eighth poem not only criticizes the strict hierarchical society of the Western Jin, but also suggests a way for the talented poor to survive changing times. This mentality is a reflection of the broader social zeitgeist after the fall of the Han dynasty. The disintegration and instability of the empire led to mass migrations of the elite population and deprived many of the protection of a close kinship network. In this situation, as far as Zuo Si was concerned, the talented poor might have been better served by following a path of reclusion and self-reliance—as Zuo Si did after his supporters, such as Jia Mi and Zhang Hua, were killed in 300.[112] Zuo Si retired to concentrate on reading and writing about classical books and documents. The Prince of Qi, Sima Jiong 司馬冏 (d. 302), offered him a position as his secretary, but Zuo did not accept the post. When the forces of Zhang Fang 張方 raided the capital in 302, Zuo Si and his family fled to Jizhou 冀州 (in modern Hebei Province), where he died a few years later of an unspecified illness.[113]

Conclusion

In discussing the doctrine of "seeking out likeminded men in the past" 尚友, Mencius said,

> That scholar, whose goodness is most outstanding in the village, will become a friend to all the good scholars of the village. That scholar, whose goodness is most outstanding in the state, will become a friend to all the good scholars of the state. That scholar, whose goodness is the most outstanding in the world, will become a friend to all the good scholars of the world. When he feels that being a friend of all the good scholars of the world is not enough, he will go back in time to consider the people of antiquity, repeating their poems and reading their books. Not knowing what they were like as persons, he considers what they were like in their own time. This is to go back in time and make friends.[114]

> 一鄉之善士斯友一鄉之善士，一國之善士斯友一國之善士，天下之善士斯友天下之善士。以友天下之善士爲未足，又尚論古之人，頌其詩，讀其書，不知其人可乎？是以論其世也。是尚友也。[115]

The passage from the *Mencius* tells readers that one should make friends with people at the same level. However, if befriending all the good people in the world is not enough, one should seek friends from ancient times. In Zuo Si's "Yongshi," he passes over his contemporaries and goes directly to commune with ancient figures to express his ideals and concerns.

This chapter investigates how Zuo Si made full (and often free) use of historical figures to help embellish his own biography and to shape his reputation in his eight "Yongshi." By comparing his deeds and ambitions favorably with those of historical figures, these poems elevate Zuo's status and provide the enduring means through which he can disseminate his ideas, present his ideal self, and influence the later reception of his image and literary works. He seemed to expect that his readers would share the traditional notion of a poem as an authentic, transparent, and trustworthy representation of the self, and would therefore receive the poems as the reflection of his life and values.

Zuo Si makes an interesting case study, as he adopts three major ways to engage in retrospective memory to secure his reputation through *yongshi shi*. First, Zuo depicts himself as having lofty visions to assure later readers that his actions stem from virtuous motivations. These visions include indifference towards material well-being and freedom from the desire to seek fame, qualities exemplified by figures such as Xu You, Lu Zhonglian, and Yang Xiong. Zuo Si's poems on abandoning fame help these historical figures to be remembered in the long view of history, even if they were not celebrated in their own times. But in commemorating the virtues of these figures, Zuo is also indicating to readers that he has similar characteristics and should be compared favorably to them (and remembered alongside them). Being remembered by future generations is a just compensation for the poet's failure to achieve immediate fame in his own lifetime.

The second way that Zuo Si engages in retrospective memory is to emphasize his abilities as being comparable to those of historical figures, and to demonstrate that his case of not being able to employ them adequately is not unique in history. He, as with his predecessors, was capable of handling important missions but was not given an opportunity to extend his talents due to the chaos of society or to intense factional struggles. For instance, in Zuo's second and fourth "Yongshi," Feng Tang and Yang Xiong are cited as figures who were not recognized by their contemporaries but became famous posthumously. When Zuo Si invokes their names and describes their situations, it becomes a strategy of veiled criticism towards his own society. Because these historical figures were praised and remembered after their lifetimes (partly in Zuo's own poetry), Zuo is tacitly indicating his belief that his case should be the same, and that his talents would be appreciated among his ultimate literary readership, if not among his immediate political contemporaries.

The third and final rhetorical gesture that Zuo Si makes in his "Yongshi" is irony: common tropes include the idea that those, such as Su Qin and Zhang Yi, who nakedly aspire to fame and power live short lives and die attempting to obtain glory, while those, such as Xu You and Lu Zhonglian, who seek to transcend fame and greed reap the highest honor of being permanently remembered by later generations for their virtue. Being remembered by future generations appealed to the poet more than immediate fame because he observed that one can become well known quickly, but not without consequences. Only through good virtues and moral values (and talented writing) can one be remembered forever without threat to one's life in the short term.

The self-narrative Zuo Si presents is a journey from youthful ambitions to eventual disillusionment. He gives us a condensed version of his life by recounting the fate of all educated men who had political ambitions but not the resources or connections to achieve them: after years of struggle, they gradually come to doubt the feasibility of their lofty aspirations and realize that the social hierarchy and lack of opportunity will forever bar them from achieving their goals.[116] Zuo creates a stark contrast between youthful idealism and adult realism. By expressing his intentions and frustrations through allusions and other rhetorical devices in these eight poems, he tries to persuade his readers that his motivation for seeking political patronage was not fame or power but the desire to use his talent to serve the country. After failing to achieve political success, Zuo settled for conveying his ambitions and ideals to later generations through commenting on historical figures. Ultimately, through his "Yongshi," he succeeded in crafting a self-image comparable to that of those figures and thereby was successful in his self-idealization and self-promotion.

Zuo Si's innovative use of the word "I" and occasional explicit self-references tell readers that the real intention in writing poems about other historical figures is to establish an ideal poetic self. Zuo's use of historical allusions to express his emotions allows him to assume an air of modesty and to lend his feelings legitimacy by linking them to admired figures in history. Zuo's "Yongshi" reflects the different stages of his life. In his youth, he modeled his writings after those of Confucius and Sima Xiangru, and studied the military strategies of Sima Rangju, with the goal of serving his state. After encountering political obstacles, he took Xu You and Yang Xiong as exemplars of a reclusive life that avoided the miseries of politics. He situated himself in the company of these outstanding figures, using the medium of poetry to transcend the bounds of time and space and connect with them spiritually. By the end of the "Yongshi," the extended and enduring fame of literature has gained more appeal for Zuo Si than political success, which eluded him all his life and proved dangerous for those of his friends who had achieved it. Thus, Zuo urges us to aim for loftier goals. Only by cultivating and practicing virtue—and expressing it in an enduring literary form—can one be forever remembered. In so doing, Zuo Si laid a solid foundation for his future reception.

Chapter 3

Prospective Memory and the Reception of Zuo Si's "Yongshi" in Early Medieval China

The previous chapter examined how Zuo Si used retrospective memory to strategically associate himself with historical figures, and to establish a lineage including Zuo himself, paving the way for the future reception of his poems. This chapter will seek to establish whether his efforts were effective in shaping the prospective memory of his poems.[1]

There has been extensive research into early medieval Chinese writers influenced by Zuo's "Yongshi," such as Zhang Xie 張協 (d. ca. 307), Liu Kun 劉琨 (271–318), Guo Pu 郭璞 (276–324), and Yuan Hong 袁宏 (ca. 328–ca. 376).[2] These writers' use of parallelism and comparison, sentence structure, and passionate literary style are strikingly similar to Zuo's work, although there is no direct intertextual evidence to confirm Zuo's influence. Zuo's "Yongshi" had a more direct influence over writings by Tao Yuanming 陶淵明 (ca. 365–427), Xie Lingyun 謝靈運 (385–433), Bao Zhao 鮑照 (ca. 414–466), and Jiang Yan 江淹 (444–505).[3] Tao's, Xie's, and Bao's relationship to Zuo's work have all received critical attention. Kōzen Hiroshi notes that Tao's "Poems on Impoverished Scholars" ("Yong pinshi" 詠貧士), as with Zuo's "Yongshi," select and praise impoverished scholars who held steadfast to their moral principles. There are also structural similarities—both works are series of poems where the first poem(s) serve as an introduction to the entire series.[4] Xu Chuanwu concurs with Kōzen, and points out that Zhong Rong, in *The Gradations of Poets* (*Shipin* 詩品), explicitly mentions a link between the two writers. Zuo and Tao both broke away from their contemporary societies to become recluses, and both adopted a passionate, unrestrained style in their poems on history.[5]

Because Zhong Rong quoted Xie Lingyun's effusive praise of Zuo and placed both in the top rank in *Shipin*, Xie and Zuo are linked.⁶ Xie famously stated that Zuo Si's and Pan Yue's 潘岳 (247–300) poems are almost without parallel in the past and present.⁷ Xie's "Poem on Narrating Ancestor's Virtues" ("Shu zude shi" 述祖德詩) borrows allusions from and directly quotes from Zuo's third "Yongshi" poem, also emphasizing the virtue of forgoing fame and reputation once one has achieved one's goals.

Zuo's influence on Bao Zhao's poems on historical themes is particularly clear, and has been discussed by Ming and Qing dynasty critics, such as Hu Yinglin 胡應麟 (1551–1602), Chen Zuoming 陳祚明 (1623–1674), He Zhuo 何焯 (1661–1722), and Shen Deqian 沈德潛 (1673–1769).⁸ More recently, Xu Chuanwu and Kōzen Hiroshi have pointed out that Bao's affinity for Zuo was likely rooted in their similar background and life experience.⁹ Zuo's influence can be seen in the second and third of Bao's "Imitating Ancient Poems" ("Nigu" 擬古).¹⁰ Bao also adopted Zuo's vigorous literary style for his own *yongshi shi*.¹¹ Bao's poem on Yan Junping 嚴君平 (86 BCE–10 CE), for example, shares the themes, structure, and diction of Zuo's fourth *yongshi* poem. Each poem contrasts a man who cultivated his character in reclusion, Yan Junping and Yang Xiong 揚雄 (53 BCE–18 CE), respectively, with scholars and noble men in the capital who eagerly pursued fame and reputation.¹² All of the historical figures Bao discusses in his poem on the four worthies of Shu were mentioned in Zuo's rhapsody on the Shu region, further suggesting that Zuo's works directly influenced Bao's.

This chapter does not aim to examine every single instance in which Zuo's "Yongshi" was cited or commented upon in early medieval China, but will instead focus on a few significant cases, approaching them from a new perspective: three levels of literary and cultural reception of Zuo's poems, demonstrating how readers imitated, evaluated, and responded to his "Yongshi" in early medieval China.

The first level is the intertextual links between Zuo Si's "Yongshi" and other poems in the early medieval period, focusing on the case of Jiang Yan's "Poems of Various Forms" ("Zati shi" 雜體詩). The influence of Zuo's "Yongshi" poems on Jiang Yan was just as profound as it was for other poets, such as Bao Zhao and Tao Yuanming, but Zuo's influence on Jiang has been far less studied. Current studies on this poem have largely agreed that Jiang's imitation of Zuo was unsuccessful. This chapter will reconsider this argument by providing a new reading of Jiang's imitation of Zuo's "Yongshi" poems, critically engaging in discussing the similarities and differences between Jiang's imitation and Zuo's original "Yongshi" to reveal the significance of

Jiang's imitation.¹³ Expanding our critical lens even further, Zuo Si's poems are also assessed by early medieval works of literary criticism, most notably *Literary Mind and Carving of Dragons* (*Wenxin diaolong* 文心雕龍) and *Shipin*. This chapter builds on earlier scholarship of Liu Xie and Zhong Rong's comments on Zuo's poems, particularly his "Yongshi," by providing a close reading of their literary evaluation. This close reading allows for a correction of previous misunderstandings of Zhong Rong's comments, and reconciles a seemingly contradictory comment on Zuo Si's poetry. And beyond the evaluations of these critics, an analysis of the reception of Zuo's "Yongshi" should examine how these poems were used by the educated elite in other forms of discourse, as represented in narratives in anecdotal collections or standard histories, such as the *History of the Northern Dynasties* (*Beishi* 北史). The anecdote from the *Beishi* has been rarely brought up for discussion in studies of the reception of Zuo's "Yongshi."

Jiang Yan's Imitation of Zuo Si's "Yongshi"¹⁴

The earliest extant imitations of Zuo's "Yongshi" were composed by Jiang Yan, a famous writer and an important official in the Song (420–479), Qi (479–502), and Liang (502–557) dynasties. At the end of the fifth century, he composed a series of poems imitating thirty representative poets. His models range from the anonymous authors of ancient "old style" poems to his contemporaries.¹⁵ According to the scholar Cao Daoheng 曹道衡 (1928–2005), this series of poems was composed in Jiang's later years, when he was employed by Xiao Ze 蕭賾 (440–493) and promoted to a high position.¹⁶ In Jiang's preface to his poems, he explains that his motivation for imitating others' poems was to provide exemplars of proper style to contrast with the poor literary taste of his own time, in which "each is mired in what beguiles his fancy, yet all favor the sweet and shun the bitter, love the cinnabar red and reject the plain white."¹⁷ 各滯所迷，莫不論甘而忌辛，好丹而非素。¹⁸ Specifically, Jiang criticizes his contemporaries for neglecting plain but worthy literary styles in favor of superficially attractive ones. He also notes a tendency to "value the previous poets and despise the current ones."¹⁹ 貴遠賤近。²⁰ Jiang argued for a more realistic and independent standard for evaluating poems rather than simplistic veneration of the ancients.

Jiang believed that there should be no critical bias in favor of poets from previous eras over contemporary poets, because the styles of different eras and regions each "have their own merits and advantages."²¹ 各具美兼

善.²² Jiang wanted to provide examples of a diverse range of worthy writing styles for pentasyllabic poetry across the literary tradition. The poets he selected to imitate were poets he felt wrote in an ideal literary style. Because he was a senior official, Jiang's opinions held greater authority among his scholar-official peers.

Imitation poetry was already a well-established subgenre in early medieval China.²³ Jiang Yan's imitation of the subgenre of *yongshi shi* is entitled "Record Keeper Zuo Si's Poems on History" ("Zuo jishi Si yongshi" 左記室思詠史).²⁴ Although Jiang did not directly comment on Zuo's poems, his explicit reference to them in the title indicates that he holds up Zuo's "Yongshi" as the representative of the *yongshi* subgenre.

左記室思詠史
Record Keeper Zuo Si's Poems on History[25]

	韓公淪賣藥，	Sir Han sank to selling medicine,[26]
	梅生隱市門．	Mr. Mei hid at the city gate.[27]
	百年信荏苒，	Their lives passed by quickly,
4	何爲苦心魂．	Why were their hearts and spirits so embittered?
	當學衛霍將，	One should study Generals Wei and Huo,
	建功在河源．	and complete a grand work at the head of the Yellow River.[28]
	珪組賢君眄，	Jade tablets and silk bands show the regard of the worthy ruler.
8	青紫明主恩．	Green and purple sashes demonstrate the kindness of the enlightened lord.
	終軍才始達，	Zhong Jun's talent had just begun to be realized.[29]
	賈誼位方尊．	Jia Yi's rank had only just become respected.[30]
	金張服貂冕，	Jin and Zhang wore marten caps.
12	許史乘華軒．	Xu and Shi rode in magnificent carriages.[31]
	王侯貴片議，	Princes and marquises were ennobled for the slightest suggestion,[32]
	公卿重一言．	Dukes and earls were esteemed because of a single word.[33]
	太平多歡娛，	Great peace comes with much happiness and pleasure.
16	飛蓋東都門．	Carriages with flying awnings at the capital's Eastern Gate.
	顧念張仲蔚，	I cast my thoughts back to Zhang Zhongwei,
	蓬蒿滿中園．	His garden was full of wild grass.[34]

Unusually, both for imitation poems as a genre and for Jiang's imitation poems, there are several significant differences between Jiang's imitation and Zuo's original model. Some scholars, such as Cao Daoheng 曹道衡, consider Jiang's imitation of Zuo's poem unsuccessful—in terms of aesthetics, content, and style—for this very reason.[35] Xu Chuanwu argues that the divergence between the two poems is explained by the significant differences between Jiang and Zuo's life experiences, official careers, thoughts, life goals, and ideals. In his imitation poem, Jiang expresses his desire to accomplish great deeds for the purpose of enjoying a good life—a stark contrast to Zuo's reclusive aversion to fame. Zuo admires and identifies with poor scholars, while Jiang merely pities them.[36] Nicholas Williams points out that "Zuo Si normally balances his treatment of historical figures with another contrasting theme," focusing on a limited number of historical figures, while "Jiang Yan's poem is laden with far more historical figures and lacking in natural imagery," packing more than a dozen figures into a single poem.[37] Therefore, Williams argues, "the imitation resembles its sources more than the sources themselves, because it is an amplification and intensification of certain features of its models."[38] With the stark contrast between these two poems in mind, this section will nevertheless stress Jiang's imitation of the overall theme and style of Zuo's original poems.

Jiang's imitation of Zuo's "Yongshi" uses linguistic and stylistic allusions to Zuo's work. The direct intertextual link between Zuo and Jiang's poems lies in lines eleven and twelve, which, similar to Zuo's second and fourth poems, allude to the Jin, Zhang, Xu, and Shi clans: "The Jin and Zhang relied on the legacy of their ancestors, / Seven generations wore the sables of Han." 金張藉舊業/七葉珥漢貂[39] and "At dawn they gather in Jin and Zhang's mansions, / At dusk they sleep in Xu and Shi's villas." 朝集金張館/暮宿許史廬.[40] These affluent members of the nobility ascended to high positions and held them for a long time because of their eminent family backgrounds. The Jin and Zhang enjoyed hereditary positions, and the Xu and Shi were the emperor's relatives. A critique of social injustice was an important theme of Zuo's "Yongshi."

Along with borrowing words and images directly, Jiang's poem imitates the style and theme of Zuo's "Yongshi." As with Zuo's eight poems, Jiang discusses changing attitudes towards fame and reputation, argues for meritocracy, and points to historical circumstances and family background as the key to political success in a hierarchical society. Jiang echoed the essential message of Zuo's poetry in his own poem because he found himself entangled in similarly complex court politics. Jiang examines past figures and their lessons, concluding, as Zuo did, that it is best to stay away from politics and enjoy one's life.

Jiang's imitation grasps the stages in the development of Zuo's attitudes toward life that are captured in Zuo's eight "Yongshi." The first four couplets encourage people to make contributions to the nation. However, couplets five and six focus on historical circumstances that harm one's political endeavors. John Marney tries to explain this contrast by arguing that the middle part of the poem should be considered "satirical—life is short, so why vex one's spirit on vanity."[41] Marney's interpretation is plausible, but it should be pointed out that this shift also reflects Zuo's original poems. This seeming contradiction relates to the arc of Zuo's life as related in his "Yongshi." The first of Zuo's poems describes his youthful ambitions: "Looking to the left, I would pacify the region of the Yangtze and Xiang Rivers, / Glaring to the right, I would subdue the Qiang and Xiongnu." 左眄澄江湘/右盻定羌胡.[42] The fifth poem describes how Zuo abandons his political aspirations after encountering many frustrations: "I am not a dragon-mounted guest, / Why have I suddenly come here to travel?" 自非攀龍客/何爲欻來遊.[43] Jiang condenses this arc into a few couplets. Young people, seeking to achieve great political accomplishments, model themselves after Generals Wei Qing 衛青 (d. 106 BCE) and Huo Qubing 霍去病 (140–117 BCE). After years of experiences and struggle, they gradually come to doubt the feasibility of their lofty aspirations.[44] Jiang imitates the contrast Zuo sets up between youthful idealism and mature realism.

Both Zuo and Jiang focus on the uncertainties inherent in political endeavors. Jiang employs the examples of Zhong Jun 終軍 (ca. 133–112 BCE) and Jia Yi, who died almost as soon as they achieved success, in lines nine and ten. Jiang was intimately familiar with the deadly risks of engaging in politics, living as he did in a tumultuous society. Given his own experience, it was natural that he would express his concerns over the dangers of political struggles. Jiang therefore ends his poem with a reference to Zhang Zhongwei, who, despite his talent, retired to a reclusive life on principle. These two lines of Jiang's imitation poem are not directly borrowed from Zuo Si's poems, but echo the message of his eighth poem on history.

Zuo expresses his worries about political uncertainties by commenting on Su Qin 蘇秦 (d. 284 BCE) and Li Si 李斯 (284–208 BCE), both of whom obtained and lost power quickly. I provide the relevant part of the eighth "Yongshi" poem below:

> Su Qin traveled north to spread his teachings,
> Li Si submitted his memorial in the west.
> A nod of their heads produced honor and glory,
> Yet within a breath, they withered and died.
> In drinking from a river, expect only to fill your belly,
> Cherish sufficiency, and do not long for more.
> Make a nest in the woods to roost on a single tree branch:
> This can be a model for all enlightened scholars.⁴⁵

Zuo suggests that one should not invest in mercurial fame, but instead be like the proverbial mole and wren in the *Zhuangzi*, and value self-sufficiency above all. Both Zuo and Jiang argue that people should cherish their lives and avoid the dangers of politics.

Zuo's and Jiang's poems both highlight the critical role that historical circumstances play in the rise and fall of one's official career. Lines thirteen and fourteen of Jiang's poem describe how Lou Jing and Tian Qianqiu were promoted to senior positions because, as luck would have it, their proposals were favored by the emperor. Jiang's two fortunate cases contrast with Zuo's negative example of the neglected talent of Feng Tang: "How could Sir Feng not be great? / Even in old age, he was not summoned by the Emperor." 馮公豈不偉/白首不見招.⁴⁶

Jiang's imitation poem borrows not only from Zuo, but also from other poets who composed *yongshi shi*, such as Zhang Xie 張協 (d. ca. 307) and Tao Yuanming 陶淵明 (ca. 365–427). Lines fifteen and sixteen of Jiang's poem imitate the first two couplets of Zhang Xie's "On History" (*Yongshi* 詠史):⁴⁷

	昔在西京時，	In the past, in the Western capital,
	朝野多歡娛．	Among the court and the public were much happiness and pleasure.
	藹藹東都門，	Many thronged to the capital's Eastern Gate,
4	群公祖二疎．	Where gathered lords bade farewell to the two Shus.⁴⁸

Jiang borrows Zhang's exact words: "much happiness and pleasure" 多歡娛 and "the capital's Eastern Gate" 東都門. These couplets refer to the way in which Shu Guang 疏廣 (d. 45 BCE) and Shu Shou 疏受 (d. 48 BCE), beloved by both officials and populace alike, were seen off by both groups when they left the capital.⁴⁹ Although Zhang's approach to historical lore is different from Zuo's—Zhang summarizes historical accounts, saving his commentary for the final lines, while Zuo is more focused on expressing his own feelings—Zhang reiterates Zuo's basic message of self-sufficiency, being content with one's lot, and withdrawing from politics at the right moment, once one has achieved what can be achieved.

The end of Jiang's poem imitates a couplet from Tao Yuanming's "Poem on Impoverished Scholars" ("Yong pinshi" 詠貧士): "Zhongwei loved to live alone, / around his house wild grass grew." 仲蔚愛窮居/遶宅生蒿蓬. Among historical figures, Jiang identified with Zhang Zhongwei, as Tao did. The ultimate goal of literati life, according to Zuo Si's "Yongshi" poems, was to become a recluse safely removed from the political center. The path for poor talented scholars in an aristocratic system was limited and, in a period characterized by rapid sociopolitical change, the future was unpredictable. Both Tao and Jiang address the idea of aristocracy versus meritocracy using a voice very similar to that found in Zuo's poems. For example, in Zuo's fourth poem,[50] he praises the lonely scholar Yang Xiong, who, in a world filled with educated men eagerly pursuing fame, held fast to his moral principles and focused on his scholarly endeavors:

> How quiet and silent Master Yang's residence was!
> No high officials' carriages stopped at his home.[51]
> Isolated and lonely, he remained in his empty house.
> What he taught was shrouded in *Mystery*.[52]

Under the guise of imitating Zuo Si, Jiang is actually grouping Zuo Si's poems together with those of Zhang Xie and Tao Yuanming, whose works share some of the same themes and stylistic features with Zuo's. Jiang, nevertheless, explicitly refers to Zuo's "Yongshi" in the title of his imitation, marking them as the paragon of this subgenre. In doing so, Jiang responds to and continues a lineage of transmission and reception of Zuo's poems, thus securing their place in the canon.

Jiang's imitation of Zuo's "Yongshi" may very well have influenced Zhong Rong's comments on Zuo's poems in the *Shipin* and Xiao Tong's (501–531) selection and prominent placement of these poems in *Wen xuan*. Zhong was a student in the imperial academy when Jiang Yan was an instructor there. Zhong might have been Jiang's student and have been influenced by Jiang's writings; thus, the poets that Jiang imitated received high praise in Zhong's *Shipin*. In addition, the preface to *Shipin* and the preface to Jiang's imitation poems mention almost identical representative poets and poems. All of this evidence suggests that Zhong read and was familiar with Jiang's writings, and used them to inform his comments on the poetry he evaluates in *Shipin*.[53] Xiao Tong thought so highly of Jiang's imitation poems that he selected all thirty for *Wen xuan*. Furthermore, Xiao included in *Wen xuan* twenty-four of the thirty subgenres employed by Jiang. "Yongshi," for example, is included as a subgenre heading in *Wen xuan*, which collects twenty-one poems under it, including eight by Zuo Si.[54]

Judging by Zhong's and Xiao's reception, Jiang evidently succeeded in setting up critical models for later writers. In his imitation poem, Jiang imitates Zuo's poems as well as Zhang Xie's and Tao Yuanming's poems in the same subgenre, thus shaping the historical development of *yongshi* poems. At the same time, through this gesture, Jiang established his authority as a senior scholar able to correctly appraise and interpret *yongshi shi* from before his era. Jiang Yan's opinions evidently had a swift and profound effect, as the important work of literary criticism *Shipin* and the canonical anthology *Wen xuan* both accepted the literary standards Jiang established through his own poetic works.

Liu Xie's and Zhong Rong's Literary Criticism of Zuo's "Yongshi"

Although the positive reception of literary works is a slow process that plays out over decades, even centuries, "the first reader" plays a crucial role in shaping later reception.[55] The process of canonizing Zuo Si's "Yongshi" began in early medieval China with *Wenxin diaolong* and *Shipin*. As "the first readers," Liu Xie and Zhong Rong largely determined through their comments how we view the status of the poet and his poems today. Modern studies on early medieval Chinese literature have shown that *Wenxin diaolong* and *Shipin* may not have been as important or influential for their contemporary readers in early medieval China as we might have expected.[56] However, as the only extant works of literary criticism from that era, these works are still valuable as a reflection of the literary values of scholars and the literary tradition they constructed. Furthermore, modern and contemporary histories of classical Chinese literature have mainly followed their lead in assessing Zuo Si's "Yongshi."[57] The reception of these poems not only began in the early medieval period, but, to a certain extent, reached a critical plateau at that time.

In *Wenxin diaolong*, Liu Xie 劉勰 (ca. 465–520) gives high praise to Zuo's poems: "Zuo Si was a man of extraordinary talent, deeply accomplished in his literary works, and of profound vision. He was completely focused on writing the 'Rhapsody on the Three Capitals' and outstanding in his 'Poems on History,' exhausting all his energy in them."[58] 左思奇才, 業深覃思, 盡銳於三都, 拔萃於詠史, 無遺力矣.[59] From the quote above, we can see that Liu considered Zuo to be a dedicated writer. His "Sandu fu" became popular after Zhang Hua and Huangfu Mi endorsed it. Liu elevates the status of Zuo's "Yongshi" by mentioning them alongside his better known "Sandu fu." Furthermore, while Liu only mentions the enormous effort Zuo expended writing his rhapsodies, he uses exceptionally positive words to praise the "Yongshi," which suggests that he felt the latter was an even greater achievement. Liu's enthusiastic praise likely heightened the expectations of his contemporary readers.

Some fifteen years after *Wenxin diaolong* was composed, Zhong Rong wrote *Shipin*,[60] in which he discusses pentasyllabic poems from previous periods, giving short comments on their provenance, strengths, shortcomings, and ranking.[61] In the main preface to *Shipin*, Zhong identifies various subgenres and selects the best and most representative examples of each. He uses Zuo's "Yongshi" as the paragon of the *yongshi shi* subgenre, and compares them to other poetic masterpieces of the early medieval period:

> The works, Zuo Si's "Yongshi," Yan Yanzhi's [poem on] going to Luoyang, Tao Yuanming's composition on poverty, and Xie Huilian's "Pounding Clothes," are all "spurring whips" among poems written in five-character lines. These "pearls in the marsh" of writing are the [mythical] Deng Forest of glorious literature.[62]

> 太沖《詠史》, 顏延入洛, 陶公詠貧之製, 惠連《擣衣》之作: 斯皆五言之警策者也. 所謂篇章之珠澤, 文彩之鄧林.[63]

This high praise places Zuo in an exalted literary lineage. *Shipin* was where Zuo's poems were first put in the context of the development of pentasyllabic poems overall, thus making his work an integral part of a larger historical evolution.

In *Shipin*, the origin of Zuo's poems is identified for the first time. Zhong Rong claims that Zuo Si's style originates from the work of Liu Zhen (劉楨, d. 217), who himself was influenced by the "Old Poems" (*gushi* 古詩), which in turn evolved out of the tradition of the "Airs of the States"

(*Guofeng* 國風) in the *Shijing*. These "airs" of the *Shijing* are traditionally defined as poems that deal with "the affairs of a single state, rooted in [the experience of] a single person."[64] 是以一國之事，繫一人之本，謂之風.[65] Zhong thus gives Zuo's poetry a lineage that explains its emotional power despite its density of allusion. Akin to the *Guofeng*, Zuo's poems show a strong emotional investment in the society in which he lives. By employing historical allusions, Zuo articulates his private thoughts, expresses his ambitions, and criticizes his society as a whole.[66]

In *Shipin*, Zhong places 122 famous poets into three tiers according to talent: top, middle, and bottom. Zhong placed Zuo Si's pentasyllabic poems in the top tier: "His poems stem from those by Gonggan [Liu Zhen]. In their use of refined language to express his grievances and dissatisfaction, they are quite lucid and penetrating, achieving the peak of admonition through allegory."[67] 其源出於公幹.文典以怨, 頗爲清切, 得諷諭之致.[68] Many scholars believe that these comments mainly refer to Zuo's eight "Yongshi."[69] However, some of Zuo's other extant poems also demonstrate the features that Zhong mentions, such as "Miscellaneous Poem" ("Zashi" 雜詩) and "Summoning the Recluse" ("Zhaoyin" 招隱). Only Zuo's fourteen poems and an incomplete poem attributed to him have been preserved until now, but Zhong likely had access to far more of Zuo's poems. Therefore, Zhong is probably commenting on Zuo's pentasyllabic poems as a whole, including his representative "Yongshi" poems. Zhong uses the term *dian* 典 to denote literary quality. Scholars have often interpreted *dian* in this context as "allusions," because Zuo is well-known for his "Yongshi" with allusions to historical figures and events.[70] However, early medieval Chinese literati used the word *yongshi* 用事 instead of *yongdian* 用典 to refer to allusions or references.[71] *Dian* here instead refers to the refined language and plain style that Zuo adopts. Zhong Rong's contemporary Pei Ziye's 裴子野 (469–530) poems were also praised for being *dian*, and as David Knechtges proposes: "The term 'classically chaste' (*dian* 典) as applied to Pei's writings probably refers to his adherence to the classical ideal that stressed a sober, plain style in which content was more important than form."[72] In Zuo's case, *dian* denotes his plain, straightforward, but also sufficiently substantial style. Zhong's use of *yuan* 怨, dissatisfaction or resentment, to comment on Zuo's poetry, follows in a long tradition of linking poetry to *yuan*. This tradition appears in *Analects of Confucius*:

> The Master said, "Why is it none of you, my young friends, study the *Shijing*? An apt quotation from the *Shijing* may stimulate the

imagination, allow one to engage in observation, enable one to live in a community and express resentment. Inside the family there is the serving of one's father; outside, there is the serving of one's lord; there is also the acquiring of a wide knowledge of the names of birds and beasts, plants and trees."

子曰："小子何莫學夫《詩》？《詩》，可以興，可以觀，可以羣，可以怨. 邇之事父，遠之事君；多識於鳥獸草木之名."[73]

Confucius here encourages young people to study the *Shijing* and discusses the literary, social, familial, and political functions of citing *Shijing*, functions which include expressing *yuan*. The *Shipin* continues this tradition of using poetry to express *yuan*. In the first preface, Zhong writes, "At fine gatherings, one entrusts one's feelings to poetry in order to express affections; separated from others, one depends on poetry to express resentment."[74] 嘉會寄詩以親，離羣託詩以怨.[75] *Yuan* in Zhong's comments on Zuo Si is connected with the practice of *fengyu* 諷喻 (admonition, often through allegory or parable), which proves his eloquence and softens the emotions prompted by sociopolitical problems. Zhong has a nuanced critical understanding of the use of allusion or making references, which he details in the second preface to the *Shipin*:

When it comes to chanting one's feelings and nature, what value is there in making references? "I long for you like the flowing water" is just what was before the eyes. "On the high terrace much mournful wind" is also only what was seen. "In the clear morning I climbed Longshou" has nothing to do with anything that happened in the past. "Bright moonlight shines on drifts of snow"—did that come from the Classics or histories? If you observe the finest phrases of past and present, most are not patched or borrowed; all follow from direct encounters.[76]

至乎吟詠情性，亦何貴於用事？"思君如流水，"既是即目；"高臺多悲風，"亦唯所見；"清晨登隴首，"羌無故實；"明月照積雪，"詎出經史？觀古今勝語，多非補假，皆由直尋.[77]

Since Zhong considered "direct encounters" so important, why did Zhong place Zuo's allusion-filled poems in the top tier of *Shipin*? Zhong did not unconditionally oppose using allusions in writing. He mentions in the second preface to the *Shipin* that some types of writing he feels are appropriate for the use of allusions:

> Making parallel references in composition is now a matter of general discussion. When it comes to things like official documents in managing the state, they should be endowed with broad knowledge of precedent; critiques and memorials giving account of virtue ought to give all the outstanding cases of those now dead.⁷⁸

> 夫屬詞比事, 乃爲通談, 若乃經國文符, 應資博古; 撰德駁奏, 宜窮往烈.⁷⁹

With this comment, Zhong emphasizes that he has no problem with allusions in some practical writings. But with respect to poetry, Zhong much prefers direct expression of emotions. Although Zhong was critical of allusion in poetry, the poetic style of *yongshi shi* itself requires allusions to past figures and events, and Zuo Si's use of allusions was not in excess of what the genre demands. In addition, as Stephen Owen argues, although Zhong claims not to favor the usage of allusion in poetry, almost all the poems Zhong praises in the preface make use of allusions.⁸⁰ Zhong does not seem to see any inherent contradiction between the allusions in Zuo's "Yongshi" and the direct expression of emotion he favors.

Zuo's poems also fit other preferences Zhong states in his preface. One of the critical standards Zhong sets out is "force of inspiration" (*fengli* 風力). As Ye Jiaying 葉嘉瑩 writes, Zuo's poems are characterized by that "which arises from the depths of the heart in order to stir up and support the poetic effect [*fengli*]."⁸¹ Gu Nong 顧農 builds upon this concept, outlining three components of Zuo Si's "force of inspiration":

> [T]he will to pursue great accomplishments, a dissatisfaction with influential families, and a new reclusive mode of life where, having no alternative, the writer withdraws and finds contentment in the individual spiritual freedom within the small world of one's own mind. All of these factors are relevant to Zuo Si's particular family background and individual experience.

追求建功立業之志、不滿門閥觀念之意和不得已而退避並安於
個人心靈自由小天地的新式隱居模式,都與左思個人特殊的家世
及個人經歷有關。[82]

Zhong Rong explicitly cites the *fengli* found in Zuo's poems as a major influence on the poetry of Tao Yuanming: "It stems from Ying Qu, and is guided by Zuo Si's force of inspiration." 其源出於應璩,又協左思風力。[83] The appearance of historical figures enhances and intensifies the strong feelings that Zuo expresses. Through historical figures, Zuo demonstrates to his audience that many cultural icons shared his experience of failing to fulfill his ambitions due to an unfair social system and the mercurial nature of politics.

Xue Cheng Articulates His Frustrations through Zuo's "Yongshi"

Along with imitation poems and literary criticism, another source for understanding the reception of Zuo's "Yongshi" is historical narrative—anecdotal collections and standard histories. For example, the biography of Xue Cheng 薛憕 (fl. 520) in the *Beishi* provides a window through which one can see how Zuo's "Yongshi" were adopted and received by scholars to express their own difficulties and frustrations.

> Xue Cheng, with the capping name Jingyou, was a native of Fenyin, Hedong [east of the Yellow River]. During Helian's rebellion, Cheng's great-grandfather Hongchang led members of his lineage to escape from the chaos to Xiangyang. Cheng's father died in his youth and his family was poor. He ploughed the land himself in order to support his grandmother. When he had spare time, he flipped through books. He was free and unrestrained, so his contemporaries did not consider him marvelous. The southern area mostly selected officials from influential hereditary families. Cheng's family did not have noble scholars, or official positions higher than assistant minister. Since he had migrated from elsewhere, he was not promoted. He often sighed, saying, "How could I wear a turban for fifty years and die in the position of field officer, lowering and leaning my head, bending and lifting it towards people!" He often felt melancholic and

his ambitions remained unfulfilled. When dealing with people, he was arrogant and contemptuous of others; he relied on his talents, acted on impulse, and was never inclined to run to the door of influential and wealthy families. The left military officer in charge of security of the royal palace, Wei Qiandu, a native of Jingzhao, said to him, "Your family status is not low, and your talent is not inferior. Why do you not try to obtain a position in the Ministry of Official Personal Affairs?" Cheng replied, "'The descendants of nobility ascend to high positions, / While the talented sink to lower offices.' Even people in ancient times lamented over this situation—I cannot change it." Qiandu told other people, "This young man is indeed passionate, but his day has not yet arrived."

薛憕字景猷, 河東汾陰人也. 曾祖弘敞, 逢赫連之亂, 率宗人避地襄陽. 憕早喪父, 家貧. 躬耕以養祖母, 有暇則覽文籍. 疏宕不拘, 時人未之奇也. 江表取人, 多以世族. 憕世無貴仕, 解褐不過侍郎. 既羈旅, 不被擢用. 常歎曰: "豈能五十年戴幘, 死一校尉, 低頭傾首, 俯仰而向人也!" 常鬱鬱不得志, 每在人間, 輒陵架勝達, 負才使氣, 未嘗趨世祿之門. 左中郎將京兆韋潛度謂曰: "君門地非下, 身材不劣, 何不褧裾數參吏部?" 憕曰: "'世冑躡高位, 英俊沈下僚,' 古人以為歎息, 竊所未能也." 潛度告人曰: "此年少實慷慨, 但不遭時耳."[84]

The narrative above tells us that Xue read extensively, and was knowledgeable, but was not offered a good position because power was held by aristocratic families. When asked why he did not try to obtain a position in the Ministry of Official Personal Affairs, he quoted a couplet from Zuo Si's second "Yongshi": "The descendants of nobility ascend to high positions, / While the talented sink to lower offices." Xue was frustrated by his contemporary political situation during the Northern Wei (386–534), but did not yield his principles for a position. Wang Liqun 王立群 situates Xue Cheng's depression just before the Putai 普泰 reign of Emperor Min 閔 (531–532), when Xue held a minor position. Xue had a similar background and experiences as Zuo Si, so expressing his emotions through Zuo's poem came naturally to him.[85]

In his second "Yongshi," Zuo complained that this unfair situation had existed in society for a long time, which led to noble family members controlling politics and occupying important positions, and the talented poor sinking to the bottom of society. Zuo further identified with the figure of

Feng Tang, who, despite being a great person according to Zuo's belief, was not given the opportunity to demonstrate his abilities in service. Through Feng's story, Zuo seems to insinuate that he possesses equally remarkable potential and was also stymied by an unfair system. Zuo Si had high ambitions in his early years, and expressed his ideals in the first "Yongshi shi": "Looking to the left, I would pacify the region of the Yangtze and Xiang Rivers, / Glaring to the right, I would subdue the Qiang and Xiongnu."[86] As his first "Yongshi" suggests, he had ambitions of becoming both an influential writer and a military leader as a young man. These ideals were increasingly apparent after he and his family moved to the capital, Luoyang, as Michael Farmer observes: "The major turning point in Zuo's early life was the appointment of his younger sister, Fen, to the imperial harem of Sima Yan (posthumous name Emperor Wu) of the Jin dynasty (265–419) as a lady-in-waiting in 272."[87] However, Zuo Fen did not enjoy a happy palace life, largely because the Emperor appreciated her poetic abilities more than her appearance. As a result, Zuo Fen probably lacked the influence to help her brother's career, and Zuo Si only ever obtained minor positions.

Feng Tang's story easily becomes a reflection of Zuo's own life; though he was capable of both civil and military service, he felt both unappreciated and abandoned by the powers of the day. Zuo used poems as a medium to articulate his frustrations, and adapted his literary talents to express his criticism about aristocratic society; his "Yongshi" became the vehicle by which to vindicate his own poetic, far-ranging talent. Zuo's "Yongshi" speaks for the talented poor in a straightforward, passionate, and memorable style, and for this reason his poetry became popular among scholars. Xue Cheng's bitter citation of the key lines from Zuo's poem provide a potent critique of injustice in a society where a man was chosen as a high official not because of his ability but because of his family's status. That Xue would readily cite Zuo's line above all others shows how prevalent knowledge of Zuo Si's poetry had become.

Conclusion

Zuo's efforts in establishing a poetic, idealized self in his "Yongshi" helped form a positive prospective memory of him and his poetry. Placing Zuo Si's "Yongshi" in the context of early medieval China, we can see that an important early reader, Jiang Yan, considered Zuo's "Yongshi" the most representative of this subgenre. Liu Xie both praised Zuo's talent and considered these poems among the best in Zuo's corpus. Shortly after Liu, Zhong Rong, in his *Shipin*, placed Zuo in the top tier of Chinese poets and, concurring with Jiang Yan, chose Zuo's "Yongshi" as the best example of this subgenre. Many scholars, especially those from humble origins such as Xue Cheng, recited Zuo's "Yongshi" to articulate their criticism against a society that neglected the talented poor. These poets, literary critics, and scholars were actively engaged in shaping the reputation of Zuo's "Yongshi." The imitation of, comments on, and citation of these poems surely influenced Xiao Tong's selection of these eight poems for his grand anthology of literature, thus ensuring their preservation and transmission.[88] Because *Wen xuan* became the most important anthology of pre-Tang literature, the choices made by its editors shaped subsequent critical understanding of all pre-Tang poems—even the poems not included in the anthology were still read against the standards of taste articulated and practiced in that collection.

The reception of Zuo's "Yongshi" shows us how changing horizons of expectation can lead to shifts in interpretation. Scholars of the Western Jin generally attached more importance to ornamental amplification of emotion and beautiful diction. In his "Rhapsody on Literature" ("Wen fu" 文賦), Lu Ji 陸機 (261–303), one of Zuo's contemporaries, writes, "Poetry ought to follow the poet's feelings and be ornate, / Rhapsody should consist of physical descriptions of objects and be markedly eloquent."[89] 詩緣情而綺靡, 賦體物而瀏亮.[90] Zuo Si's style is dramatically different, as has been noted by Kōzen Hiroshi:

> We are unlikely to find in his works the superior writing skills favored by contemporary tastes and fashion. Generally speaking, Zuo Si's works have little to do with beautiful ornamentation and complex parallel couplets. He did not prize restrained emotional expression; his writing style and diction are instead very direct and clear.[91]

Chris Connery concurs:

> Although he [Zuo Si] is often grouped with the so-called Taikang Poets (named after the reign period, 280–89), Zuo's poetry stands apart from that of his contemporaries like Lu Ji or Pan Yue, showing little of their emphasis on embellishment and intricate verbal refinement.[92]

Zuo was an outlier to mainstream contemporary tastes, but he was not in a class of his own. He is often paired later with Liu Kun 劉琨 (270–318) as representatives of an alternative poetic style of the Western Jin. This style is described as a continuation of the Jian'an 建安 (196–220) style, focused on poetic substance rather than ornament and form. This group of poets was distinctly a minority of those writing in the Western Jin.

However, in the Southern Dynasties (420–589), many literary scholars held an open attitude towards the literary past and advocated different styles. This eclectic attitude allowed Zuo's bold, direct, and passionate style to emerge as an attractive alternative to the decorousness of his contemporaries. Zuo's "Yongshi" were imitated by Jiang Yan, interpreted by Liu Xie and Zhong Rong, and cited as attested by the anecdote about Xue Cheng. Thus, we can identify three factors that went into shaping the reception of Zuo Si's "Yongshi": compositions by other poets, critical appraisals of poems, and the use of poems in other forms of writing and general discourse among the educated elite.

The prospective memory of Zuo Si's "Yongshi" cannot be captured in a snapshot of a static literary masterpiece, but is a complex process of literary reception, selection, and transmission. It is an unfolding of changing literary interpretations and collective opinions held among early medieval Chinese elites regarding their literary past and those who inhabited it.

Chapter 4

Tao Yuanming's Perspectives on Life as Reflected in His Poems on History

While chapters 2 and 3 apply the concepts of retrospective and prospective memory to Zuo Si's *yongshi shi* to describe the interrelation between poetry and reputation construction on a political stage, this chapter focuses on how Tao Yuanming 陶淵明 (ca. 365–427) reflections in his *yongshi shi* carried on cultural memory in a way that also conveyed his personal perspective on life, moving the *yongshi* subgenre from the political realm into the individual realm.

Tao, a native of Xunyang 潯陽 (modern Jiujiang 九江, Jiangxi), is one of the best-known and most-studied pre-Tang Chinese poets. His extant corpus, comprising 125 poems and 12 prose works, is one of the few complete collections to survive from early medieval China, largely thanks to Xiao Tong 蕭統 (501–531), a prince of the Liang dynasty, who collected Tao's works, wrote a preface, and composed one of his extant biographies.[1] Scholars have examined the factors that impacted Tao's personality, lifestyle, and stylistic choices, focusing on the influence of "dark learning" or Neo-Daoism (*xuanxue* 玄學) on Tao's perspective on life and his pastoral poems.[2] This chapter complements these current directions in research and investigates Tao's perspective on life as reflected and established in his *yongshi shi*.

Tao's *yongshi shi* are quite different from his pastoral poems in terms of language, style, and tone. Whereas his poems about fields and gardens are famous for their simple, natural language and their pure and subtle style, his *yongshi shi*, like those of his contemporaries, are dotted with allusions, which demonstrate Tao's rich historical knowledge. Tao in fact has the greatest number of surviving *yongshi shi* of any early medieval Chinese poet; Wei Chunxi 韋春喜 lists twenty-five *yongshi shi* attributed to Tao, which in his count include

"Poem on Jing Ke," "Poem on the Two Shus," "Poem on the Three Good Men," the seven "Poems on Impoverished Scholars," and the "Nine Poems after Reading *Shiji*." In addition, "Drinking Wine" and "Imitating the Ancients" are about wine-drinking or imitating ancient poems to express one's cares and mind—but the second, eleventh, twelfth, and eighteenth "Drinking Wine" poems, as well as the second and fifth poems of "Imitating Ancient Poems," all use history to express their concerns. These poems all strongly resemble the nature and quality of *yongshi shi*, so they can be considered as such. Thus, we can count twenty-five [*yongshi*] poems in total.

《詠荊軻》、《詠二疏》、《詠三良》、《詠貧士》七首、《讀史述九章》九首; 又《飲酒》和《擬古》雖爲飲酒或擬古詠懷之作, 然《飲酒》其二、十一、十二、十八、《擬古》其二、其五均借史抒懷, 具有強烈的詠史性質, 也可劃歸詠史詩.這樣共計25首.[3]

These poems constitute roughly one-fourth of Tao's extant oeuvre. Through writing *yongshi shi*, Tao synthesized relevant historical materials with his own perception of various aspects of life, including but not limited to his views on political careers, poetry composition, the experience of reclusion, and family life. Tao developed this perception by discussing three main issues in his *yongshi shi*: the desire for the proper appreciation of scholars, the problem of following the Dao in poverty, and the idea of withdrawing from politics after achieving results. Tao's views on these issues hinge on his understanding of "timeliness" (*shi* 時). Although Tao was not the first writer to discuss these problems, his innovation was to connect these different issues and to internalize and individualize principles drawn from the lives of the ancients, which he applied not only to his poetry but also to his life.[4] This innovation of practicing the values that he discussed in his *yongshi shi* in turn heightened the significance and understanding of these ancient figures.

Tao Yuanming's Profound Knowledge of History

Tao Yuanming read widely in history, so he could interpret ancient figures from a variety of perspectives. Scholars have widely acknowledged that Tao was exceptionally well read in history. Qi Yishou 齊益壽 believes that Tao

Yuanming's erudition likely stems from the influence and environment of his family, which possessed a large private collection of books.[5] Tao Yuanming was described by Yan Yanzhi as someone "fond of rare books" (*xinhao yishu* 心好異書). Tian Xiaofei believes that "yishu" here refers to "precious or rare books" 珍貴或罕見的書籍, "books that were generally not easily available, in terms of the regional circulation of books" 一般不容易得到的書籍，而且都和書籍的地域性流通有關.[6] As she further explains, "The meaning of the word 'yishu' is fixed ('rare books'), but its specific meaning is variable. In other words, we must take into account for whom, where, and when a book was rare." "異書"一詞的意義雖然是固定的（"難得一見之書"），但是其具體內涵卻是一個變量，換句話說，我們必須看是對誰、在哪裡難得一見，也必須看是在什麼時期難得一見.[7]

According to Qi Yishou's analysis of the ancient books cited in Tao's *yongshi shi*, he had read *Shiji*, *Hanshu*, *Continuation of the History of the Han Dynasty* (*Xu Hanshu* 續漢書), *Annals of the Later Han Dynasty* (*Hou Hanji* 後漢紀), *Annals of the Jin Dynasty* (*Jinji* 晉紀), *Records of the State of Wu* (*Wu lu* 吳錄), *The Definite Record of the Three Adjuncts* (*Sanfu juelu* 三輔決錄), and *Biographies of the Former Worthies of Runan* (*Runan xianxian zhuan* 汝南先賢傳).[8] Qi Yishou and Zhong Shulin believe that Tao's mastery of history (*shicai* 史才) accounts for his appointment as the editorial director of the palace library (*Zhuzuo lang* 著作郎), though Tao refused to accept the nomination.[9]

Tao's works demonstrate a consistent respect for the craft of historiography. In the *Beishi*, Shen Yue 沈約 (441–513) states that Tao's contemporaries regarded "The Biography of Mr. Five Willows" ("Wuliu xiansheng zhuan" 五柳先生傳) as an "authentic record" (*Shilu* 實錄).[10] Tao's "Biography of His Excellency Meng, Former Chief of Staff to the Jin Generalissimo for Subduing the West" ("Jin gu Zhengxi dajiangjun Zhangshi Meng fujun zhuan" 晉故征西大將軍長史孟府君傳) was added to the official biography of Meng Jia 孟嘉 (ca. mid-fourth century).[11] Moreover, Tao's other works, such as "Nine Poems after Reading *Shiji*" ("Du *Shi* shu jiuzhang" 讀史述九章) and "In Praise of the Paintings on a Fan" ("Shanshang hua zan" 扇上畫贊), demonstrate his historical acumen. For example, although the concluding remarks sometimes differ from those in the standard histories in terms of their perspective and content, "Du *Shi* shu jiuzhang" continues the historiographical tradition of the *Shiji* and *Hanshu* by commenting on historical figures at the end of each biography. Later compilers of official histories considered Tao's writings of high historical value. As part of his engagement with history, Tao wrote many *yongshi shi*.

The Unappreciated Scholar in Tao's *Yongshi shi*

Most of the historical figures about whom Tao wrote were talented scholars who suffered political setbacks and were therefore unable to realize their ideals in the societies in which they lived. This fate befell scholars both in periods when China was flourishing and in those when it was in decline. During the Warring States period (475–221 BCE), scholars often traveled between different states, serving rulers who, eager to gain an advantage over their rivals, actively sought talented advisers. After the Qin unified the country, scholars influenced by the Confucian classics still felt obligated to serve, but there were far fewer opportunities to serve in a unified court. Many were unsuccessful in obtaining positions, leading to the emergence of the trope of "a lack of appreciation for scholars" (*shi buyu* 士不遇).[12] A literary tradition traced this theme back to Qu Yuan's "Encountering Sorrows" ("Lisao" 離騷), Jia Yi's "Rhapsody on Lamenting Qu Yuan" ("Diao Qu Yuan fu" 弔屈原賦), Sima Qian's "Grieving the Lack of Appreciation for Scholars" ("Bei shi buyu fu" 悲士不遇賦), Wang Can's "Rhapsody on Climbing the Tower" ("Denglou fu" 登樓賦), Ruan Ji's 阮籍 (210–263) "Songs of My Cares" ("Yonghuai" 詠懷), and Zuo Si's "Yongshi." Therefore, *shi buyu* came to reflect both a persistent sociopolitical reality and a set of established literary tropes.

Tao's "Rhapsody on Being Stirred by the Lack of Appreciation for Scholars" (*Gan shi buyu fu* 感士不遇賦) clearly follows in the broader tradition.[13] The work references two rhapsodies on the same topic, written by Dong Zhongshu 董仲舒 (179–104 BCE) and Sima Qian. Dong's rhapsody focuses on the injustice of the marginalization of upright scholars in favor of lesser men who rely on sophistry. It also describes the isolation faced by men with integrity, using historical figures such as Bo Yi 伯夷 (fl. 1046 BCE), Shu Qi 叔齊 (fl. 1046 BCE), and Qu Yuan 屈原 as examples. Despite his isolation, Dong refused to compromise his principles: "Although covering up the truth could yield a hundred benefits, it does not compare to rectifying one's heart and returning to the good." 雖矯情而獲百利兮，復不如正心而歸一善。[14] Dong was not alone in his concerns; in "Bei shi buyu fu," his contemporary Sima Qian expressed his anxiety that not only was he alienated from his contemporaries, he also could not use his talents to bequeath his lofty ideals to later generations. This anxiety became one of Sima Qian's principal motivations for editing and writing the *Shiji*.

Tao saw himself as continuing this tradition, but staked out a markedly different position. Given how difficult it was to achieve something worthy of being remembered, he argued it was better to maintain one's moral values, follow Heaven's principles, and study the writing of sages in the past.¹⁵ Tao, in his rhapsody, also investigates why it is so difficult to accomplish political goals:

> An excellent strategist is said to be enchanting;
> A candid talker is called absurd.
> The straightforward person is unbiased and innocent,
> But in the end suffers humiliation and slander.
> 妙算者謂迷, 直道者云妄.坦至公而無猜, 卒蒙恥以受謗.¹⁶

As for the difficulties they faced in accomplishing their political goals, Tao argues that, given the fickleness of public opinion, timeliness plays a key role in determining one's success.¹⁷ For Tao, timeliness refers to both conditions that one can control—speaking or writing the right message, with the right delivery, at the right moment—and conditions beyond one's control, such as whether one was born into a harmonious society and has the opportunity to serve a virtuous ruler. In the following poem on Qu Yuan 屈原 (ca. 340–278 BCE) and Jia Yi 賈誼 (200–168 BCE), Tao emphasizes the role of timeliness in the careers of the two scholars:

屈賈　Qu Yuan and Jia Yi¹⁸

	進德修業,	One advances virtues and refines achievements,
	將以及時.	In order to arrive at a moment of timeliness.¹⁹
	如彼稷契,	Such was the case with Ji and Xie,²⁰
4	孰不願之?	Who would not wish to be like them?
	嗟乎二賢,	Alas! The two virtuous scholars,²¹
	逢世多疑.	They encountered a distrustful world.
	候詹寫志,	Visiting Zhanyin, [Qu] wrote down his intentions,²²
8	感鵩獻辭.	Shaken by the arrival of the owl, Jia Yi presented his rhetoric reasoning.²³

The four-character lines of this short poem resemble the commentary historians traditionally placed at the end of biographies in standard histories. Tao's preface to this series of poems states, "I was moved by reading *Shiji* and wrote poems to express my feelings." 余讀《史記》有所感而述之.²⁴ Qu Yuan and Jia Yi were discussed together in one biography in Sima Qian's *Shiji*, which likely influenced Tao's choice to pair them together in this poem.

At the beginning of this poem, Tao seems to espouse a conventional Confucian teaching: that timeliness is essential to success in cultivating one's moral values and advancing one's career. He cites Ji and Xie as examples of men who encountered a time when their abilities were appreciated by virtuous rulers and put to a good use. By way of contrast, Qu Yuan and Jia Yi were virtuous and willing to serve, but they had the misfortune of not being born at the right time and not encountering worthy rulers. Despite having abilities comparable to the exemplary officials Ji and Xie, Qu and Jia were doubted, slandered, and forced into exile. Consequently, their potential was never fully realized, and they were instead forced to use literature to articulate their thoughts and vent their frustrations with respect to society and politics. Tao composed this poem after reading the *Shiji*, which suggests that Tao's understanding of the function of literature commenting on social reality was inspired by Sima Qian's theory of venting frustrations (*fafen* 發憤) from "The Letter to Ren Shaoqing" ("Bao Ren Shaoqing shu" 報任少卿書). In the letter, Sima Qian writes,

> In fact, King Wen was imprisoned when he elaborated on the *Classic of Changes* [or *Yijing*]. Zhongni [Confucius] suffered hardship before he wrote the *Spring and Autumn Annals*. Qu Yuan was exiled and thus composed the *Li Sao*. Zuo Qiu lost his eyesight and wrote the *Conversations of the States*. Sunzi's feet were amputated before he compiled his *Art of War*. [Lü] Buwei was demoted to Shu, and his *Synopticon of Lü* was then transmitted. Han Fei was imprisoned by the Qin before he wrote "On the Difficulties of Persuasion" and "Solitary Frustration." The three hundred Odes were, overall, products of sages and worthies expressing their frustrations. All these men had pent-up frustrations that could not be resolved.[25]

> 蓋文王拘而演《周易》；仲尼厄而作《春秋》；屈原放逐，乃賦《離騷》；左丘失明，厥有《國語》；孫子臏腳，《兵法》脩列；不韋遷蜀，世傳《呂覽》；韓非囚秦，《說難》《孤憤》；《詩》三百篇，大底聖賢發憤之所爲作也。[26]

Sima here proposes that masterpieces are produced through this impulse of *fafen*, and he tapped into that impulse to compose the *Shiji*. In expressing sentiments similar to Sima's, Tao may have been signaling his desire to use his writings to transmit his reputation to future readers and compensate for his political frustrations. This poem shows that Tao believed that opportune timing was essential for cultivating moral values and advancing one's career; otherwise, the difficulties and frustrations would be insurmountable. In this difficult situation, what is Tao's perspective on a scholars' choices and development? Should they continue expending effort to become politically successful?

In the following poem on Han Fei, Tao insists that no matter how ingenious and assiduous a scholar is, if the time is not right, he will fail in his endeavors, or even undermine his own goals:

韓非　Han Fei[27]

	豐狐隱穴，	The sleek-furred fox conceals himself in a den,
	以文自殘．	because of his patterning, he brings harm on himself.[28]
	君子失時，	If a gentleman loses his moment,
4	白首抱關．	he will still be a gatekeeper even when his hair is white.
	巧行居災，	Clever actions harbor disaster;
	忮辯召患．	Shrewd arguments invite worry.
	哀矣韓生，	How sorrowful Master Han was!
8	竟死說難．	Unexpectedly, he died from "Difficulties of Persuasion."[29]

The paradox at the heart of this poem demonstrates that the pursuit of political success, social status, and even a fulfilling life can lead to ruin in the end. In Han Fei's case, his cleverness and eloquence led directly to a tragic fate. Han Fei was a statesman during the Warring States period, who moved to the state of Qin when the King of Han did not adopt his recommendations. Han was initially favored by the Qin king, but when he opposed Li Si's 李斯 (ca. 284–208 BCE) plan to annex the other six states, Li slandered Han in front of the king, which led to Han Fei's imprisonment and poisoning.[30] In the end, Han's talent led to his own demise. In his work "Shuinan" ("Difficulties of Persuasion"), Han discussed methods for persuading rulers, but he failed to persuade the ruler of Qin of his own worth and was persecuted for irritating a major official. Tao therefore uses Han's life experience to express his perspective on losing one's moment. If someone misses their moment, regardless of their effort and dedication, they cannot achieve anything, and in fact, ironically, the more effort they put in, the quicker and more dramatic their failure will be.

Yet, while Tao believes that timeliness is indispensable, he also believes that compromising one's principles is never acceptable under any circumstances. This principle is made clear in Tao's poem on the two recluses of Lu, a reworking of a story from the *Shiji*:

魯二儒　The Two Confucian Scholars from the State of Lu[31]

	易代隨時，	"The change of dynasties follows the passage of time,[32]
	迷變則愚．	If puzzled by changes, one is truly confounded."
	介介若人，	Upright gentlemen the two Confucian scholars were,
4	特為貞夫．	They were especially lofty and resolute.
	德不百年，	"When virtue has not been present for a hundred years,
	汙我詩書．	It will taint our *Poetry* and *Documents*."[33]
	逝然不顧，	They resolutely ignored [Shusun's invitation],
8	被褐幽居．	Wearing coarse clothes, they lived in reclusion.

The first couplet initially seems to be Tao's own commentary, but is actually a subtle citation of an observation by Shusun Tong 叔孫通 (d. ca. 188 BCE) as recorded in the *Shiji* biographies of the Western Han officials Liu Jing 劉敬 (fl. 200 BCE) and Shusun Tong. The couplet cites Shusun's opinion that two Confucian scholars who refused to participate in the reformation of rites and procedures for the new Han dynasty held antiquated beliefs.[34] However, the second couplet shows that Tao does not consider these scholars to be backward; instead, Tao praises the two scholars for their integrity, overlooking their seemingly eccentric behavior, because the two Confucian scholars spurned Shusun, stating, "You served almost ten rulers, and obtained each one's favor through obsequiousness." 公所事者且十主，皆面諛以得親貴．[35]

With respect to Shusun Tong, Tao's opinion diverges from that of Sima Qian, who praised Shusun: "Shusun Tong observed the world and adjusted his approach to affairs, establishing and adapting rituals in accordance with the changing times. Eventually, he became the Confucian great master of the Han dynastic house." 叔孫通希世度務，制禮進退，與時變化，卒為漢家儒宗．[36] Tao, however, advocates holding steadfast to one's principles, regardless of the changing times. He emphasizes the virtuous words and deeds of the two scholars. For instance, the third couplet changes to the first person, mimicking the two scholars' tone as they refused to help reform ritual and music for the new dynasty, believing that such reforms should only be conducted after a long period of ascending virtue, lest the ancient knowledge in the Classics be tainted by them. Tao revered the way in which the two scholars from Lu maintained their integrity. In other poems dealing with personal choice in a fast-changing, transitional environment, Tao advocated for withdrawing from public life and "delighting in the Dao in poverty" (*anpin ledao* 安貧樂道) instead of changing with the times.

Tao's Understanding of Delighting in the Dao in Poverty

As discussed above, timeliness is a key prerequisite for the exercise of virtue. If the moment is right, a virtuous scholar should serve the state, but if the moment is not right, those who do not want to sacrifice principles should, according to Tao, *anpin ledao*. Tao not only advocated this principle in his writing but also tried to practice this ideal in his own life, despite knowing the difficulty and drudgery that this lifestyle would entail. As he wrote in his "Rhapsody on Being Stirred by Unappreciated Scholars" ("Gan shi buyu fu" 感士不遇賦), "I would rather suffer poverty to achieve my intentions, / neither compromising nor burdening myself." 寧固窮以濟意, 不委曲而累己.[37] Tao motivated himself to delight in poverty and enjoy a life suited to his nature by reflecting on figures from history who followed a similar path. In a poem composed in 403, Tao praises the concept of *anpin ledao* and demonstrates how he applied it to his own life.

癸卯歲始春懷古田舍 其二
Meditating on the Past in a Farmhouse at the
Beginning of Spring in the Guimao Year II[38]

	先師有遺訓,	The Old Teacher left us the lesson,
	憂道不憂貧.	"Worry about the Dao, not about poverty."[39]
	瞻望邈難逮,	I see this lesson from afar, too distant to grasp.
4	轉欲志長勤.	I deflect desire and toil long at my aims.
	秉耒歡時務,	Grasping a plow, I take joy in seasonal work.
	解顏勸農人.	Letting out a smile, I encourage the farmers.
	平疇交遠風,	The level farmland meets distant winds,
8	良苗亦懷新.	Good sprouts also embrace new things.

The "Old Teacher" Tao refers to is Confucius, a substantial influence on Tao's writings and thought, whose injunction from the *Analects* he quotes: "Worry about the Dao, not about poverty!" 憂道不憂貧. Given a hypothetical extreme situation, Confucius advocates that a gentleman should seek and follow the Dao no matter what poverty or misfortune he encounters:

The Master said, "The gentleman devotes his mind to attaining the Dao and not to securing food. Go and till the land and you will end up by being hungry, as a matter of course; study, and you will end up with the salary of an official, as a matter of course. The gentleman worries about the Dao, not about poverty."[40]

子曰: "君子謀道不謀食. 耕也, 餒在其中矣. 學也, 祿在其中矣. 君子憂道不憂貧."[41]

Here Confucius emphasizes the importance of the Dao, which is achieved through cultivating virtues and moral values, over material needs like food. Tao understood Confucius as believing that study was a reliable key to the Dao. Because his impoverishment was an obstacle to study, Tao farmed for a living, providing himself with a physical and financial foundation for studying the Classics.[42] Eventually, Tao's personal way of dealing with difficult situations shaped his perspective on ancient figures, which in return contributed to his decision to live a reclusive life and practice his firm belief in *anpin ledao*.

Alan Berkowitz has noted that "recluses" in early medieval China were actually highly sociable and "reclusion" often served as a shortcut for seeking remunerative official positions.[43] By way of contrast, Tao advocated sincere reclusion aimed at adhering to the Dao. His position was expressed through a series of seven poems on ancient scholars who were materially poor but spiritually rich.[44] In each of these poems, he starts with the theme of the brutality of the natural world—a severe winter or gloomy weather—then discusses the effects of poverty the scholars suffered, such as a lack of proper food and clothes, before finally posing a rhetorical question to show that despite this unfavorable situation, these poor scholars cited ancient figures as role models, and ultimately found contentment by delighting in the Dao.

In this section, I will closely examine three poems from Tao Yuanming's series of "Poems on Impoverished Scholars" ("Yong pinshi" 詠貧士) to further explore his belief in *anpin ledao*. The scholars Tao profiled in this series were often virtuous recluses. Analyzing such official histories as *Hou Hanshu*, *Songshu*, and the *History of Southern Dynasties* (*Nanshi* 南史), Wendy Swartz identifies several categories of early medieval reclusion: "those who live in obscurity in search of an ideal; those who retire to preserve their integrity; those who retreat in order to avoid harm; those who withdraw out of protest against an unrighteous government; those who withdraw for 'not having met with their time' (*bu yu shi* 不遇時, which means that, in the absence of favorable circumstances, a worthy man is unable to realize his political ambitions); and those who follow their innate nature."[45] Tao Yuanming and the historical figures he praised easily fit into these categories.

In the second poem of his series on impoverished scholars, we get a glimpse of Tao's life:

其二　II[46]

	淒厲歲雲暮，	Fiercely cold, nearing the end of the year,
	擁褐曝前軒．	Wearing coarse clothes, I bask at my front window.
	南圃無遺秀，	The southern garden has nothing left to yield,
4	枯條盈北園．	Withered twigs fill the northern garden.
	傾壺絕餘瀝，	Pouring out the jug, not one drop is left,
	闚竈不見煙．	Peering into the stove, I see no smoke.[47]
	詩書塞座外，	*Poetry* and *Documents* are crammed around my seat,
8	日昃不遑研．	The sun slants, there is not enough time to study.
	閑居非陳厄，	Loafing at home is not encountering hardship in Chen,[48]
	竊有慍見言．	Privately, I still harbor words of resentment.
	何以慰吾懷？	How can I console the feelings in my heart?
12	賴古多此賢．	I depend on these many virtuous men from the past.

Tao seems to live in constant want of clothes, food, and wine. He dealt with these quotidian worries by reading books, including such Confucian classics as the *Shijing* and the *Shangshu*. Reading books, enjoying music (in particular, playing the zither and singing), and engaging in conversation created cultural capital which compensated for the material deprivation of the lifestyle of the recluse. However, the extreme poverty Tao suffered made it difficult to engage in even these activities. As Robert Ashmore discusses, the central irony of the poem is "a tension between an ideal and a person who confronts that ideal and questions whether it is adequate to his experience or his experience adequate to it."[49] Tao is surrounded by books and yet is unable to engage in the study that is indispensable to his literati identity and ideals of moral cultivation. The continuous use of strong negative words, such as "has/have no" (*wu* 無), "absolute/absolutely" (*jue* 絕), and "no/not" (*bu* 不 and *fei* 非), reveals Tao's helplessness and embarrassment, and engenders compassion within the reader. Tao's embarrassment is also revealed through self-effacing comic detail: "basking" because he lacks clothes in winter, pouring out an empty jar, peering into the stove. To mitigate the tension between ideal and reality, and to console himself, Tao looks to figures from history. Tao adopts the character *ci* 此 ("these") in the last line to refer not only to the virtuous men of antiquity but also to himself, placing himself in their lineage. Furthermore, Ashmore argues, "By writing this sequence of poems and framing them in this way within his own life and reading, Tao Yuanming invites future readers to add him to the number of those who have managed to remain steadfast in adversity and, through understanding the poems, to enter in turn into community with them."[50]

This is not the only occasion in which Tao weathered dire poverty by focusing on the example of ancient virtuous figures and their works. In the poem "Presented to My Cousin Jingyuan in the Twelfth Month of the Guimao Year" ("Guimao sui shier yue zhong zuo yu congdi Jingyuan" 癸卯歲十二月中作與從弟敬遠), Tao describes a period spent in his poor and empty house surveying ancient books.[51] Although the sages were gone, the writings that recorded their words and deeds remained. The books were Tao's companions as he actively sought to follow in the footsteps of the sages.

Tao's aim in following the example of the sages was to adhere to the Dao, even in a moment of great difficulty. The Dao in Tao's mind was not abstract, but was instead realized in the virtuous lives his predecessors had led. He depended for spiritual support on the deeds and ideals of ancient worthies, who, although they encountered enormous constraints and difficulties, appeared calm, detached, and still focused on their ideals. A poem on Rong Qiqi 榮啓期 (571–474 BCE) and Yuan Xian 原憲 (fl. 515 BCE) illustrates Tao's psychological dependence on models of *anpin ledao*:

其三   III[52]

	榮叟老帶索，	Old Mr. Rong often wore rope as a belt,
	欣然方彈琴．	But he delighted in playing the zither.
	原生納決履，	Scholar Yuan mended his broken sandals,
4	清歌暢商音．	But he sang "The Hymns of Shang" melodiously.[53]
	重華去我久，	Chonghua left us long ago,[54]
	貧士世相尋．	Impoverished scholars have sought each other for generations.
	弊襟不掩肘，	His tattered garment could not cover his elbow,
8	藜羹常乏斟．	His goosefoot leaf soup was too meager to ladle.
	豈忘襲輕裘？	How could he forget wearing light furs?

	苟得非所欽.	Obtaining it improperly is not something to be admired.
	賜也徒能辯,	Ci was only good at sophistry.⁵⁵
12	乃不見吾心.	Thus, he does not apprehend my heart.

In the first couplet, Tao praises Rong Qiqi, a character in the *Liezi*, whose life and personality Confucius apparently admired. Although Rong lived in poverty, he was nevertheless happy. As Rong explains to Confucius,

> My joys are very many. Heaven gives birth to the Ten Thousand Things, but people alone are noble. I had the luck to become a person; this is my first joy. In the distinction between men and women, a man is noble and a woman base, so to be a man is considered noble. I had the luck to become a man; this is my second joy. In human life, some do not [live to] see a day or a month, or do not even escape their swaddling clothes. I have already lived for ninety years; this is my third joy.⁵⁶

> 吾樂甚多: 天生萬物, 唯人爲貴. 而吾得爲人, 是一樂也. 男女之別, 男尊女卑, 故以男爲貴. 吾既得爲男矣, 是二樂也. 人生有不見日月、不免襁褓者, 吾既已行年九十矣, 是三樂也.⁵⁷

Rong was optimistic, and found value in such ordinary activities as playing musical instruments and singing. The *Liezi*'s Confucius approved of his outlook on life. Tao then provides another example of an honorable poor scholar, Yuan Xian 原憲 (b. 515 BCE), a disciple of Confucius who suffered from poverty but was unwilling to compromise his principles to acquire wealth. Through his austerity, Yuan adhered to Confucius's position on the relationship between poverty, wealth, and the Dao, articulated in the following passage from the *Analects*:

> The Master said, "Wealth and high station are what men desire, but unless I obtain them in the right way, I would not remain in them. Poverty and low station are what men despise, but even if I did not obtain them in the right way I would depart from them."⁵⁸

> 子曰: "富與貴, 是人之所欲也, 不以其道得之, 不處也. 貧與賤, 是人之所惡也, 不以其道得之, 不去也."⁵⁹

Confucius acknowledges the commonsense position that wealth and social status are desirable, but insists that obeying the Dao, the guiding principle in life, must come first. Furthermore, he emphasizes that the proper way to confront and even overcome poverty is through benevolence and virtues. Tao alludes not only to Yuan's commitment to this principle, but also to Yuan's conversation with Zigong, another of Confucius's disciples, regarding the difference between poverty (*pin* 貧) and distress (*bing* 病). In that conversation, Yuan disputes Zigong's assessment of Yuan as "distressed," arguing,

> I, Xian, have heard that if one lacks wealth, it is called "poverty." If one studies the Dao, yet is not able to put it into practice, it is called "distress." As for me, Xian, I am in poverty, but I am not distressed.[60]

> 吾聞之，無財者謂之貧，學道而不能行者謂之病. 若憲，貧也，非病也.[61]

In discussing the importance of adhering to the Dao in poverty, Ashmore asserts, "The idea of steadfastness in adversity plays a central role in Tao Qian's poetry, not only as a recurrent theme in the poet's reflections on ethical values but also as a shaping influence on the situation of address that the poems create vis-a-vis their readers."[62] In these allusions, Tao references two scholars whose physical poverty did not prevent them from enjoying meaningful and virtuous lives. Tao alludes to these figures not only to praise their values, but also to actively associate himself with them.

For similar reasons, Tao dedicated a poem to Zhang Zhongwei of the Eastern Han (25–220). The poem directly expresses Tao's deep appreciation of Zhang's personality and moral worth. Zhang's way of life was an example of following the Dao in which Tao delighted:

其六   VI[63]

	仲蔚愛窮居，	Zhongwei liked living a poor life,
	遶宅生蒿蓬.	All around his residence grew wild grasses.
	翳然絕交游，	Concealing himself, he broke from society,
4	賦詩頗能工.	He was quite skilled at composing poetry.
	舉世無知者，	In all the world, there was no one who understood him,
	止有一劉龔.	Save for one Liu Gong.
	此士胡獨然？	Why was this scholar so lonely?

8	寔由罕所同.	Indeed, because he could seldom find others like himself.
	介然安其業,	He was steadfast and content with his deeds,
	所樂非窮通.	What he enjoyed was neither failure nor success.
	人事固以拙,	I am certainly clumsy in dealing with the affairs of men,
12	聊得長相從.	I just want to follow him for a long time.

Few historical records documenting Zhang Zhongwei survive, and his presence in Tao's *yongshi shi* is another element that distinguishes Tao's work from other poets in the genre, who focused on better-known figures. In his "Yong pinshi," Tao Yuanming often combines references to several scholars, but this poem exclusively praises Zhang Zhongwei, demonstrating his profound admiration of Zhang.

One of the few accounts of Zhang's life can be found in *Biographies of Lofty Figures* (*Gaoshi zhuan* 高士傳):

> Zhang Zhongwei was a native of Pingling [northwest of modern Xianyang, Shanxi]. Together with Wei Jingqing of the same commandery, he cultivated the Dao and moral virtue. He lived as a recluse and did not hold an official position. He understood astronomy and natural sciences; he was skilled in prose composition and delighted in *shi* and *fu* poems. He lived simply and in constant poverty; where he lived was overwhelmed by wild grasses. He shut his gate and nourished his nature; he did not concern himself with glory or fame. None of the men of his time acknowledged him; only Liu Gong knew him.[64]

> 張仲蔚者, 平陵人也. 與同郡魏景卿俱修道德, 隱身不仕. 明天官博物, 善屬文, 好詩賦. 常居窮素, 所處蓬蒿沒人. 閉門養性, 不治榮名. 時人莫識, 惟劉龔知之.[65]

Tao believed that because Zhang Zhongwei's happiness did not rely on conventional definitions of success and failure, a person like Zhang was close to the Dao. Zhang also offered a model for achieving one's goals even in an environment of scarcity. Zhang's example shows the influence on Tao of Confucian values—namely, the idea that righteousness, not worldly success or failure, is the path to spiritual affluence and satisfaction. If one does not follow this righteous path and instead pursues wealth and status for its own sake, it stains the conscience.

In the *Analects*, Confucius compares these ill-gotten gains to a transitory cloud:

> The Master said, "In the eating of coarse rice and the drinking of water, the using of one's elbow for a pillow, joy is to be found. Wealth and rank attained through immoral means have as much to do with me as passing clouds."[66]

子曰：" 飯疏食飲水，曲肱而枕之，樂亦在其中矣. 不義而富且貴，於我如浮雲。"[67]

As Confucius sees it, material possessions and status are transient, but the virtues of the Dao are permanent. Zhang Zhongwei's adherence to this model epitomizes Tao's belief of *anpin ledao*, to the point where Tao dedicates the entirety of a poem to him. Zhang's dedication to principle was not common among his contemporaries, so he had few people who truly understood him (*zhiyin* 知音), but literature helped him to cope with poverty.[68] Tao identified with Zhang Zhongwei so strongly that he chose to distance himself from his contemporaries and "communicate" with Zhang instead. Tao clearly demonstrates this desire in the final couplet. James Hightower points out the function of the word *zhuo* 拙 ("clumsy") in the penultimate line: "[Tao] is not just pleading ineptitude as an excuse for staying out of worldly affairs, he is also claiming the kind of natural simplicity he spoke of in the first of the 'Back to the Farm' poems, 'Simplicity intact, I have come back to the fields.'"[69] For Tao, Zhang's reclusion and focus on self-cultivation represented an ideal model of simple virtue, and he paid particular attention to Zhang's close relationship with Liu Gong (who was also known as Menggong): "There is no Menggong here for me, / And so I hide my feelings in the end. 孟公不在茲 / 終以翳吾情."[70] Even more isolated than Zhang, Tao could only seek consolation and spiritual support in virtuous figures from antiquity.

Given that *anpin ledao* was neither a comfortable nor an easy lifestyle to adopt, why was Tao drawn to it? Tao's embrace of the ideal is likely related to the fate of his own political pursuits in a complicated and tumultuous political environment.[71] Tao had entered the service of Huan Xuan 桓玄 (369–404) in the second year of the Long'an 隆安 reign (398), when the latter was appointed governor of Jiangzhou (*Jiangzhou Cishi* 江州刺史). Tao served him for two years until his mother's death in the fourth year of the Long'an reign (400). In the spring of the third year of the Yuanxing 元興 reign (404), Tao returned to politics, serving Liu Yu 劉裕 (363–422), the future emperor of the Liu Song dynasty (420–479), as adjutant to the general in command of defense (*Zhenjun canjun* 鎮軍參軍). In the third month of the first year of the Yixi 義熙 reign (405), Tao assumed the position of adjutant in Liu Jingxuan's 劉敬宣 (371–415) camp. In the eighth month of the same year, Tao became magistrate of Pengze County (*Pengze ling* 彭澤令), abandoning the position abruptly three months later, possibly due to his sister's death in Wuchang. The fast-changing and ruthless political environment Tao experienced over the course of his career likely influenced his decision to permanently become a recluse. Tao, who had worked with Liu Yu before Liu rebelled, may have sensed his ambition. Tao also witnessed the rise and fall of Huan Xuan, one of Liu's major competitors, whom Tao regarded highly. After experiencing so many disappointments, Tao's dream of achieving his ideals through politics began to fade. Reflecting on his life in his later years, Tao was keenly aware that he had not fulfilled the political aspirations expressed in the poetry he composed as a young man, and instead consoled himself by pointing to his steadfast principles. As Wendy Swartz notes, the elegy of Tao written by Yan Yanzhi emphasizes this moral quality: "All the descriptions of his life and character in the elegy point to the same pair of ideas: contentment in poverty and steadfastness in reclusion."[72] Tao's sentiments were vindicated by later critics, most notably the influential late imperial literati Gui Youguang 歸有光 (1506–1571) and Wen Runeng 溫汝能 (1748–1811), who praised his embrace of *anpin ledao*.[73] Through his espousal of this ideal, Tao successfully secured his place in Chinese literary and cultural history.

Yet Tao's *yongshi shi* do not always focus on unsuccessful scholars. Tao also examines several historical figures who were able to achieve their goals. Tao advocates for those successful in achieving their goals to "withdraw after making contributions" (*gongcheng shentui* 功成身退). The concept is to achieve something (*gongcheng* 功成), and then, as the wheel of fortune is always turning, especially in a chaotic era, to avoid potential disasters by withdrawing from politics (*shentui* 身退). While it is less preferable than achieving one's ideals in a golden era, *gongcheng shentui* represents a path toward engaging in worldly affairs without sacrificing one's principles.

"Withdraw after Making Contributions" in Tao Yuanming's *Yongshi shi*

Gongcheng shentui comes from chapter 2 of the *Dao de jing*, which challenges the conventional wisdom around duality and contrasts, and explains the attitude a sage should hold toward achievements:

是以聖人處無爲之事，	Therefore, the sage keeps to the deed that consists in taking no
行不言之教.	action and practices the teaching that uses no words.
萬物作焉而不辭(司);	The myriad creatures rise from it, yet it claims no authority;
生而不有;	It gives them life yet claims no possession;
爲而不恃;	It benefits them yet exacts no gratitude;
功成而弗居.	It accomplishes its task yet lays claim to no merit.
夫唯弗居，	It is because it lays claim to no merit
是以不去.	That its merit never deserts it.[74]

The sage follows nature and allows everything to proceed according to the Dao.[75] The sage does not interfere with this process, nor claim ownership over it, but instead seeks to be remembered for his wise restraint in allowing the Dao to realize itself. By not deliberately seeking fame, the ethical person avoids acting too intentionally and going against the Dao, and passes down their deeds and virtues.

Chapter 9 of the *Dao de jing* uses the metaphors of water and a blade for the problems of wealth and fame, highlighting the importance of *gongcheng shentui*—knowing satisfaction and avoiding excesses which will only bring the opposite of one's desires.[76] In Tao's time, this idea provided a way to maintain one's principles, engage in public life, and yet still avoid the perils of political treachery and instability. Tao's poem on the two Shus explicitly delineates Tao's understanding of this idea:

詠二疏　Poem on the Two Shus[77]

	大象轉四時，	The Great Image turns the four seasons,[78]
	功成者自去.	Its achievement complete, it withdraws itself.
	借問衰周來，	May I ask, since the decline of the Zhou,
4	幾人得其趣?	How many have followed this impulse?
	游目漢廷中，	Looking around the Han court,
	二疏復此舉.	The two Shus revived this action.
	高嘯返舊居，	With a high whistle, they returned to their former residence,
8	長揖儲君傅.	Bowing deeply to the Crown Prince's Tutor.
	......	...
	誰云其人亡，	Who would say those men have passed away?
24	久而道彌著!	After so long, their Dao is fully manifest.

This poem is very similar, in both structure and content, to Zhang Xie's 張協 (d. ca. 307) poem on the topic of the Two Shus.[79] Tao may have read both Zhang's poem and historical accounts and been moved by their adherence to *gongcheng shetui*. Indeed, Tao's second line is practically a restatement of this idea. *Ziqu* 自去 in that line referring to withdrawal after achievement—an impulse of nature worthy of emulation in the world of human politics: once results are achieved, one should discard fame and reputation, and withdraw from public life.

To explain *gongcheng shentui*, Tao raises the issue of dynastic transitions and then focuses on the two Shus, whom he considered to be the best representatives of how to approach that problem. Most of the poem celebrates the actions that result from their Daoist-influenced worldview: their abdication of official duties, and their indifference to fame and to leaving a material legacy for their descendants. Tao praises the two Shus for understanding the idea of *gongcheng shentui* as the true meaning of the Dao. After contributing to the state by tutoring the crown prince, they withdrew from politics and enjoyed a quiet life in their home village. They understood that trying to achieve more would have defied the will of nature and only undermined their aims. Their lack of interest in fame and material possessions made them influential models for later generations of scholars and officials. The last couplet places the two Shus' deeds in a longer historical context, asserting that the Dao the two Shus adhered to will last forever.

Where Tao's poem on the two Shus demonstrates the advantages of *gongcheng shentui*, his poem on the three good men (*sanliang* 三良) reveals what happens when historical figures exert and invest enormous effort in their political pursuits:

詠三良　Poem on the Three Good Men[80]

	彈冠乘通津，	"Dusting off our caps, we boarded the ferry in all directions.[81]
	但懼時我遺。	We only feared that we missed our moment.
	服勤盡歲月，	Working hard the whole year through,
4	常恐功愈微。	We always worried our achievements were shrinking ever more."
	……	…
	一朝長逝後，	Once [their lord] passed away forever,
12	願言同此歸。	They were eager to go with him.
	厚恩固難忘，	Great kindness was indeed difficult to forget.
	君命安可違？	How could they defy their lord's command?

The story of the three good men can be found in many literary and historical accounts. Two representative historical accounts appear in the *Zuozhuan* and *Shiji*. The *Zuozhuan* contains the earliest extant account:

> Renhao, the Duke of Qin died. With him were buried alive the three sons of the Ziju clan: Yanxi, Zhonghang, and Qianhu. All three were among the finest men of the Qin. People of the state lamented over their fate and composed the poem "Yellow Bird."[82]

> 秦伯任好卒，以子車氏之三子奄息、仲行、鍼虎爲殉，皆秦之良也。國人哀之，爲之賦《黃鳥》.[83]

The account in *Shiji* is similar:

> In the thirty-ninth year [of his reign], Duke Mu died. He was interred at Yong. Those who followed him in death numbered one hundred seventy-seven. Three members of the Qin's fine official Ziyu clan, named Yanxi, Zhonghang, and Qianhu, were among those who followed him in death. The people of Qin mourned them, and composed and sang for them the poem "Yellow Bird."[84]

> 三十九年，繆公卒，葬雍。從死者百七十七人，秦之良臣子輿氏三人名曰奄息，仲行，鍼虎，亦在從死之中. 秦人哀之，爲作歌黃鳥之詩.[85]

Both the *Zuo zhuan* and *Shiji* accounts record that after Lord Mu of Qin died, the three good men were buried alive with him. The people of Qin lamented their fate and composed the poem "Huangniao" to commemorate them. Tao's poem demonstrates that the three good men were eager to serve their country and diligently worked for their ruler. During their moment, they were highly favored, treated with dignity, and achieved great political success. However, their success was tightly bound to Lord Mu, and they were therefore unable to withdraw from the political world before they met a grim fate.

Gongcheng shentui requires the courage and willingness to abandon one's immediate interests, and the wisdom to leave the service of a ruler safely and smoothly. Practically speaking, such a withdrawal is often hard to achieve because a ruler is loath to relinquish a loyal and effective official.

Gongcheng shentui profoundly influenced the course of Tao's life. It appears not only in his *yongshi shi*, but also in his poems addressed to family members. In his poem "Command to My Son" ("Mingzi" 命子),[86] Tao offers his forebears, particularly his great-grandfather Tao Kan 陶侃 (259–334), to his son as models, depicting them as calm, resourceful, virtuous, and aloof from worldly fame:

	桓桓長沙,	How mighty and powerful Changsha was,[87]
	伊勳伊德.	His great deeds and his virtues!
	天子疇我,	The emperor rewarded us with farmland,
4	專征南國.	He commanded a campaign against the South.
	功遂辭歸,	After his accomplishments, he withdrew from politics and returned home.
	臨寵不忒.	Receiving favor, he did not stray.
	孰謂斯心,	Who would say that this spirit
8	而近可得.	Can be found in recent times?[88]

Tao's great-grandfather Tao Kan helped found the Eastern Jin dynasty (316–420) and held such high-ranking positions as grand marshal (*da sima* 大司馬). But after reaching this level of success, he retreated from political life, refusing even important positions bestowed upon him personally by the emperor. Tao therefore saw *gongcheng shentui* as part of his family legacy, a legacy he wanted his sons to continue.

Conclusion

This chapter investigates Tao's perspective on life as expressed in his *yongshi shi*. Tao was well read, and his rich understanding of Chinese culture is deeply rooted in that reading. The historical figures that Tao commented on are distributed across many centuries, from Ji and Xie in the mythical reigns of Yao and Shun to several figures from the Eastern Han. For the most part, the subjects of these poems were not majestic rulers or major officials, but virtuous and upright scholars whom Tao saw as men worthy of emulation. By analyzing Tao's interpretation of the legacies of these scholars, we can better understand his perspective on life and his personality, which in turn augments our ability to interpret his other writings.

Tao's *yongshi shi* emphasize a series of values and concepts he felt were key to leading a successful, ethical life. Tao believed that timeliness was essential to the political success of the scholar. Ji and Xie became virtuous models of great officials because they arrived at the right historical moment, whereas the equally virtuous Qu Yuan and Jia Yi were suspected and slandered because they arrived on the political stage at the wrong time. Tao felt that without timeliness, regardless of one's efforts and dedication, it would be nearly impossible to achieve lasting political accomplishments, and he therefore encouraged literati not to try to manufacture opportunities through clever schemes and artful rhetoric. Such tactics would not only be unseemly but ultimately counterproductive, as was tragically the case for Han Fei. Tao sometimes contradicted the verdicts of the historical accounts he alluded to, and re-evaluated these figures according to his own ideals, as in the case of the two Confucian scholars and Shusun Tong described in the *Shiji*. Tao sought to use literature to circulate accounts of "unappreciated scholars" and, in doing so, make a space for them and for himself in literary history. For Tao, writing *yongshi shi* was a way to achieve many aspirations: expressing emotions, making up for political failure, transmitting his ideas and intentions to later readers, and achieving literary immortality.

Along with advocating for the achievement of one's goals by means of literature, Tao was committed to the ideal of *anpin ledao*. Adhering to the Dao was not an abstract concept in Tao's poems, but was rather made concrete through the example of praiseworthy ancient figures, and the lived cultural practices such as reading, writing, and making and appreciating music that figures like Zhang Zhongwei, Yuan Xian, and Rong Qiqi exemplified. Living in poverty was neither easy nor comfortable, but the historical figures that Tao praised overcame these difficulties and were able to uphold the principles of the Dao. As was the case with Tao himself, most of these historical figures lived through transitional and chaotic periods and consequently withdrew from politics, abandoned efforts to pursue fame and reputation, and focused instead on cultivating their moral values. Tao projected himself onto these historical figures, and his vivid depictions of professed moral values in turn influenced later readers' understanding of Tao's own personality and output.

With respect to those successful in their career, Tao used the examples of Shu Guang and Shu Shou to advocate withdrawing after making contributions. The three good men, in contrast, serve as a case study of officials who choose not to withdraw from the court due to such reasons as loyalty or binding interests and inevitably encounter a tragic fate. Tao's idea of withdrawing after making contributions did not only appear in his *yongshi shi* but was also a principle he followed in his own personal life. Tao used this principle to evaluate his forebears and advocated it to his sons. Tao integrated this value into his personal life and his individual interpretation of it into his literary works.

Although some of Tao's *yongshi shi* discuss life on the farm, for Tao, farming was a channel for putting his ideals into practice, or he was at least adopting the persona of a farmer in his poetry to demonstrate his credentials as one who was able to practice *anpin ledao* and keep his focus on cultivating virtue. By commemorating historical figures in poems, Tao kept these figures alive in the spiritual world and the imaginations of scholars long after they would have otherwise been forgotten. Tao's *yongshi shi* have served as a medium for passing down the deeds and virtues of historical figures to future generations. Tao connected ancient figures with a future audience and, in doing so, he placed himself in this lineage.

Some aspects of Tao's perspective on life are based on more widespread concepts such as the importance of timeliness, delighting in the Dao in poverty, and withdrawing after making contributions, but Tao individualized and internalized these concepts by practicing his own understandings of these concepts gleaned from the examples of ancient figures in his own life, making them more concrete and personal. In addition, these seemingly unrelated concepts demonstrate an internal and connected logic in Tao's *yongshi shi* as discussed above, which reflected his rationale behind his writing. In reading history and writing *yongshi shi*, Tao developed a sophisticated perspective on life.

Chapter Five

Cultural Memory and Xie Zhan's Poem on Zhang Liang

Chapters 2 to 4 largely focus on *yongshi shi* inspired by the poets' experience of reading historical accounts. To complement these cases, this chapter discusses poems inspired by visiting historical places or relics. This chapter begins with a fully annotated translation and close reading of Xie Zhan's 謝瞻 (385–421, courtesy name Xuanyuan 宣遠) poem about Zhang Zifang (Zhang Liang 張良 [ca. 250–186 BCE]), entitled "Poem on Zhang Zifang" ("Zhang Zifang shi" 張子房詩). It then uses a cultural memory framework to explain this poem, comparing the poem with Zheng Xianzhi's (364–427), Fan Tai's (355–428), and Xie Lingyun's (385–433) writings and reading it together with Xie Zhan's own poems presented to Kong Jing 孔靖 (347–422) and Xie Lingyun, to provide a larger literary and historical context for "Poem on Zhang Zifang." It investigates how Xie Zhan and Liu Yu 劉裕 (363–422), the future founding emperor of the Liu Song dynasty, construct the cultural memory of Zhang Liang and harness that cultural memory to achieve their own political goals. The theoretical framework of cultural memory can illuminate how contemporary appropriation of memories of the past were used to establish the legitimacy of a new regime as well as reveal Xie Zhan's subtle psychological state during the dynastic transition from the Eastern Jin to the Liu Song dynasty.

Historical Context

Xie Zhan was an Eastern Jin dynasty (317–420) scholar-official from the famous Xie clan.[1] Commenting on his "Zhang Zifang shi," Wang Jian's 王

儉 (452–489) *Seven Categories* (*Qizhi* 七志) states, "Gaozu [Liu Yu] visited the Zhang Liang temple, ordering the officials accompanying him to compose poems. On this occasion, Xie Zhan's poem won the laurels." 高祖遊張良廟, 並命僚佐賦詩, 瞻之所造, 冠于一時.² Although this poem was well received by his contemporaries, it was largely dismissed by critics of later centuries, who objected to its obsequiousness toward Liu Yu, who ordered its composition. He Zhuo 何焯 (1661–1722) appreciated how the first half of the poem situates Zhang Liang in history and comments on his achievement, but argued that the second part of the poem, which treats Liu Yu as an emperor even though he was still just an official at the time it was composed, shows a lack of moral judgment and responsibility on the part of Xie Zhan. He therefore felt that only the first part of the poem should be selected for anthologies, and that the second part should be discarded.³ Fang Dongshu 方東樹 (1772–1851) criticized the poem for its lack of personal feeling and poor quality.⁴ This chapter argues against the traditional dismissal of this poem as mere flattery, unworthy of further study. On the contrary, when seen through the lens of cultural memory, the cultural significance and value of this poem becomes apparent. It reveals Liu Yu's efforts to obtain cultural capital through literature by proxy as well as win the confidence of aristocratic families. This chapter centers on Xie Zhan's long poem on Zhang Liang, but also illustrates the broader context of Liu Yu's use of the past during his northern expedition between the twelfth and thirteenth years of the Yixi 義熙 reign (416–417), as well as the writings of Zheng Xianzhi 鄭鮮之 (364–427), Fan Tai 范泰 (355–428), and Xie Lingyun 謝靈運 (385–433) on Zhang Liang and Liu Bang.

Xie Zhan composed "Zhang Zifang shi" during a period of considerable political turbulence. The background of this poem is recorded in several accounts. In one example, an annotated version of *Wen xuan* records the following:

> Yao Hong (388–417) had just been enthroned [as ruler of the state of Later Qin], and the Guanzhong region was rebelling. In the first month of the thirteenth year of the Yixi reign (417), Liu Yu moved his army by boat to attack [Yao Hong]. [Liu Yu's] troops stopped at Xiangcheng and passed the Zhang Liang temple.
>
> 姚泓新立, 關中亂. 義熙十三年正月, 公以舟師進討, 軍頓留項城, 經張良廟也.⁵

Liu Yu was a general in the service of the waning Eastern Jin dynasty during the Yixi 義熙 (405–418) reign. In the eleventh year of that reign (415), he defeated several renegade military commanders and conquered several rival states in the south. The very next year (416), he launched a military campaign against the Eastern Jin's rivals in the north. When Liu's troops passed Zhang Liang's temple, he asked Fu Liang 傅亮 (374–426) to write a piece, entitled "Composed on Behalf of Duke Song, Instructions on Repairing Zhang Liang's Temple" ("Wei Songgong xiu Zhang Liang miao jiao" 爲宋公修張良廟教), which demonstrates Liu's commemoration and admiration of Zhang's virtues, righteousness, and political contributions.[6] Liu ordered the temple repaired, and called on his courtiers to compose poems in Zhang's honor.

Cultural Memory and Poems on Zhang Liang and Liu Bang

As a major adviser and strategist to Liu Bang 劉邦 (emperor Gaozu 高祖, the founding emperor of the Han dynasty, 256–195 BCE), Zhang Liang became a popular cultural icon in China shortly after his death and has had a profound influence over Chinese culture ever since.[7] Xie Zhan's "Zhang Zifang shi" demonstrates how ritual and ceremony continued the cultural memory of the Han dynasty general Zhang Liang, a tradition that had profound political implications. Xie's use of this cultural memory allowed him to prospectively shape the literati's communicative memory of Liu Yu as the future first emperor of the Liu Song dynasty; to promote Liu's governance, ability, and virtue; and to pave the way for legitimating Liu's rule. At the same time, this poem also reveals Xie Zhan's psychological state during a period of social transition and transformation. I have provided a complete translation of the poem below:[8]

張子房詩　Poem on Zhang Zifang

王風哀以思,	The airs of the royal domains were mournful and pensive,[9]
周道蕩無章.	From the Zhou way they strayed, and all order was lost.
卜洛易隆替,	The omens for Luoyang changed from glory to decline,

4	興亂罔不亡.	Giving rise to rebellion: all would perish in the end.[10]
	力政吞九鼎,	A regime of force swallowed the nine tripods,[11]
	苛慝暴三殤.	Violence and wickedness caused the demise of three generations.[12]
	息肩纏民思,	Easing the yoke lingered in the minds of the people,[13]
8	靈鑒集朱光.	Numinous insight alighted on the Red Shining [Liu Bang].[14]
	伊人感代工,	That [Zhang Liang] sensed this and acted on his behalf,
	聿來扶興王.	And so, he came to support the ascending king.[15]
	婉婉幄中畫,	Gentle and graceful, he strategized within the tent,
12	輝輝天業昌.	Bright and splendid, the cause of heaven prospered.
	鴻門消薄蝕,	At the Grand Gate, the eclipse was dispelled,[16]
	垓下殞攙搶.	At Gaixia, the Chanqiang comet perished.[17]
	爵仇建蕭宰,	He ennobled the enemy and set up Xiao He as prime minister,[18]
16	定都護儲皇.	He established the capital[19] and protected the crown prince.[20]
	肇允契幽叟,	Sincere from the beginning, he made a pact with the Mysterious Old Man,[21]
	翻飛指帝鄉.	He fluttered off to the place where the Emperor of Heaven abides.[22]
	惠心奮千祀,	This kind heart rose up for a thousand years,
20	清埃播無疆.	Cleansing the dust beyond all bounds.[23]
	神武睦三正,	The divine warrior aligned the three realms,[24]
	裁成被八荒.	His [Liu Yu] achievements extended over the eight lands.[25]
	明兩燭河陰,	Double brightness shone south of the Yellow River,[26]
24	慶霄薄汾陽.	Auspicious clouds enveloped everything north of the Fen.
	鑾旆歷頹寢,	The flags of carriages passed the ruined chamber,[27]
	飾像薦嘉嘗.	He adorned the statue and presented great offerings to it.
	聖心豈徒甄,	How could he only be known for his sagely heart?
28	惟德在無忘.	His virtue also lies in not forgetting [virtuous figures from the past].
	逝者如可作,	If the deceased could be revived,[28]
	揆子慕周行.	Perhaps Sir [Zhang Liang] would admire the processions of the officials of Zhou.[29]
	濟濟屬車士,	Many were the carriages of the retainers,

32	粲粲翰墨場．	Brilliant, what those men accomplished with ink and brush.[30]
	瞽夫違盛觀，	This blind man was not present at this magnificent spectacle,[31]
	竦踴企一方．	He craned and jumped up to look at it from the side.
	四達雖平直，	Although the four thoroughfares were flat and straight,
36	蹇步愧無良．	I limped along, regretting my lack of talent.
	飡和忘微遠，	Living in harmony, forgetting how insignificant and remote I am,
	延首詠太康．	I stretched my neck forward, to sing of great peace and prosperity.

This poem can be divided into four sections based on the shifts in narrative focus. The first section, from the first to the third couplets, summarizes Chinese history from the Zhou dynasty to the Han—how Zhou society fell into chaos, and how the Qin were able to unify the empire militarily, but only by relying on severely oppressive laws and regulations. The second section, from the fourth to the tenth couplets, narrates how the Han received the Mandate of Heaven to overthrow the Qin and established a long-lasting empire, a historical process in which Zhang Liang played an essential role. The third section, from the eleventh to the sixteenth couplets, switches the focus of the poem to Liu Yu, praising both his merits and his veneration of history. The last section explains why Xie composed the poem in the first place and expresses his own emotions at being absent from a ceremony he admires.

Xie Zhan's poem combines four narratives of three different individuals: retrospective memory of Zhang Liang's personal charisma, prospective memory of Zhang Liang's legacy and reputation, communicative memory of Liu Yu's visit to the Zhang Liang temple, and documentation of Xie's psychological state shortly before a dynastic transition.

Liu Yu's selection of Zhang Liang as a figure to be venerated was very much deliberate and strategic. To understand the nuances of Xie Zhan's poem, we can compare it with another poem inspired by visiting the Zhang Liang temple, written by Zheng Xianzhi. As a loyal follower of Liu Yu, Zheng was known for his straightforward personality. He admonished his superior without fear or hesitation, and because of his sincerity he was favored and trusted by Liu.[32] Zheng participated in the northern expedition, asking only for a short leave to visit his great-grandfather's tomb. After returning to Liu's camp, Zheng participated in the composition of poetry in honor of Zhang Liang.[33] A translation of Zheng's poem is provided below:

行經張子房廟詩　　Poem on Passing the Zhang Liang Temple[34]

七雄裂周紐.	Seven powerful states severed the knot of the Zhou.
道盡鼎亦淪.	The Dao was exhausted, and the tripods were destroyed.[35]
長風晦崑溟.	A great storm obscured the bright sea.[36]
4　潛龍動泗濱.	A hidden dragon stirred the Si River.[37]
紫煙翼丹虬.	Purple smoke aided the young red wyrm.[38]
靈媼悲素鱗.	A divine sorceress mourned white snake scales.[39]

These couplets mainly focus on the historical context of Liu Bang's rise, as adapted from his biography.[40] The poem first provides the historical background of the end of the Eastern Zhou. Although the Zhou king was still the nominal ruler, local lords held much of the power and competed to bring more land under their individual control. The word *lie* 裂 ("split; break") vividly evokes how the different states divided the Zhou kingdom into pieces, plunging society into chaos, as symbolized by the destruction of both the Dao and tripod of sovereign power. Liu Bang emerged as a strong potential ruler among different competing powers at the end of the Qin dynasty and attracted talented men such as Zhang Liang to join forces with him and assist him in unifying the country. This poem is very similar to lines 1–4 of Xie Zhan's, emphasizing the chaos at the end of the Zhou dynasty. The account of social decline and social unrest described in the first two couplets of Zheng's poem lays the groundwork for the introduction of Zhang Liang, and the restoration of peace and prosperity in the empire by Liu Bang, who was guided by Zhang's advice. Both Xie's poem and Zheng's poem adopt retrospective memory to depict Zhang Liang and Liu Bang as heroes. Xie depicts a Zhang Liang who helped Liu Bang obtain the Mandate of Heaven and who seeks to rescue the people from their dangers and burdens. Zheng alludes to a story about Liu Bang killing a magical white snake, probably invented by Liu or his officials to exaggerate his charisma and power and to legitimate his rebellion. In Liu Bang's subsequent military campaigns, Zhang Liang became one of his major advisers.

　　The retrospective memory of Zhang Liang represented a number of values which appealed to the Chinese scholars whom Liu Yu was trying to persuade to join his cause. Zhang's narrative contained the tropes of the "scholar encountering a confidant" 士遇知己 and an official "withdrawing after making contributions" 功成身退, both of which were long celebrated by Chinese scholars. Most significantly, Zhang Liang represented the rare case of a scholar being allowed to put his talents to use. Such a situation was far from the norm, to the point where the "unappreciated scholar" 士不遇 was already a popular theme in Chinese literature, the subject of such classic works as Dong Zhongshu's 董仲舒 (179–104 BCE) "Rhapsody on the Unappreciated Scholar" ("Shibuyu fu" 士不遇賦), Sima Qian's 司馬遷 (ca. 145–ca. 90 BCE) "Lament for the Unappreciated Scholar" ("Bei shibuyu fu" 悲士不遇賦), and Tao Yuanming's 陶淵明 (ca. 365–427) "Rhapsody on Being Moved by the Plight of the Unappreciated Scholar" ("Gan shibuyu fu" 感士不遇賦). Liu Yu, on the other hand, was suggesting that his military and political campaigns would give scholars the opportunity to use their talents, just as Zhang Liang was able to assist Liu Bang in establishing the Han dynasty. Liu's choice of Zhang was also a signal to his contemporaries that any officials who loyally served him would be secure.

In the ninth and tenth couplets of Xie Zhan's poem, having described Zhang Liang's military and political acumen, the poem draws attention to how Zhang avoided hubris, and retired at the peak of his career, securing his historical reputation. The *Shiji* records Zhang Liang's explanation for withdrawing from the political arena:

> My family served as ministers to the state of Han for generations. When Han was destroyed, we spared no expense in rousing the world in revolt against the rapacious Qin to avenge Han. Now, by the wagging of my meager tongue, I have become a teacher to an emperor, enfeoffed with ten thousand households and placed among the ranks of the nobility. A common man can reach no greater heights; here I am content to rest in this good deed. I wish now to lay aside the affairs of this world and want to join Master Red Pine in roaming.[41]

> 家世相韓, 及韓滅, 不愛萬金之資, 爲韓報讎彊秦, 天下振動. 今以三寸舌爲帝者師, 封萬戶, 位列侯, 此布衣之極, 於良足矣. 願弃人閒事, 欲從赤松子游耳.[42]

The ninth couplet of Xie Zhan's poem returns to an episode early in Zhang's career, in which his sincerity and humility endeared him to a mysterious old man, who rewarded him with a magical guide for political and military success.⁴³ Xie Zhan follows this couplet by asserting that Zhang will be remembered both across time ("a thousand years" 千祀) and space ("beyond all bounds" 無疆). The prospective memory the poet invokes is that Zhang will be remembered by future generations not only because of the contribution that he made to the establishment and consolidation of the Han dynasty but also because he was wise and courageous enough to relinquish power when the time came. Zhang withdrew from politics after achieving political success, and for that reason he was able to avoid the persecution and misfortune suffered by figures such as Han Xin 韓信 (196 BCE). Xie was therefore suggesting not only that officials who followed Liu Yu would be able to make use of their talents but also that they would be allowed to enjoy a safe and quiet retirement once their work was finished. Liu Yu indeed kept his promise. For example, Kong Jing was a key official who supported Liu Yu from the beginning and presented strategies to defeat Huan Xuan 桓玄 (369–404).⁴⁴ When Kong Jing was preparing to withdraw from politics, Liu Yu held a banquet for him at Xima Terrace 戲馬臺 on the Chongyang Festival 重陽節 (the ninth day of the ninth month in the lunar calendar) in the fourteenth year of the Yixi reign (418).

The prospective memory of Zhang Liang was particularly useful for Liu Yu's political agenda. In the thirteenth and fourteenth couplets of Xie Zhan's poem, Xie turns to Liu Yu and the magnificent ritual commemorating Zhang Liang. Liu Yu's reconsecration of the Zhang Liang temple demonstrated his commitment to restoring stability to the empire and to regaining the confidence of the literati in the state. For this reason, Ding Fulin 丁福林 reads Xie Zhan's poem primarily as an astute political maneuver: "This poem praises Zhang Liang, and through it Xie Zhan expresses his eagerness to make great achievements during the transition between the Jin and Song dynasties."⁴⁵ Wang Xiaomeng 王曉萌 has also noted the way in which the poem reflects a political problem faced by Liu Yu, the "longing for talented officials and strategists like Zhang Liang."⁴⁶ The latter view is particularly worthy of consideration. At the time of the northern expedition, Liu Yu eagerly wished to find gifted counselors and strategists like Zhang Liang, and though he had successfully recruited a number of officials, he did not necessarily trust in their loyalty or competence.

When Liu Yu set off on the northern expedition, he asked Liu Muzhi 劉穆之 (360–417) to stay in Jiankang (modern Nanjing in Jiangsu Province) and entrusted him with many responsibilities, which Liu diligently and skillfully carried out. However, an unfortunate event disturbed Liu Yu's original plan. As the *Songshu* records,

In the eleventh month, the former general Liu Muzhi died. Liu Yu temporarily placed the left minister of war, Xu Xianzhi, in charge of Liu Muzhi's duties. All the major issues that were previously decided by Liu Muzhi now had to be made in consultation with Liu Yu. Liu Yu had wanted to stop and have a rest in Chang'an to make plans for managing the Zhao and Wei regions. However, after Liu Muzhi's untimely death, Liu Yu returned [to Jiankang].

十一月, 前將軍劉穆之卒, 以左司馬徐羨之代掌留任. 大事昔所決於穆之者皆悉以諮. 公欲息駕長安, 經略趙、魏, 會穆之卒, 乃歸.⁴⁷

When Liu Yu learned of Liu Muzhi's death in 417, he immediately put a stop to the northern expedition and returned to Jiankang. From then on, Liu Yu asked that every major matter be reported directly to him and made all important decisions personally, a clear indication that he could not find many officials he felt he could trust.

The prospective memory of Zhang Liang was also a useful tool for expressing Liu Yu's ambitions in a politically sensitive way. When Emperor An of Jin 晉安 (Sima Dezong 司馬德宗, 382–419) learned of Liu Yu's good deeds, including restoring the Zhang Liang temple, he bestowed honors upon Liu's ancestors, as the *Songshu* records: "The emperor bestowed the posthumous title of Minister of Ceremonies upon Duke Song's grandfather, and the title of Left Grand Master for Splendid Happiness upon his father, which he modestly declined" 天子追贈公祖爲太常, 父爲左光祿大夫, 讓不受.⁴⁸ After Liu occupied Chang'an in 417, Emperor An praised Liu's accomplishments, and raised Liu's status to Prince 王, an honor Liu initially declined.⁴⁹ These gestures of modesty signaled to officials that he was a man of humility and moral principle, and helped him to establish his own authority. Liu cleverly and patiently managed his ascension to power, making concessions when it would allow him to make advances later in his political career.

However, Liu acted decisively when his moment arrived. In the first month of the reign of Emperor Gong of the Jin dynasty 晉恭帝 (386–421; r. 419–420), he also bestowed the title of prince to Liu. This time Liu accepted it, after a six-month delay for the sake of propriety.⁵⁰ After this act, Liu's political ambitions became increasingly apparent, and he did not hesitate to accept the same treatment as the emperor. Once he had secured his grip on power, Liu saw no need to continue to feign modesty. Xie Zhan's "Zhang Zifang shi" was very much in line with Liu's canny positioning. Ostensibly dedicated to a loyal official, it also focused on the doctrine of the Mandate of Heaven, preemptively justifying the legitimacy of Liu's political actions. Zhang Liang was a vessel that allowed Xie to present Liu's ambitions in an acceptable form, and to win over public opinion by demonstrating his commitment to a Sinitic moral order and cultural identity.

The fifteenth and sixteenth couplets of Xie Zhan's poem connect the past with the present and combine history with reality in the very same frame. Xie Zhan adopted the subjunctive mood to describe the magnificent and solemn atmosphere of the ceremony commemorating Zhang Liang. Xie highly praises both the orderliness of the procession and the accomplishments of the participating officials. Liu Yu's commemoration of Zhang Liang earned him the admiration of the literati and demonstrated his consideration for the talented. Liu made full use of the prospective memory of Zhang Liang as shaped by Xie Zhan. As Jan Assmann explains, cultural memory plays a key role in the formation of cultural identity:

> Cultural memory is imbued with an element of the sacred. The figures are endowed with religious significance, and commemoration often takes the form of a festival. This, along with various other functions, serves to keep the foundational past alive in the present, and this connection to the past provides a basis for the identity of the remembering group. By recalling its history and reenacting its special events, the group constantly reaffirms its own image; but this is not an everyday identity. The collective identity needs ceremony—something to take it out of the daily routine. To a degree, it is larger than life. The ceremony as a means of communication is itself a forming influence, as it shapes memory by means of texts, dances, images, rituals, and so on.[51]

The festive ritual of commemorating Zhang Liang depicted in lines 26–32 of Xie Zhan's poem was essential to the maintenance of his memory, and it drew on the participation and collective performance of Liu's entourage, members of the educated scholar class who, during this period, largely monopolized the cultural resources necessary to construct and continue cultural memory.

Liu further legitimated his power by associating himself with the illustrious Western Han dynasty. Liu claimed to be a descendant of Liu Bang's younger brother Liu Jiao 劉交 (d. 179 BCE), King Yuan of Chu 楚元王. As Andrew Chittick notes, Liu Yu's military expeditions were largely successful:

> Liu Yu engaged in a series of successful campaigns, including the conquest of the small state of Southern Yan (in modern Shandong) in 409–410 and the seizure of the south bank of the Yellow River during the Guanzhong campaign in 416–417, thereby establishing the frontier line along the Yellow River for the first time.[52]

Liu's forces conquered Luoyang and Chang'an, and Liu captured and executed Yao Hong 姚泓 (388–417), the ruler of the Later Qin dynasty 後秦 (384–417), in 417. Liu's army passed through many places of interest on the northern campaign of 416–417, but according to the extant historical records, Liu only asked officials to pay homage and compose poetry at two sites: the Zhang Liang Temple and the Liu Bang Temple.[53] In both cases, the political and cultural message Liu Yu intended to send was clear.

Although we have both Xie Zhan's and Zheng Xianzhi's poems commemorating the visit to the Zhang Liang Temple, the only poem we have on visiting the Liu Bang temple is one written by Fan Tai. The location of the Liu Bang temple was Liu Yu's birthplace of Pengcheng, in what is now Xuzhou, Jiangsu province. Because Liu Yu claimed to be descended from the royal family of the Han, it was to his benefit to visit the Liu Bang temple and make a sacrifice to his supposed ancestor. A translation of Fan's poem is provided below:

經漢高廟詩　Poem on Passing the Temple of Emperor Gao of the Han[54]

	嘯吒英豪萃.	Whistling and shouting, the powerful heroes were assembled,
	指揮五岳分.	His command split the Five Sacred Peaks.[55]
	乘彼道消勢.	Taking advantage of the decreasing Dao of the Qin,
4	遂廓宇宙氛.	[Liu Bang] expanded the *qi* of the universe.
	重瞳豈不偉.	With double pupils, how could [Xiang Yu] not be great?[56]
	奮臂騰群雄.	Raising his arms, he sprang against a host of warriors.
	壯力拔高山.	His mighty power toppled a tall mountain,[57]

8	猛氣烈迅風．	A brave spirit violently stirred a quick wind.
	恃勇終必撓．	But, relying on courage, one will eventually be hindered.[58]
	道勝業自隆．	The Dao won and [Liu Bang's] enterprise naturally flourished.[59]

In the ninth month of 417, Liu led his army and accompanying officials in commemorating Liu Bang. Fan Tai likely composed this poem on this occasion, a few months after the visit to the Zhang Liang temple that inspired Xie Zhan's and Zheng Xianzhi's poems. The first couplet of this poem depicts Liu's gallant actions, and does not mention any historical figures, but the title naturally prompts readers to think of Liu Bang. The poem describes the personality and awe-inspiring prestige that drew powerful men to Liu Bang. Liu's greatest rival was Xiang Yu, who appears in the third and fourth couplets. The poet uses a rhetorical question and a vivid depiction of Xiang Yu's deportment to emphasize his greatness and courage, in turn allowing him to heap even more praise on Liu Bang, who defeated even this marvelous general. This poem does not explicitly discuss major episodes of Liu Bang's life, instead focusing on the historical lessons of the Qin–Han transition. The poet's conclusion is that ultimately the Dao determines the outcome of history.

After visiting the Liu Bang temple, Liu Yu met with both civil and military officials in the Weiyang Palace 未央殿, the residential palace of the Western Han emperors and a place where many important edicts were issued and political decisions were made.[60] Both visiting the Liu Bang temple and receiving officials in the Weiyang Palace were signals of Liu Yu's ambition to become emperor himself. In the first year of the Yongchu 永初 reign (420), Liu Yu seized the throne, issuing an edict in imperial language that provided a pretext for his usurpation: "The Jin dynasty has suffered myriad disasters. The stars have shifted. Respectful and obedient to former kings and their sound edicts and laws, We have received the Mandate of Heaven" 晉氏以多難仍遘，曆運已移，欽若前王，憲章令軌，用集大命于朕躬．[61] Liu Yu staked his claim on the inability of the Jin emperors to address the difficulties that arose in the last few decades of the dynasty, which, according to Liu, were proof that the Jin had lost the Mandate of Heaven. Liu had gradually accumulated enough political, military, and cultural capital to take the throne. The emperors had long been his puppets, he had risen through the ranks to become a powerful general who had defeated major enemies, and he had organized and participated in many cultural activities. His employment of retrospective and prospective memory of Zhang Liang demonstrated his respect for important historical figures, winning over literati, and the connection he claimed with the Han dynasty conferred some legitimacy on his accession to the throne.

The cultural memory of Zhang Liang and Liu Bang in the discussion above resonates with Liu Yu's ambitions; it is a cultural memory that is used by Xie Zhan to frame his communicative memory of Liu's tribute to Zhang Liang as a means of conveying Liu's subtle psychological state at a time of dynastic transition. For those who participated in the ceremony and the cultural production surrounding it, Liu Yu's celebration of Zhang Liang built up Liu Yu's personal image, his taste, and his treatment of civil officials and military commanders. The political and military strategies Zhang provided to Liu Bang were key to his success. Zhang was a major adviser to Liu, and Liu credited him in part for his triumph over his rival Xiang Yu:

> When it comes to sitting within the tents of command and devising strategies that will assure us victory a thousand miles away, I am no match for Zhang Liang. In ordering the state and caring for the people, in providing rations for the troops and seeing to it that the lines of supply are not cut off, I cannot compare to Xiao He. In leading an army of a million men, achieving success with every battle and victory with every attack, I cannot come up to Han Xin. These three are all men of extraordinary ability, and it is because I was able to make use of them that I gained possession of the world. Xiang Yu had his one Fan Zeng, but he did not know how to use him and thus he ended as my prisoner.[62]

> 夫運籌策帷帳之中，決勝於千里之外，吾不如子房. 鎮國家，撫百姓，給餽饟，不絕糧道，吾不如蕭何. 連百萬之軍，戰必勝，攻必取，吾不如韓信. 此三者，皆人傑也，吾能用之，此吾所以取天下也. 項羽有一范增而不能用，此其所以爲我擒也.[63]

Liu Bang here explains his success in establishing the Han dynasty as a result of his skill as a wise ruler appreciative of talent, able to make use of talented men to make up for his own shortcomings. Xie Zhan's poem succinctly summarizes Zhang's achievements in the fourth to eighth couplets. Zhang played a major role in the banquet at Hongmen 鴻門 and the encirclement at Gaixia 垓下 before the founding of the Han. At the banquet of Hongmen, Xiang Yu intended to kill Liu Bang, but Zhang Liang was given advance warning because of his good friendship with Xiang Bo 項伯 (d. 192 BCE) and helped Liu escape.[64] At Gaixia 垓下, Zhang Liang proposed that the troops sing the songs of Chu, so Xiang Yu's army would believe that their homeland had already been conquered and their retreat cut off. This tactic forced Xiang Yu to finally commit suicide in the Wu River 烏江.[65] The banquet at Hongmen and the encirclement at Gaixia are famous allusions, and Xie Zhan is able to use these allusions to concisely summarize Zhang's contributions to Liu's rise in only four lines.

After the dynasty was established, Zhang advised Liu to enfeoff Yong Chi 雍齒 (d. 192 BCE), protected the heir apparent, recommended Xiao He 蕭何 (257–193 BCE) as prime minister, and chose Chang'an as the capital.[66] In the early days of the dynasty, Liu Bang faced many difficult questions of policy such as how to reward meritorious officials and how to ensure that his orders would be carried out. The first event in line 15 is recorded in the *Shiji*:

> When your majesty [Liu Bang] rose from among the common people, it was through these men that you seized control of the empire. You have become the Son of Heaven, but those whom you have enfeoffed have all been close friends from old days, such as Xiao He and Cao Can, while all your former enemies you have ordered executed. . . . The emperor thereupon held a feast and enfeoffed Yong Chi as marquis of Shifang, ordering the prime minister and imperial secretary to act with all dispatch in settling the question of recognizing merit and carrying out the remainder of the enfeoffments. When the other ministers left the banquet, they said to each other happily, "If even Yong Chi can become a marquis, the rest of us have nothing to worry about!"[67]

> 陛下起布衣，以此屬取天下，今陛下爲天子，而所封皆蕭、曹故人所親愛，而所誅者皆生平所仇怨……於是上乃置酒，封雍齒爲什方侯，而急趣丞相、御史定功行封。羣臣罷酒，皆喜曰："雍齒尚爲侯，我屬無患矣。"[68]

This passage explains that Zhang urged Liu Bang to reward Yong Chi, so that all officials would feel that Liu was fair-minded and impartial. Line

16 refers to Zhang Liang's advice in choosing the capital and protecting the crown prince. Zhang's advice in the first matter was decisive. Liu Bang wanted to make Luoyang the capital of the dynasty, but Lou Jing 婁敬 (fl. ca. 202 BCE) argued that Chang'an was preferable, and Zhang supported Lou.⁶⁹ With regard to the crown prince, Liu Bang wanted to replace him with his third son, Ruyi 如意 (d. 194 BCE), the king of Zhao. The crown prince's mother, Empress Lü 呂后 (241–180 BCE), panicked and sought help from Zhang Liang, who was initially evasive, saying that he did not wish to interfere in the private affairs of the royal family. After several requests from Empress Lü, Zhang Liang presented his strategy:

> There are four men in the world whom the emperor has not succeeded in attracting to his court. . . . Now if you are willing to spare no expense in gold and precious gifts, you might have the heir apparent write them a letter offering in the humblest possible terms to send carriages to fetch them, and at the same time dispatch some artful talker to press the invitation. In that case I think they would come. If they came, you could entertain them as your guests and from time to time take them with you to court. The emperor will be sure to wonder who they are and ask about them. When he discovers that they are worthy men, this will help you to somewhat strengthen the position of the heir apparent.⁷⁰

> 顧上有不能致者，天下有四人……今公誠能無愛金玉璧帛，令太子爲書，卑辭安車，因使辯士固請，宜來。來，以爲客，時時從入朝，令上見之，則必異而問之.問之，上知此四人賢，則一助也。⁷¹

Zhang told Empress Lü that it would be difficult to persuade or impress the emperor with words, but that if the crown prince were able to gain the backing of the Four Old Men of Mount Shang 商山四皓, four famously virtuous hermits whom Liu Bang tried and failed to seek council from, it would prove the prince's virtues and ensure his position. Indeed, when the Four Old Men of Mount Shang appeared together with the prince before Liu Bang, it secured the crown prince's position.⁷² Xie Zhan's description of Zhang Liang's many achievements is remarkably terse, and the poet is able to emphatically signal Liu's own virtues through his use of the strong, active verbs "dispel" 消, "perish" 殞, "suggest" 建, and "protect" 護. The ascension of the Liu Song dynasty marked a shift away from the political dynamics that dominated the Eastern Jin, namely, governance as a delicate collaboration between the emperor and aristocratic families 士族. As Wang Ping explains,

> Their [common men's] sudden ascension to the top of the social pyramid encroached on the prestige and prerogatives of the old aristocratic class, which was not yet ready to accept a new hierarchical order. Ensuing contention between the "rootless" emperors and big-clan members during the fifth century was a manifestation of the power and terror of absolute rule.[73]

Liu Yu and other powerful men, who came from humble backgrounds, were gradually able to gain political and military power, and their ascent was in line with a growing consensus that the elite aristocratic families had to be reined in.[74] In the last three couplets of Xie Zhan's poem, he finally introduces his own position relative to Liu Yu's remembrance of Zhang Liang. Although Xie Zhan did not have the opportunity to participate in the ceremony, he imagined it, and wrote this poem to celebrate the virtue of Liu. Through this imaginary journey to the Zhang Liang temple, Xie praises Zhang's contribution to the establishment of the Western Han dynasty (202 BCE–8 CE), and at the same time demonstrates his communicative memory of Liu Yu. In the second half of the poem, Xie is self-deprecating, referring to himself as a "blind man" 瞽夫, and claiming that he is "without talents" 無良 and "insignificant and remote" 微遠.[75]

By the reign of Yixi, Liu Yu, who had been a common soldier and risen through the ranks, had become the de facto ruler of the Eastern Jin dynasty. The legitimate Jin emperor was merely Liu's puppet, and Liu was tireless in suppressing dissent to his rule. Aristocratic families who stood in his way were often punished, and sometimes even eradicated. By this era, the aristocratic families which had so dominated Jin society had lost much of their political and military power, but they were still able to maintain their cultural influence. For instance, the percentage of military positions held by members of the Xie clan decreased during the transition between the Eastern Jin and Liu Song dynasty, from 41 percent of all military position to 20 percent. Xie clan members generally entered the bureaucracy at a higher rank, but they rarely held real power. In other words, in a shift forced by lower-ranked generals and staff, they held prestigious sinecures. Retrospective memory of Zhang Liang helped Liu Yu establish his status and legitimate his power in the context of the decline of aristocratic families during the Jin–Song transition. The Xie clan members were still able to use their cultural capital to influence the state.[76] The largely uneducated Liu Yu needed the assistance of elite courtiers to confer cultural legitimacy upon his regime.[77] According to the *History of the Southern Dynasties* (*Nanshi* 南史), Xie Hui 謝晦 (390–426) once wrote a poem on Liu's behalf to save him from the embarrassment of making mistakes;[78] on another occasion, Liu Muzhi suggested that he write in large characters because his calligraphy was otherwise rather unattractive.[79] Liu Yu was savvy enough to recognize that he needed a degree of cultural capital to successfully establish his own dynasty.

Xie Zhan, in the eleventh and twelfth couplets of his "Zhang Zifang shi," praised Liu's benevolence and righteousness in organizing a ceremony and sacrifice for Zhang Liang. Xie Zhan understood Liu's aims well, and therefore only discussed the more sophisticated, positive elements of Zhang Liang's cultural memory. He omitted Zhang's more controversial actions, such as the hiring of a strongman to assassinate Qin Shihuang 秦始皇 (259–210 BCE) with an iron bludgeon. As the *Shiji* records:

> Zhang Liang once journeyed to Huaiyang to study ritual and there met the lord of Canghai. Through him he obtained the services of a man renowned for his great strength. Zhang Liang had an iron bludgeon made which weighed 120 catties and, when the Qin emperor came east on a tour, he and the assassin lay in wait for him. When the emperor reached the area of Bolangsha they made their attack, but mistakenly struck the carriage of his attendants. The emperor was enraged and ordered an immediate search throughout the empire for the rebels, hoping to seize Zhang Liang. Zhang Liang assumed a false name and fled into hiding in Xiapi.[80]

> 良嘗學禮淮陽.東見倉海君.得力士，爲鐵椎重百二十斤.秦皇帝東游，良與客狙擊秦皇帝博浪沙中，誤中副車.秦皇帝大怒，大索天下，求賊甚急，爲張良故也.良乃更名姓，亡匿下邳.[81]

Because this anecdote was present in the same Sima Qian biography Xie uses as a source for other events of Zhang's life, its omission is deliberate.[82] Knowing that Liu Yu wanted to establish legitimacy for his political pursuits, Xie focuses on Zhang Liang's more fruitful strategies rather than his seditiousness.

By way of contrast, another member of the Xie clan, Xie Lingyun, emphasized the more violent aspects of Zhang Liang's biography, a rhetorical misstep which eventually cost him his life. According to the *Nanshi*, in the eighth year of the Yuanjia 元嘉 reign (431), Xie Lingyun was demoted to governor of Linchuan 臨川 (modern-day Fuzhou 撫州, Jiangxi Province). Xie seems to have been ashamed of not being assigned a more important position. Unhappy with his new assignment and duties, he neglected them in favor of traveling, wandering, engaging in "pure talk," and composing literary works inspired by his beautiful natural surroundings. Xie's behavior enraged local officials, who brought him up on charges of misconduct; Xie responded to their impeachment by having the local officials arrested. He articulated his frustrations in four lines of poetry:[83]

	韓亡子房奮,	The state of Han declined and Zifang surged,[84]
	秦帝魯連恥.	Conferring imperial dignity to the Qin would humiliate Zhonglian.[85]
	本自江海人,	They originally led a wandering life,[86]
4	忠義感君子.	Their loyalty and righteousness touched noble men.

The style, rhetoric, and tone of this poem are very different from Xie Lingyun's landscape poetry and fully demonstrate his fury. The poet associates himself with Zhang Liang and Lu Zhonglian to demonstrate his disdain for the Liu Song dynasty and his discomfort with the society and political landscape in which he lived. The poem suggests an equivalence between the powerful but brutal Qin and the Liu Song dynasty, which also rose to power through military force and brutality. Both Zhang Liang and Lu Zhonglian fiercely opposed Qin tyranny. Xie insinuates his shame at serving the Song dynasty and not avenging the Eastern Jin dynasty. The poem was perhaps just a case of carelessness brought on by profound vexation, but the consequences were very serious. When Emperor Wen 宋文帝 (407–453; r. 424–453) found out about these verses, he demoted Xie to an office in Nanhai 南海 (what is now Guangzhou, Guangdong Province). Rather than obey the emperor's orders, Xie arranged for people to rescue him, which irritated the emperor so much he condemned Xie to death.[87] When compared with Xie Lingyun's recklessness, Xie Zhan's circumspection in choosing which aspects of the Zhang Liang story to use seems wise. In hindsight, Xie Zhan understood his political milieu and was appropriately concerned about the position of his clan. He came from a powerful and prominent family, and hoped that his clan would preserve their status through the fast-changing society, but he feared that he would share the fate of some literati of previous transitions who had done a poor job of positioning themselves politically and suffered the consequences.⁸⁸ The "Poem on Zhang Zifang" is therefore only one of several poems in which Xie signals his political loyalty (or, at least, acquiescence) to Liu Yu.

In the fourteenth year of the Yixi reign (418), on the Chongyang Festival 重陽節 (the ninth day of the ninth month in the lunar calendar), Xie Zhan attended a banquet for Kong Jing 孔靖 (347–422), who was about to withdraw from politics, held at Xima Terrace. On that occasion, Liu Yu ordered the officials in attendance to compose poems in Kong's honor.⁸⁹ Xie's contribution was the following poem:

九日從宋公戲馬臺集送孔令詩⁹⁰
A Valediction for Director Kong of the Imperial Secretariat Written at the Command of the Duke of Song on the Ninth Day at a Gathering at Xima Terrace⁹¹

	風至授寒服，	When winter arrives, winter clothes are passed out;
	霜降休百工．	When frost falls, workers of all trades cease to work.
	繁林收陽彩，	Dense forests withdraw their brilliant hues,
4	密苑解華叢．	Lush gardens shed their colorful foliage.
	巢幕無留鷰，	No swallows remain in their nests by the curtains,
	遵渚有來鴻．	There are migrating geese arriving at the waterfront.
	輕霞冠秋日，	Light evening glow caps this autumn day,
8	迅商薄清穹．	Swift western wind reaches the clear sky.
	聖心眷嘉節，	His ruler's heart is touched by the fine season,
	揚鑾戾行宮．	Riding the imperial carriage, he came to the traveling palace.
	四筵霑芳醴，	The side mats are spread with fragrant wines,
12	中堂起絲桐．	The central court rings with beautiful music.
	扶光迫西汜，	The waning sun approaches the western edge,
	歡餘讌有窮．	The banquet comes to a close, but pleasures remain.
	逝矣將歸客，	The departing guest is taking his leave,
16	養素克有終．	His cultivation remains constant to the end.
	臨流怨莫從，	By the flowing river I regret I am unable to follow him.
	歡心歎飛蓬．	In admiration I sigh over the windblown grass.

Kong Jing was a key official who supported Liu Yu from the beginning and presented strategies to defeat Huan Xuan 桓玄 (369–404).⁹² This poem begins by depicting the natural environment at the time of this seasonal occasion, namely autumn's Chongyang Festival. Autumn in traditional Chinese literature and culture has been often associated with melancholy and sadness, but this poem adopts a merry tone. Wu Fusheng argues that this unusual choice of tone was dictated by the context of poetic composition—namely, a farewell banquet. Furthermore, this choice also indicates that the appearance of Liu Yu was such an auspicious event that it transformed the seasonal mood from the depression and unhappiness that was traditional to cheerful joy. After depicting the natural landscape, the poem praises the lavish banquet Liu Yu organized for this festival. Only in the last section does the poem turn to the subject indicated by the title: Kong Jing's retirement and moral values. The subtext of the poem conveyed by the last couplet is Xie's own situation, and the anxiety he feels over the lack of control he has over his life and fate. The tone is that of eulogy, particularly the mournful lines "His ruler's heart is touched by the fine season, / Riding the imperial carriage he came to the traveling palace." This tone is in part dictated by the conventions of the occasion, and the genre of panegyric poetry (*yingzhi shi* 應制詩). To the extent that this poem expresses Xie's own feelings, it does so only subtly, maintaining the conventions of courtly poetry.

Xie Zhan's reticence was shaped by his adherence to self-preservation. Xie's family was unable to restore their previous level of power and influence, and could only look on in fear at the rise of the Liu Song *homines novi*.[93] Xie, in fact, actively appealed to Liu Yu for a demotion, so that he and his family would be a safe distance from the dangerous whirlpool of politics.[94] Xie openly expressed his commitment to self-preservation in conversations with his family members. According to the *Nanshi*, on one occasion, Xie Lingyun, Xie Hui, and Xie Zhan discussed the lives of several literati of the Wei–Jin transition: Jia Chong 賈充 (217–282), Pan Yue 潘岳 (247–300), and Lu Ji 陸機 (261–303). Xie Zhan's view was expressed as follows:

> Let us suppose you'd be able to forget about your power when occupying a place of honor. Even so, criticisms will inevitably arise, and you would find yourself cast into danger without reason. How can a gentleman's use of wisdom to protect his life possibly inhere in this [idea of yours]?[95]

若處貴而能遺權, 斯則是非不得而生, 傾危無因而至. 君子以明哲保身, 其在此乎.[96]

This statement reflects a Confucian adherence to the "doctrine of the mean," and a cautious approach to his life and career. Xie understood this arc clearly, so he deliberately withdrew from a position of political power, an act aimed at preserving both himself and his family.

This conversation is not the only one in which Xie expressed his principle of self-preservation. He also tactfully articulated this principle in his poetic exchanges with family members. For example, in his "Response to Lingyun at Ancheng" ("Yu Ancheng da Lingyun" 於安城答靈運), a poem written in the eleventh year of the Yixi reign (415) in response to a poem by his family member Xie Lingyun 謝靈運 (385–433), Xie Zhan emphasizes staying away from high political positions:

	跰行安步武,	Hobbling on one leg, how could I walk in your traces?
	鎩翮周數仞.	Wounded in one wing, I flew around for a few yards.
	豈不識高遠,	How could I not know how far and high one could fly?
4	違方往有吝.	But to go against my heart would have led to humiliation,
	歲寒霜雪嚴,	In the cold of the year, frost and snow are bitter,
	過半路愈峻.	Halfway along, the road grows steeper still.
	量己畏友朋,	I have taken my own measure and stand in awe of my friends,
8	勇退不敢進.	I am bent on retiring since I dare not advance.
	行矣勵令猷,	Now I will go! Strive to set a good example!
	寫誠訊來訊.	In all sincerity I write this reply to your letter.[97]

Although Xie Zhan, adopting a self-deprecating tone, acknowledges Xie Lingyun's talent, Xie Zhan, speaking as a close family member, also reminds Xie Lingyun of the importance of self-preservation.[98]

Xie Zhan was far from the first intellectual to stress self-preservation. In the fast-changing political environment of a dynastic transition, literati strove to keep themselves safe and avoid political persecution. Xie Zhan, however, was not simply concerned with protecting himself—he expounded this principle to his clan members, at times even placing the interest of the whole clan higher than himself. Xie Zhan's biography records that when he came down with a serious illness in Yuzhang—an illness that would eventually claim his life—he did not want his family members to pay him a visit.[99] This behavior can be interpreted as an expression of his consideration of the interests of the whole clan, who might come under suspicion if they were to visit him. Xie Hui, for example, was at that time in charge of the imperial guards and not permitted to leave the palace. When Xie Hui did eventually travel to see Xie Zhan in Yuzhang, he was slandered as a rebel and had to return with Xie Zhan to the capital.[100] Xie Zhan was careful to the point of elevating the interests of the clan over his own life.

In hindsight, Xie Zhan understood his political milieu and his worries about his clan members were justified. A few decades after he composed this poem on Zhang Liang, some of Xie Zhan's fears were realized. Xie Hui, who cut an imposing figure and excelled in rhetoric and writing, did not heed Xie Zhan's advice of keeping a low profile. Xie Hui was trusted by Liu Yu, who made him one of the executors of his will. At the same time, Xie Hui's outspokenness exposed him to danger. He frequently disagreed with Liu Muzhi, who tried to exclude him from the government, and was eventually killed in the political struggles that followed Liu Yu's death.[101] Discussing the tragic fate of Xie clan members, Tian Yuqin 田余慶 (1924–2014) writes,

> Since the end of the Jin dynasty, the Xie clan was the most influential and talented of all the elite aristocratic clans, and they therefore were given more opportunities to participate in the government. With the restoration of imperial power during the Eastern Jin and Liu Song dynasties, the support of aristocratic clans like the Xie were a valuable resource for establishing imperial authority, but they were also the greatest threat to that authority. Therefore, beginning in the Yixi reign when Liu Yu seized power and extending into the Liu Song dynasty, more members of the Xie clan—Xie Hun, Xie Hui, Xie Lingyun, Xie Zong 謝綜 (d. 446), and Xie Yue 謝約 (b. ca. 423), etc.—were executed by Liu Song than from any other aristocratic clan.
>
> 晉末以來，幾家最高的門閥士族，以謝氏影響最深，潛力最大，所以謝氏人物參預政治的機會，也較其它家族爲多. 在晉宋皇權復興之際，謝氏這樣的家族，對於皇權說來，既最有利用的價值，又最具生事的危險. 所以自東晉義熙年間劉裕當權以後，以迄劉宋之間，謝氏家族人物被劉宋殺戮者，比其它高門都要多，計有謝混、謝晦、謝靈運、謝綜、謝約等人.[102]

The story of the Xie clan was a classic tragedy of hubris: a rise to immense power during the early medieval period, and an equally dramatic fall.[103] Although many of these events happened after Xie Zhan's poem on Zhang Liang, his discernment surpassed his contemporaries' and demonstrated a very subtle literati psychological state. His outlook on official life, fame, and reputation, and his understanding of the course of development of a major aristocratic clan, were prescient.

Conclusion

This chapter applies the concept of cultural memory to explain Xie Zhan's "Zhang Zifang shi," Zheng Xianzhi's parallel poem on Zhang Liang, Fan Tai's poem on Liu Bang, and Xie Lingyun's poem on Zhang Liang and Lu Zhonglian. Xie Zhan, Zheng Xianzhi, and Fan Tai made use of the past to secure the present for their patron Liu Yu. What is important is the repertoire of historical tropes used to prefigure Liu's imperial authority. By contrast, Xie Lingyun sacrificed his life by writing on historical figures. These literati not only adopted retrospective memory and prospective memory to commemorate historical figures and place their ruler in a great lineage but also contemplated the ethics of those historical figures. Retrospective memory helps us to understand how historical figures came to be memorialized through poetry, and prospective memory aids us in understanding how poets ensured that their patron would be remembered. Righteous behavior and moral values convey one's reputation to future generations. When poets compose poems about historical figures and their stories, they do not simply reiterate longer historical accounts, but rather select which parts of the stories they wish to lyricize, a choice which speaks to both their own agenda and/or contemporary views of historical figures and events.

Liu Yu used retrospective and prospective memories of famous Han figures as a guide for the present and an indicator of the future. Assmann discusses the role that genealogy played in identify formation, stating, "The genealogy is a form that bridges the gap between the present and the time of origin, legitimizing a current order or aspiration by providing an unbroken link with the very beginning."[104] Liu Yu claimed (and likely fabricated) descent from King Yuan of Chu in the Western Han. In addition to embellishing his genealogy, Liu Yu arranged for cultural elites to compose poems on his great deeds in visiting the Liu Bang temple and restoring the Zhang Liang temple. The communicative memory of Liu Yu, along with his successful northern military campaign, earned him much legitimacy, which not only allowed him to overthrow the Jin, but even allowed him to claim that he received the Mandate of Heaven from the glorious Han dynasty. Liu Yu retrospectively used the past to establish his legitimacy and prospectively used his good deeds and virtues to promote his status and convey the message that his rule would restore social order. Liu Yu directly linked his present moment and his activities to the Han. Through visiting the temples, Liu Yu brought the remote past into his contemporary environment, demonstrating and consolidating his identity and values. Liu's behavior, in turn, shaped the communicative memory conveyed by his officials about him and his virtues.

By commemorating these historical figures and events, these Jin–Song literati felt the powerful weight of history as it was passed down through texts and memory. The past was stronger than the present: what was gone carried more weight and ironically felt more present than the actual present for the early medieval Chinese literati. Liu Yu's visits to the Zhang Liang and Liu Bang temples, and the poems he commissioned in honor of the dead, not only demonstrated his deep admiration and respect for the cultural heritage of the Western Han but also were calculated efforts to use that heritage to win the respect of literati and confer cultural legitimacy upon his imminent seizure of power. Liu's demonstration of reverence for culture heroes like Zhang Liang and Liu Bang sent the signal that he would seek to legitimize his own authority, which was particularly critical in an era of political turmoil. It was also a gesture meant to reflect Liu's own virtues: his noble character and sentiments, and particularly the fact that, although he was a relatively uneducated military man, he was committed to cultural refinement and eager to recruit talented officials. Through poems like those written by Xie Zhan, Zheng Xianzhi, and Fan Tai, Liu Yu eulogized the past and seemed to attempt a restoration of the strength and traditions of the Han dynasty.

But while Xie Zhan's "Poem on Zhang Zifang," his poem dedicated to Kong Jing, and "Response to Lingyun at Ancheng" were a testament to Liu's confidence, they revealed Xie's ambivalence. Xie wanted to participate in politics and establish himself as an official, but he was also anxious about making the wrong move in a fast-changing political environment. He was well aware of the historical example of scholars in the Wei–Jin (220–420) period who strove to protect themselves in a similar situation and often failed. In the Xie Zhan poems discussed above, Xie demonstrates his desire for self-preservation. The fast-changing and unstable sociopolitical environment was the primary factor shaping the image the Xie family members presented of themselves in writing, and prevented scholars like Xie Zhan from directly addressing contemporary social issues and moral questions. Although Xie Zhan is compelled to sing the praises of Liu, a careful reading of his writings reveals his pain and trepidation. Such was the nature of Xie and Liu's collaboration: Liu, whose power was based in military force, needed Xie's cultural capital, and Xie, aware of his own vulnerability, could not but lend it to him. This dynamic epitomized the anxieties of the age.

Chapter Six

Approaches to Lore in the "Yongshi" Section of the *Wen xuan*

The end of the early medieval era, particularly the Qi–Liang period, witnessed major developments in literary criticism and the compilation of literary anthologies. During this period, *Wen xuan* established *yongshi shi* as a poetic subgenre. *Wen xuan* was compiled by Xiao Tong 蕭統 (501–531) and his editorial team, which likely included Liu Xiaochuo 劉孝綽 (481–539) and He Xun 何遜 (d. 518). It contains 761 pieces of prose and verse composed by 130 writers, ranging from the late Zhou to Liang eras, representing literary writings from thirty-seven different genres.[1] In the Song, a popular saying reveals its importance among the literati: "The *Wen xuan* thoroughly done, / Half a licentiate won."[2] It is the first extant anthology of Chinese literature arranged into categories, and was a crucial text for scholars preparing for the civil service examination in the Tang dynasty (618–907).[3] This anthology contains a section entitled "[Poems] on History" ("Yongshi" 詠史), with twenty-one poems written by nine poets between the Jian'an 建安 era (196–220) and the Liu Song dynasty (420–479). It provides an important angle from which to examine the types and features of *yongshi shi* in early medieval China, as it was the first time that *yongshi shi* was established as an explicitly labeled literary subgenre in an anthology based on extant materials. Although the selections reflect the personal tastes of Xiao and his editorial team, they were influenced by the intellectual atmosphere of the Southern Dynasties (420–589).

In writing *yongshi shi*, early medieval Chinese poets recalled and selected certain aspects of historical figures and wrote them into their poetry. This remembered history contributes to the formation of the cultural memory of the historical figures; as Jan Assmann argues, "What counts for cultural memory is not factual but remembered history. One might even say that cultural memory transforms factual into remembered history, thus turning it into myth."[4] Given that remembered history plays a definitive role in shaping cultural memory, it is important to note which parts of historical accounts poets chose to become remembered history. How did poets approach complex historical records on particular historical figures?

This chapter investigates the ways in which Xiao's editorial team conceptualized the features and content of *yongshi shi* in the "Yongshi" section of *Wen xuan* and examines the relationship between lore in various forms, such as historical, official, and anecdotal accounts and what is represented in *yongshi shi*.[5] This chapter takes these accounts collectively as lore to which the poets could refer or allude. I have identified three approaches that the poets who composed the *yongshi shi* in *Wen xuan* adopted in appropriating lore from various accounts. In each case, the poet uses lore to express his own opinions and emotions, but the degree to which the poet's own opinion is foregrounded is different. In the first case, the lore is emphasized, while the poet's opinion is tacitly expressed through the historical figures and events that he chooses to select and emphasize. The poet often waits to express an opinion in the closing lines. In the second case, the lore is used to bolster the poet's opinion by providing relevant examples. In the last case, the poet stresses his personal feelings, and lore is only briefly alluded to, serving as the background for the articulation of his views, or as a broader cultural context and tradition for the poet's situation. In this case, *yongshi shi* are very similar to the genre of poems known as "songs of my cares" (*yonghuai shi* 詠懷詩).

Close Citation of Accounts of Lore

The first approach toward integrating accounts of lore a reader encounters in the "Yongshi" section of *Wen xuan* is that of paraphrasing these records. A prime example of this approach is Zhang Xie's "Poem on History" ("Yongshi" 詠史), which sings of the two Shus 二疏. The major account of these figures during Zhang's time is *History of the Han Dynasty* (*Hanshu* 漢書); other materials on them seem to have been limited. Zhang's poem, the first extant poem on the two Shus, captures the main developments of their lives, which appears to be based on passages in the *Hanshu*. It mimics the format of standard histories by narrating a biography, then providing comments in closing.

	昔在西京時，	In the past, in the Western capital,
	朝野多歡娛．	Among the court and the public were much happiness and pleasure.
	藹藹東都門，	Many thronged to the capital's Eastern Gate,
4	羣公祖二疎．	Where gathered lords bade farewell to the two Shus.
	朱軒曜金城，	Vermillion carriages lit up the invincible city,
	供帳臨長衢．	Tents were raised by the long thoroughfare.
	達人知止足，	Learned men knew their limits,
8	遺榮忽如無．	Glories and rewards seemed to mean nothing to them.
	抽簪解朝衣，	Taking out hairpins, removing court robes,
	散髮歸海隅．	They spread their hair and returned to a corner of the sea.
	行人爲隕涕，	Passers-by shed tears [for the two Shus],
12	賢哉此丈夫！	"How virtuous these two masters are!"
	揮金樂當年，	Throwing money around, reveling through those days,
	歲暮不留儲．	They exhausted their savings in their twilight years.
	顧謂四座賓，	They told their surrounding guests,
16	多財爲累愚．	"Excessive wealth could become a burden for fools."
	清風激萬代，	Cool breezes[6] surged for ten thousand generations,
	名與天壤俱．	Their fame is as everlasting as Heaven and Earth.
	咄此蟬冕客，	How impressive are these sable-capped guests!
20	君紳宜見書．	Their words should be inscribed on officials' sashes.[7]

This poem praises Shu Guang 疏廣 (d. 45 BCE) and his nephew Shu Shou 疏受 (d. 48 BCE), both of whom were tutors to Emperor Xuan 宣 (r. 74–48 BCE). A detailed account of their lives can be found in *Hanshu*, which predates Zhang Xie's poem. When they decided to retire to their home village, people and officials in the capital saw them off. After they returned home, they spent their fortunes on their fellow villagers and did not leave anything for their descendants.[8] Their story was revered by later generations for the moral it imparted: after contributing to the court and achieving affluence, one should shun fame and reputation, and leave the court to enjoy one's life rather than continually seeking a higher station.

In this poem, Zhang Xie paraphrases the historical source in different ways, using compact literary images to evoke the larger story from which they are drawn. The fifth couplet depicts the two Shus' resignation of their high positions with the metonymy of taking off robes and removing hairpins. In the historical source from which this poem was likely drawn, we find details not included in the poem: the pretext of their withdrawal from court and the favor they received from the emperor and the heir apparent:

> On the very same day both uncle and nephew reported that they were suffering from illness. When the customary three months waiting period had passed, they were granted a leave of absence, but Shu Guang, pleading that his illness was critical, submitted a memorial asking to be released from government service. In view of his age and precarious health, the emperor agreed to release both him and his nephew, in addition presenting them with a gift of twenty catties of gold. The heir apparent for his part presented them with fifty catties.[9]

> 即日父子俱移病. 滿三月賜告, 廣遂稱篤, 上疏乞骸骨. 上以其年篤老, 皆許之, 加賜黃金二十斤, 皇太子贈以五十斤.[10]

Zhang's poem is an aesthetically pleasing encapsulation of that longer historical narrative, employing concise literary images to express the ideas of the historical in just a few lines.

Another summarizing strategy employed by Zhang Xie is using a synoptic view to summarize the behavior of the main characters, leaving out the supporting figures and narrative details. For instance, the seventh couplet's mention of Shu Guang and Shu Shou enjoying their retirement in their hometown is a synopsis of the relatively long historical description in *Hanshu*:

> After Shu Guang had returned home, each day he would order his family to prepare wine and food, inviting relatives, old friends, and their guests to join him in making merry. From time to time he would ask his family how much gold was left and send them scurrying off to sell more of it to buy provisions. After a year or so of this, Shu Guang's sons and grandsons took one of Shu Guang's cousins aside, an elderly man whom Shu Guang loved and trusted, and said to him, "We had hoped while the old gentleman was still alive to lay the foundations for something of a family fortune, but with all this drinking and eating every day the money is almost all used up."[11]

> 廣既歸鄉里, 日令家共具設酒食, 請族人故舊賓客, 與相娛樂. 數問其家金餘尚有幾所, 趣賣以共具. 居歲餘, 廣子孫竊謂其昆弟老

人廣所愛信者曰:"子孫幾及君時頗立產業基阯, 今日飲食 (廢) [費]且盡。"[12]

Zhang Xie, unable to include all the details of the narrative in a much shorter poem, ignores the story of how the two Shus entertained relatives and guests, and the dialogue between Shu Guang's relatives. However, Zhang Xie does select some comments from supporting figures in the *Hanshu* which highlight the virtues of the two Shus. The sixth couplet comments on the reaction of the people to the two Shus leaving the capital. Although this comment may seem like the poet directly imagining and mimicking the voice of the people, it is in fact borrowed directly from the *Hanshu*: "Those who saw them passing along the road all exclaimed, 'How virtuous the two masters are!' and some sighed and shed tears for them."[13] 及道路觀者皆曰: "賢哉二大夫!" 或歎息爲之下泣。[14] The poem and the historical narrative use the same or similar phrases: "passers-by" 行人 in the poem versus "those who saw them" 道路觀者 in the narrative; "shed tears for the two Shus" 爲隕涕 in the poem and "shed tears for them" 爲之下泣 in the narrative; and "how virtuous these masters are" 賢哉此大夫 in the poem and "how virtuous the two masters are" 賢哉二大夫 in the narrative. It seems that Zhang Xie closely read and directly cited the historical source (or an urtext which serves as source for them both). The function of the direct quotation seems to be to assure readers that his poem is based on established sources and authentically represents the deeds of the two Shus.

The poem closely follows the version found in *Hanshu*. The poem even has a strong narrative element, and incorporates dialogue and commentary found in the historical source. It is as if the poet rehearsed and reimagined history as he read it, moved by its echoes, subsuming his emotional response into the language of poetry. Although it is not stated explicitly, Zhang Xie's poetic vision of history probably reflected his personal experience, which was in some ways similar to that of the two Shus. Talented as a young man, Zhang Xie held a series of different official positions and then abandoned the official life and withdrew to become a recluse at the chaotic end of the reign of Emperor Hui of Jin 晉惠帝 (259–307; r. 290–307). Historical accounts describe Zhang as a devotee of the Dao, who did not compete for political power and instead entertained himself by composing poems.[15] It is tempting to relate this poem to later stories of Zhang Xie's life; as Pauline Lin points out, "Praise for and desire of retirement is a prominent theme in Zhang's poetry. . . . Alongside the desire for reclusion, however, there is a sense of loneliness, longing, regret, frustration, unachieved ambition, and unmet aspirations and goals, reflecting Zhang's inability to attain a powerful official position."[16] It is not implausible that Zhang Xie meant his depiction of the lofty vision, unassailable virtues, and pure motivations of the two Shus as a reflection of his own ideals. Even if he does not explicitly claim an affinity with the two Shus, the specific words, language, and stories from the historical record he adopts fit his personal context.

Another example of poets paraphrasing accounts of lore in their poems is Lu Chen's 盧諶 (ca. 285–ca. 351) "Poem on Surveying the Ancient" ("Langu" 覽古).[17] This poem focuses on the historical figure Lin Xiangru 藺相如 (ca. 329 BCE–ca. 259 BCE), who skillfully maintained the security of the state of Zhao when it was threatened by Qin. Although Zhao was weak, Lin was not afraid of the powerful Qin, and was prepared to die for his state. Lin maintained a working relationship with the Zhao general Lian Po 廉頗 (d. ca. 250 BCE). Lian had initially despised Lin because, as a general, although he had defeated enemies and conquered cities, he held a lower position than Lin, whom he felt won his position only through his oratory. Lian therefore insulted Lin on several occasions, but the latter devised different pretexts for not confronting him, which allowed Zhao to have a harmonious court focused on external threats.[18] Lian later understood Lin's intentions and apologized to Lin for his narrow-mindedness and outrageousness, and they were then able to amicably collaborate to safeguard the state. The vulnerable position of Zhao is the context for the poem I provide below:

	覽古	Poem on Surveying Ancient History
	趙氏有和璧，	The state of Zhao had Bian He's jade,
	天下無不傳。	Its reputation spread throughout the world.
	秦人來求市，	A Qin official came seeking an exchange,
4	厥價徒空言。	The price they offered was only empty words.
	與之將見賣，	If the jade were relinquished, Zhao would be sold.
	不與恐致患。	If it were not, they feared it would bring calamity.
	簡才備行李，	Zhao selected a talent and prepared an envoy,
8	圖令國命全。	With plans to preserve the destiny of the state.
	藺生在下位，	Mr. Lin was an inferior,
	繆子稱其賢。	Sir Miao praised him as virtuous.
	奉辭馳出境，	Accepting the order, galloping across the border,
12	伏軾遄入關。	He bent over the chariot brace and hastened to the pass.

	秦王御殿坐，	The Qin King sat in the Imperial Hall,
	趙使擁節前．	Zhao's envoy advanced with the tally.
	揮袂睨金柱，	Flinging his sleeve, glancing at the bronze pillar.
16	身玉要俱捐．	Lin wanted to sacrifice both himself and the jade.
	連城既僞往，	The promise of a series of cities turned out to be false,
	荊玉亦眞還．	Indeed, the Chu jade was also returned to the Zhao.
	爰在澠池會，	The two rulers later met at Mianchi,
20	二主克交歡．	So that they could exchange pleasantries.
	昭襄欲負力，	King Zhaoxiang wanted to rely on his power,
	相如折其端．	Xiangru broke his will at the source.[19]
	眥血下霑衿，	Blood welled in his eyes, falling to stain his robe,
24	怒髮上衝冠．	Furious, his hair pushed up his hat.
	西缶終雙擊，	Finally [the Qin King] struck the western *fou*[20] in accompaniment,
	東瑟不隻彈．	The [Zhao King] did not play the eastern *se*[21] alone.
	捨生豈不易，	How could abandoning life be easy?
28	處死誠獨難．	Facing death is indeed uniquely difficult.
	稜威章臺顚，	The power and prestige of Zhang Terrace[22] were shaken,
	彊禦亦不干．	And strong defenses cannot be violated.
	屈節邯鄲中，	Bending his principles in the capital Handan,
32	俛首忍迴軒．	Lowering his head, he bore the return home.
	廉公何爲者？	Why did Sir Lian do this?
	負荊謝厥譽．	Bearing thorns on his back and apologizing for his faults.
	智勇蓋當代，	Lin's intelligence and courage surpassed his age,
36	弛張使我歎．	His flexibility makes me sigh with praise.[23]

The quasi-narrative elements and title indicate that the poem is based on a historical account. Before Lu Chen's time, the story of Lin Xiangru appeared in such texts as *Master Shen* (*Shenzi* 慎子), *Records of the Han from Eastern Library* (*Dongguan Hanji* 東觀漢記), *Exemplary Words* (*Fayan* 法言), *Treatise on Human Character* (*Renwu zhi* 人物志), and *Records of the Three Kingdoms* (*Sanguo zhi* 三國志). Most of these accounts allude to Lin's story in one or a few brief sentences and focus on his diplomatic success in dealing with the Qin king and/or lowering his status to Lian Po for the benefit of the state of Zhao. Jia Yi's *New Writings* (*Xinshu* 新書) and Liu Xiang's 劉向 (77–6 BCE) *Garden of Tales* (*Shuoyuan* 說苑) also mention Lin's story briefly as evidence to argue for the importance of virtuous figures for a state. The story of Lin asking the king of Qin to play a musical instrument for the king of Zhao appears in Ying Shao's 應劭 (153–196) *Comprehensive Meaning of Customs and Mores* (*Fengsu tongyi* 風俗通議). This story is borrowed directly from the *Shiji*, which contains the most complete account of Lin's biography before Lu's time. All the accounts discussed above collectively constituted the lore from which Lu Chen drew. His depiction of Lin suggests that he probably read the *Shiji* or a very similar account. The plot of the poem follows that of Lin Xiangru's biography in the *Shiji* exactly: the first two couplets highlight the famous treasure of Bian He's jade, which came into the possession of the Zhao and was the immediate trigger and pretext for the Qin's aggression. As the *Shiji* records:

> During the time of King Huiwen, Zhao acquired Chu's jade of the He Clan. King Zhao of Qin (r. 306–251 B.C.) heard of this and sent a messenger to deliver a letter to the King of Zhao, saying that he wished to offer fifteen walled cities in exchange for the jade.[24]
>
> 趙惠文王時, 得楚和氏璧. 秦昭王聞之, 使人遺趙王書, 願以十五城請易璧.[25]

In the first two couplets, the poet summarizes how the Qin king's implausible offer indicated his true unwillingness to compensate Zhao for the jade. The fifth couplet is the turning point for the first half of the poem, as it introduces Lin and establishes a contrast between Lin's low position and the nobleman Miao Xian's 繆賢 high confidence in him. This couplet paraphrases *Shiji*:

> Lin Xiangru was a native of Zhao. He was a houseman of Mou [Miao] Xian, Zhao's Prefect of Eunuchs. . . . [who said of him,] "Your servant personally considers him a brave knight, gifted with wisdom and cunning, fit to undertake this mission."[26]
>
> 藺相如者, 趙人也, 爲趙宦者令繆賢舍人⋯⋯臣竊以爲其人勇士, 有智謀, 宜可使.[27]

The fifth couplet is a direct synopsis of Sima Qian's narration, merely replacing key words with synonyms. Not only does the poem mirror *Shiji*'s plot and diction, but the poet's comments are also the same as those Sima Qian appends at the end of the biography. After narrating the stories of protecting the jade and the meeting at Mianchi, the fourteenth couplet comments on Lin's behavior. This commentary strongly resembles Sima Qian's: "To face death knowing full well one must die, surely this is courage! But as for dying itself, that is no difficult matter; it is using one's death to good purpose that is difficult!"[28] 太史公曰: 知死必勇, 非死者難也, 處死者難.[29] Both the poet and Sima Qian praise Lin's competent management of foreign affairs, and stress that living up to one's principles as Lin did is a rarity.

The eighteenth couplet is also a comment on Lin's character, and although it may seem as if it were Lu Chen's own reflection on history, it in fact echoes Sima Qian's praise of Lin: "Using wisdom and courage to good purpose—he might be said to have done both at once."[30] 其處智勇, 可謂兼之矣![31] Lu uses the first part of Sima's final commentary in the fourteenth couplet to discuss the difficulty of facing death, after narrating Lin's first two deeds.[32] He uses the passage quoted above in the eighteenth couplet to comment on Lin's abilities at the end of the poem. The poet follows the standard format of *Shiji*: first narrating the deeds of the main character, then providing commentary. This imitation allows the poet to demonstrate his skills at condensing a long narrative into a poem, while maintaining its power.

Lu uses descriptive words to underline Lin's heroic personality, dramatizing Lin's actions in critical moments. When the king of Qin was reluctant to play a musical instrument for the king of Zhao at the meeting at Mianchi, Lin warned the king of Qin to be careful, since Lin could throw the musical instrument at him. The twelfth couplet's dramatization of Lin's gallantry at this critical moment is not found in *Shiji*, but the poet's description conveys Lin's fury at the king of Qin's rejection of his polite and reasonable request. The line "blood welled in his eyes" in the twelfth couplet and the description of Lin's hair standing on end exaggerate Lin's anger, highlighting his laudable action. In the *Shiji* account, Lin threatens to kill the king of Qin, but even if Lin really did threaten the king of Qin in this way, it does not leave as deep an impression for the reader. This vivid description contributes to the cultural memory of Lin Xiangru, who was highly respected in the Chinese tradition.[33]

Since the poem is focused on Lin's deeds, it is difficult to fathom when and why Lu Chen composed this poem and what emotions were stirred within him by reading the historical accounts of Lin's life. There are several intertextual clues within this poem, however, which indicate the rationale and rough time of composition of the poems. After the capital of

Western Jin was occupied, Lu Chen, accompanying his father Lu Zhi 盧志 (d. 312), joined the army of the general and influential official Liu Kun 劉琨 (271–318). However, both men were captured by Liu Can 劉粲 (d. 318), who provided an adjutant (*canjun* 參軍) position for Lu Chen. Later, Liu Kun defeated Liu Can, so Lu Chen rejoined Liu Kun, who appointed him as attendant gentleman of the household (*zhubu* 主簿). At the end of the Jianxing reign 建興 (313–317), Lu Chen left Liu Kun's service and joined Duan Pidi 段匹磾 (d. 322). During their extended and close relationship, Lu Chen and Liu Kun exchanged several poems.[34] These poems express their opinions about the current political situation, recall their relationship, and discuss their personal concerns.

It is likely that Lu Chen wrote the above poem around, or shortly after, the time he composed one for Liu Kun titled "Presented to Liu Kun with a Letter" 贈劉琨並書. In this poem, Lu mentions that he previously did not appreciate strong-willed, devoted people:

	昔在暇日.	Formerly, during idle days,
	妙尋通理.	I delved deep into principles of comprehensiveness.
	尤彼意氣.	I condemned those with strong will and spirit,
4	狹是節士.	And belittled those men of uncompromising integrity.
	情以體生.	Now I know that feeling springs from personal experience,
	感以情起.	And arousal rises from personal feeling.[35]

Those men Lu formerly "condemned" would certainly include Lin Xiangru. Another intertextual link is that his other poems sent to Liu Kun allude to the precious jade of Bian He.[36] From these intertextual links, the composition date of "Poem on Surveying Ancient History" can be inferred as sometime between the fourth year of the Jianxing reign (the year 316) and the first year of the Taixing 太興 reign (the year 318).[37]

Lu selected Lin, from among many great historical figures, as a topic for a poem because he was moved by Lin's qualities and personality. In 318, when Lu Chen was appointed as Duan Pidi's mounted escort,[38] he found himself in a dilemma, as the appointment by a new and not fully trusted Xianbei official forced him to leave his former liege, Liu Kun, whom Lu had highly praised and cherished.[39] The last couplet states that Lu was impressed by Lin's success in both foreign and domestic affairs—namely, dealing with both the powerful king of Qin and the general Lian Po—which may have inspired him to compose "Poem on Surveying Ancient History." As with Lin in the poem, Lu was forced to make a difficult choice. As David Knechtges argues, there seems to have been a personal rift between Lu Chen and Liu Kun at this time, which pushed Lu to Duan Pidi.[40] At the same time, the poems he exchanged with Liu Kun portray a degree of ambivalence towards this alliance with Duan.[41] Read as a reflection of Lu Chen's attitude, this poem on Lin Xiangru sets up a flattering comparison between Lin and Lu himself. Enmeshed in a network of complex relationships in a fast-changing political environment, Lu Chen admired Lin Xiangru's talents and hoped he could play as essential a role as Lin did in handling complicated issues adeptly. This poem is an example of how historical figures can stir the emotions of a poet. Through commemorating the past, the poet found solace in the idea that there was historical precedent for the problems he faced. This poem, and the others in the "Yong shi" section of Wen xuan that adopt this associative approach, open a new way to understand history and its significance through a more reflective and expressive subgenre of poetry.[42]

Short Accounts of Lore as Supporting Commentary

The first approach of integrating accounts of lore into poetry is to provide a summary of events largely faithful to the historical record, including a poet's final comment. By way of contrast, in the second approach found in the *yongshi* poems in *Wen xuan*, poets, inspired by certain historical events or people, make their own opinions known through their commentary. Assuming that their readers already possess a firm grasp of lore, these poets do not take the time to narrate it they are referencing in great detail. Wang Can's 王粲 (177–217) "Poem on History" ("Yongshi shi" 詠史詩) and Cao Zhi's 曹植 (192–232) "Poem on the Three Good Men" ("Sanliang shi" 三良詩), both of which comment on the story of the "three good men" of Qin and Lord Mu of Qin's 秦穆公 (d. 621 BCE) command that they be buried alive with him, are illuminating examples of this second approach. Before discussing these two poems, it is necessary to summarize the story on which they are based and the reception of that story prior to these two poems.

The story of the three good men can be found in texts that predate Wang Can and Cao Zhi, such as the *Shijing*, *Zuozhuan*, and *Shiji*. These accounts formed the collective lore before the poets. The story raises controversial moral issues, and the different accounts offer a variety of narrative perspectives that fueled further debate. The "Huangniao" poem in the *Shijing* is the first extant version of the story of the three good men buried with Lord

Mu of Qin. The *Shijing* has a preface, composed by Han dynasty scholars, which provides a context for the poem: "It laments the three good men. The Qin people criticized Lord Mu for [burying people alive] to accompany him in death, and composed this poem." 哀三良也. 國人刺穆公以人從死, 而作是詩.⁴³ I have provided the first stanza of the poem below:

	交交黃鳥,	They flit about, the yellow birds,
	止于棘.	And rest upon the jujube trees.
	誰從穆公,	Who followed Lord Mu [to the grave]?
4	子車奄息.	Ziche Yanxi.
	維此奄息,	And this Yanxi,
	百夫之特.	Was a man above a hundred.
	臨其穴,	When he came to the grave,
8	惴惴其慄.	He looked terrified and trembled.
	彼蒼者天,	Thou azure Heaven there!
	殲我良人.	Thou art destroying our good men.
	如可贖兮,	Could he have been redeemed,
12	人百其身.	We should have given a hundred lives for him.⁴⁴

The following two stanzas adopt the same rhetoric and style, building on the image of yellow birds resting on thorny trees, to describe the other two men who were terrified and sacrificed themselves for Lord Mu. The narrator condemns heaven for this tragedy and praises the three good men, to the point of saying that others should have been sacrificed in their place. When later scholars commented on the *Shijing* and wrote a short preface (*xiaoxu* 小序) to contextualize this poem, they emphasized the link between the three good men and the "Huangniao" poem.⁴⁵

The *Zuozhuan* provides another early account of this story:

> Renhao, the Liege of Qin, died. They took Yanxi, Zhonghang, and Qianhu, three sons of the Ziju lineage, and buried them with him. All were good men of Qin. The inhabitants of the capital grieved over them and composed in their honor the ode "The Oriole."
>
> The noble man said, "It is indeed fitting that Lord Mu of Qin did not become leader of the covenant. In death, he discarded his people. When the former kings departed from the world, they would leave behind proper norms. How could they ever take away the good men of the domain!"⁴⁶

秦伯任好卒,以子車氏之三子奄息、仲行、鍼虎爲殉,皆秦之良也。
國人哀之,爲之賦《黃鳥》. 君子曰: "秦穆之不爲盟主也宜哉! 死
而棄民. 先王違世,猶詒之法,而況奪之善人乎?"⁴⁷

The *Zuozhuan* confirms the connection of the poem "Huangniao" to this story, and similar to "Huangniao," emphasizes the people's reaction to their sacrifice, and criticizes Lord Mu for his cruelty. Because of the preface to the *Shijing* and the confirmation of that connection in *Zuozhuan*, later texts, such as *Shiji*, all accepted the relationship between the "Huangniao" poem and the three good men. Ming Dong Gu explained the stability of this association by comparing two "Huangniao" poems in the *Shijing* (poems 131 and 187, based on the received order). Gu argues that the interpretation for the former is clearer due to the specific historical context it provides, while varying explanations regarding the context of the latter are provided to make sense of the poem. By comparing these two poems, he argues that a stable outer context plays an important role in limiting a text's openness.⁴⁸

The sources above are the major versions of the three good men story that predate the two poems composed by Cao Zhi and Wang Can included in the "Yongshi" section of *Wen xuan*.⁴⁹ Robert Joe Cutter argues that Wang's and Cao's poems seem to directly reflect their experience of visiting the tomb of the three good men, which Wang Can, Cao Zhi, and Ruan Yu 阮瑀 (ca. 165–212) may have done together.⁵⁰ There is evidence that at least Cao Zhi and Ruan Yu visited the tomb in the sixteenth year of the Jian'an reign (212), but no evidence supports or rules out Wang Can's visit in the same year.⁵¹ Cutter speculates that these poets visited the tomb of the three good men on the journey back from a military campaign, and later composed poetry expressing the emotions they felt.⁵² Chen Hongtian 陳宏天, Zhao Fuhai 趙福海, and Chen Fuxing 陳復興 concur:

> In the seventh month of the sixteenth year of the Jian'an reign (211), Cao Cao led a military campaign westward against Ma Chao (176–222). Wang Can accompanied the army as a man of letters. At the end of this year, [Cao Cao's] grand army returned to Chang'an (northwest of present-day Xi'an in Shaanxi) and passed the tomb of the Three Good Men, who were buried alive with Lord Mu of Qin. Wang Can contemplated this historical event, and, thoughts thronging his mind, became the first to compose a poem titled "On History" [about the Three Good

Men], expressing the exquisite emotions evoked by meditating on the past.

> 東漢獻帝建安十六年 (211年) 七月，曹操帶兵西征馬超，王粲爲隨軍文士。這年年底，曹操大軍返回長安 (今陝西西安市西北)，途經爲秦穆公殉葬的"三良"墳墓。王粲對於這一史事有所思索，浮想聯翩，首創以《詠史》爲題，抒發思古幽情。[53]

With this background in mind, let us examine the two poems written by Wang Can and Cao Zhi to investigate how the poets used historical accounts to articulate their emotions.

The first, by Wang Can, reads as follows:

詠史詩　Poem on History[54]

	自古無殉死，	Since antiquity, none have been buried alive,[55]
	達人共所知。	All learned persons know this.[56]
	秦穆殺三良，	Lord Mu of Qin killed three good men,
4	惜哉空爾爲。	What a pity his pointless behavior was.
	結髮事明君，	Binding their hair,[57] they served an enlightened ruler,
	受恩良不訾。	They accepted innumerable favors.[58]
	臨殁要之死，	Approaching death, Lord Mu asked them to die with him.[59]
8	焉得不相隨？	How could they not follow their ruler?
	妻子當門泣，	Their wives wept at their doors,
	兄弟哭路垂。	Their brothers cried on the side of the road.
	臨穴呼蒼天，	At the edge of the grave, they shouted to the grey sky.[60]
12	涕下如綆縻。	Their tears fell down like long ropes and halters.[61]
	人生各有志，	In every human life, one has aspirations,
	終不爲此移。	In the end, they were not altered by this [sacrifice].
	同知埋身劇，	They all knew it was horrific to be buried alive.
16	心亦有所施。	But, in their minds, they also had a purpose.[62]
	生爲百夫雄，	In life, they were first among a hundred men.
	死爲壯士規。	In death, they would become examples of heroic men.[63]
	黃鳥作悲詩，	"Huangniao" was composed to lament them,[64]
20	至今聲不虧。	Even today, the sound has not faded.[65]

Wang Can alternates between narrative and commentary. He begins with a direct comment on Lord Mu's action, placing it in a historical context, then switches to narrate the story of the three good men in the third, fifth, and sixth couplets. In the rest of the poem, the poet returns to commentary in an attempt to make sense of the story of the three good men and explain the significance of their deaths.

The first couplet expresses Wang Can's strong condemnation of Lord Mu's action of forcing the three good men to follow him into the grave. Wang thought not only that this behavior was cruel but also that it did not conform to rituals and principles. He emphasizes his outrage to the point of exaggeration—the 無 (none) of the first line is an extreme, categorical way to express negation. However, Wang's comment is not historically accurate. There was a long tradition of adopting human sacrifice in the state of Qin that predated Lord Mu, and Wang would have been aware of that tradition from the historical accounts available to him.[66] As *Shiji* records, "In the 20th year (678 BCE), Lord Wu died and was buried in Pingyang of Yong. [His burial] began with people following him into death, who numbered sixty-six." 二十年, 武公卒, 葬雍平陽. 初以人從死, 從死者六十六人.[67] Wang's emotions lead him to exaggerate the historical account. In the second couplet, Wang shifts from a general moral argument focused on human sacrifice to a specific moral judgment on the fate of the three good men. The poet felt both pity for the three good men buried alive with Lord Mu and indignation at a burial practice he found incomprehensible. Wang leaves vague, however, the crucial question of whether the three good men volunteered to die for Lord Mu out of loyalty or were coerced into sacrificing themselves. Wang instead focuses on a general sense of suffering and injustice, describing Lord Mu's actions with the character 殺 "killed," a word choice that conveys brutality.

From the third to the eighth couplets, the poem switches from moral arguments to focus on narrating the story of the three good men. In this section, Wang intriguingly describes Lord Mu as an "enlightened ruler," even though he vehemently criticized him in the first two couplets. This stark contrast suggests a balanced perspective towards Lord Mu, which takes into consideration the cruelty of his final actions in light of his overall character and ambition.[68] Wang also notes the favors the three good men received from their ruler, which obligated them to obey his final command. In order to vividly and emotionally illustrate the story of the three good men, the poet invented several concrete scenes. In the fifth couplet, the poem graphically describes the emotional reaction of their family members as they left their homes to proceed to the three good men's imminent death. Where the fifth couplet focuses on other people's reactions, the sixth couplet describes the three good men's own anxious, fearful emotional state when facing death.

This state is expressed through a series of increasingly intense behaviors, from shouting to crying. Wang uses similes to emphasize the extreme grief of the three good men: "Their tears fell down continuously like long ropes and halters." In the eighth couplet, the poet explicitly speculates on the state of mind of the three good men. As human beings, they naturally feared death, but they knew they were obligated by loyalty to die for their ruler. Previous materials about the three good men do not contain this moral calculation, which is inferred from the political environment that Wang understood well from his own situation. The poet narrates this story vividly, as if he were watching it unfold before him.

Wang adopts various literary devices to fully articulate the complex emotions he feels with respect to the three good men and their relationship with Lord Mu. In the fourth couplet, he uses a rhetorical question to problematize the ethics of the compliance of the three good men. Wang's tone suggests that the three good men had no choice but to follow their ruler's order, but the rhetorical question could also imply a criticism of the three good men, who obtained so much wealth and fame that they met an untimely death. In the seventh couplet, Wang compares their tough decision to the choices faced by us all. Each person has his or her aspirations in life, including the three good men, but Lord Mu's command rendered their aspirations irrelevant. Whether they agreed to die with their ruler in advance, or felt their loyalty left them with no choice, their compliance, as Wang depicts it, testifies to their strength of will, which overcame their internal hesitations and left them determined to die for their ruler. The last three couplets discuss the significance of their deeds and death in the context of the cultural tradition surrounding them. In a reflection of the poet's strong Confucian values and morals, these couplets echo the praise of these men found in the *Shijing*. The dedication of the three good men to upholding their duty made them a lasting emblem of Confucian values.

Compare, for example, the choice made by the three good men with Mencius's attitudes towards life and a sense of duty (*yi* 義, translated here by Bloom as "rightness"):

> I desire life, and I also desire rightness. If I cannot have both of them, I will give up life and take rightness. It is true that I desire life, but there is something I desire more than life, and therefore I will not do something dishonorable in order to hold on to it. I detest death, but there is something I detest more than death, and therefore there are some dangers I may not avoid.[69]

生，亦我所欲也。義，亦我所欲也。二者不可得兼，舍生而取義者
也。生亦我所欲，所欲有甚於生者，故不爲苟得也。死亦我所惡，所
惡有甚於死者，故患有所不辟也。[70]

If a choice must be made between life and duty, Mencius advocates choosing duty. By eulogizing the same priorities in this poem, Wang Can seems to be seeking to demonstrate his loyalty to the ruling Cao family in the fast-changing political environment of the end of the Eastern Han dynasty (25–220).

Wang Can's poem on the three good men is not the only work in the "Yongshi" section of Wen xuan that, instead of recapitulating a historical event, actively comments on historical figures. Another example is Cao Zhi's 曹植 (192–232) "Poem on the Three Good Men" ("Sanliang shi" 三良詩). As discussed above, Cao Zhi may have visited the tomb of the three good men together with Wang Can, and the two poems may have been composed at the same time. Although both Wang Can's and Cao Zhi's poems adopt the same approach to historical accounts, their interpretations occasionally differ from each other. A full translation of Cao's poem is provided below:

三良詩　Poem on the Three Good Men[71]

	功名不可爲，	Merit and reputation are not to be performed,
	忠義我所安．	Loyalty and duty are where I find peace.[72]
	秦穆先下世，	When Lord Mu of Qin first passed away,
4	三臣皆自殘．	The Three Officials all gave their lives.
	生時等榮樂，	In life, they shared the same glory and joy,
	既沒同憂患．	At death, they suffered the same anxiety and misery.[73]
	誰言捐軀易？	Who says sacrificing one's body is easy?
8	殺身誠獨難．	Killing yourself is indeed uniquely difficult.
	攬涕登君墓，	Wiping away tears, they climbed into their lord's tomb,
	臨穴仰天歎．	By the grave, they looked to the heavens and sighed.
	長夜何冥冥？	How dark this long night was!
12	一往不復還．	Once gone, they would never return.
	黃鳥爲悲鳴，	Yellow birds made mournful cries,[74]
	哀哉傷肺肝！	How sad! It pains one inside!

Similarly to Wang Can, Cao Zhi alternates between moral arguments and narration, adapting the historical narrative to articulate his own views. As in the case of Wang Can's poem, the first couplet advances a moral argument.

However, whereas Wang vehemently criticizes the brutal behavior of Lord Mu, Cao Zhi mainly focuses on the loyalty and sense of duty of the three good men. Even the best efforts at accomplishing great deeds and establishing a reputation might be in vain, but the individual can always uphold the values of loyalty and duty. After offering this strong opinion, the poet switches to narration. In the fourth couplet, Cao Zhi, akin to Wang Can, uses a rhetorical question to underscore the bitterness of facing death. Again Cao Zhi portrays the decision of the three good men to sacrifice themselves as voluntary. He does not downplay how difficult the decision is, but he also does not hold Lord Mu responsible for their deaths.

Cao Zhi devotes more couplets to narration than Wang Can does, but such groundwork is necessary for expressing his view of the story, which is very different from that of most previous historical accounts and literary works. Cao Zhi does not harshly condemn Lord Mu's behavior, instead only mentioning briefly that Lord Mu died first and the three good men followed voluntarily, out of loyalty and a sense of duty. In the third couplet, Cao Zhi emphasizes the sense of obligation the three good men felt after enjoying happiness in serving Lord Mu. They enjoyed their fame and reputation and they understood the responsibilities that came with it. Due to the concise nature of classical Chinese poetry, the subject of the fifth couplet is uncertain. This narrative openness allows different interpretations of the story. One possibility is that Cao Zhi is discussing his own experience visiting the tomb of the three good men. Cao is weeping and looking to the heavens, just as the three good men did, and his poem describes both the past and his present. The other is that the three good men climbed into the tomb of Lord Mu, where they respond to their imminent death by crying and bemoaning their own fate.

The comparison of Wang Can's and Cao Zhi's poems on the same topic demonstrates both the way in which the lore of the three good men shaped the poets' understanding of history and the way in which their individual views and experiences shaped their reception of that lore. Whereas Wang Can, following the tradition of the *Zuozhuan* and *Shiji*, focuses on Lord Mu's cruelty, Cao Zhi emphasizes the loyalty and sense of duty of the three good men. Both poets redeploy the three good men as rhetorical devices, seeking their own identity and expressing their emotions through these cultural icons.

Both Wang Can's and Cao Zhi's poems on the three good men reflect their views of historical figures. In the poems of the "Yongshi" section of *Wen xuan*, using historical references as supporting commentary is the most common intervention poets make in the lore-making process. Through this approach, poets directly convey their understanding of accounts of lore and actively comment on past figures and events. This practice appears to have been influenced by the "pure talk" (*qingtan* 清談) institution of character appraisal, a form of discourse on human lives that focuses on the subjects' ephemeral spirit rather than their concrete actions, which was part of a trend of evaluation and appraisal not only of people but also of painting, calligraphy, and other art forms of this era.

A case in point is Yan Yanzhi's 顏延之 (384–456) "Poems on the Five Lords" ("Wujun yong" 五君詠), five poems which commemorate the "Seven Worthies of the Bamboo Grove" (*Zhulin qixian* 竹林七賢), a group of unconventional intellectuals who gathered together to drink wine, compose literary works, and engage in intellectual discourse during the third century, shortly after the fall of the Han dynasty. Here, Qian Nanxiu's comments on the function of wine are relevant: "Given the transformative power of wine, drinking can produce a 'famous gentleman' (*mingshi*)."[75] Wine reveals a *mingshi*'s "natural endowment and identity,"[76] and allows one to transcend worldly fame and reputation. Furthermore, heavy drinking could excuse the group members' unconventional behavior, even their subversive comments on politics. Apart from indulging in drink and composing literary works, the group members also enjoyed debating the finer points of *xuanxue*, centered on their understanding of *Laozi*, *Zhuangzi*, and the *Yijing*.

Yan Yanzhi, a poet who lived through the tumultuous Eastern Jin (317–420) and Liu Song (420–479) dynasties, was famous for his frequent use of allusions, parallel structure, and ornate style to express his political concerns.[77] Yan's biography in Shen Yue's 沈約 (441–513) *Songshu* allows readers not only to infer the composition date of these five poems (433) but also to understand their background, providing clues as to Yan's state of mind at the time:

> Deeply distressed and indignant, Yan Yanzhi [wrote] "Poems on the Five Lords," which portrays the Seven Sages of the Bamboo Grove. On account of the eminence and nobility of Shan Tao (205–283) and Wang Rong (234–305), he excluded them [from the poetry cycle]. Praising Xi [Ji] Kang (ca. 224–ca. 263) he wrote, "Though the wings of the simurgh have at times been broken, / There is none who can tame a dragon's nature." Of Ruan Ji (210–263) he wrote, "He could not explain death, / But by the end of his journey he could not be moved." Of Ruan

Xian (fl. 3rd century) he wrote, "Though recommended many times, he never took office; / Then with one wave he went out to become governor." Speaking of Liu Ling (221–300) he wrote, "Each day he concealed his inner spirit with intense drinking; / Who knew he wasn't wantonly reveling?" These four couplets likely express his personal feelings.[78]

延之甚怨憤，乃作五君詠以述竹林七賢，山濤、王戎以貴顯被黜，詠嵇康曰：「鸞翮有時鎩，龍性誰能馴。」詠阮籍曰：「物故可不論，塗窮能無慟。」詠阮咸曰：「屢薦不入官，一麾乃出守。」詠劉伶曰：「韜精日沉飲，誰知非荒宴。」此四句，蓋自序也.[79]

Yan Yanzhi was born into a low-status family, but was favored by different emperors due to his literary talents and political strategies. At the same time, his straightforward character caused him trouble many times during his life, and he was exiled several times to rural areas due to his outspokenness. Shen Yue's account suggests that Yan shared many characteristics with the Seven Worthies of the Bamboo Grove. Like the Worthies, he was an emotional, sensitive, and straightforward man, prone to excessive drinking and unconventional behavior. Yan and scholars like him had to conceal their true feelings and intentions, and behaved unconventionally in order to survive in their malicious societies. Although his poems use allusions and other indirect methods to comment on the government, Yan was not fortunate enough to escape the tragic fate of punishment and exile.

In the first of these five poems, Yan evaluates the character of Ruan Ji:[80]

阮步兵　Commandant of Infantry Ruan[81]

	阮公雖淪跡，	Although Ruan Ji concealed his footprints,
	識密鑒亦洞．	His thoughts were closely held and his insights penetrating.
	沈醉似埋照，	With intoxication, he seemed to hide his aura,
4	寓辭類託諷．	His allegorical words were like satirical jibes.
	長嘯若懷人，	His long whistling sounded as though he pined for someone,
	越禮自驚眾．	His transcendent ritual naturally shocked the masses.
	物故不可論，	Things of the past could not be discussed,
8	途窮能無慟？	At the end of the path, who would not have deep sorrow?

Before Yan, lore about Ruan Ji appears in *Jinshu*, *Annals of Master Wei* (*Weishi chunqiu* 魏氏春秋), and *Appraisals for Accounts of Jin Imperial Ministers* (*Jin zhugong zan* 晉諸公贊). These accounts often allude or refer to Ruan's maverick behavior of transcending rituals and rules, the profound meaning of his speeches, his attainments in Daoism and music, and his principle of self-preservation in an unstable political environment. These accounts also use the same or similar diction as Ruan's "Yonghuai shi." Most of these aspects of Ruan Ji's character are recorded in the *Shishuo xinyu*, which was edited by Yan's contemporary Liu Yiqing and his team. This does not necessarily mean that Yan directly borrowed or quoted from the *Shishuo xinyu*, but it does suggest that Yan and Liu likely accessed the same body of lore about Ruan Ji. For this reason, the following analysis of Yan's poem refers mostly to the *Shishuo xinyu* accounts.

Ruan Ji held three positions during the Cao–Wei period, two of which he was forced to take. Commandant of infantry was his last official position, and he only accepted it because it allowed him to fulfill his personal desires. The story is recorded in *Shishuo xinyu*, but as Richard Mather points out, it is very difficult to determine the historical veracity of many of the entries in this source. However, even if they are not completely accurate, such stories are an indication of Ruan Ji's reputation.

> There was a vacancy in the office of the commandant of infantry, in the commissary of which were stored several hundred hu of wine. It was for this reason that Ruan Ji requested to become commandant of infantry.[82]
>
> 步兵校尉缺，廚中有貯酒數百斛，阮籍乃求爲步兵校尉.[83]

Yan Yanzhi's poem first discusses the difference between Ruan Ji's external appearance and his inner life. According to the poem, Ruan concealed his political views by demonstrating his social detachment through drinking and living a reclusive life. However, his far-reaching insight allowed him to make an incisive analysis of the political situation. Yan Yanzhi does not narrate in detail any historical events associated with Ruan, but instead makes various allusions to his maverick behavior. For example, in the third couplet, Yan Yanzhi makes reference to an example of Ruan's indirect and unconventional method of conveying his feelings, as recorded in *Shishuo xinyu*:

> The wife of Ruan Ji's neighbor was very pretty. She worked as a barmaid tending the vats and selling wine. Ruan and Wang

Rong frequently drank at her place, and after Ruan became drunk he would sleep by this woman's side. Her husband at first was extraordinarily suspicious of him, but after careful investigation it was found that Ruan had no untoward intentions.[84]

阮公鄰家婦, 有美色, 當壚酤酒. 阮與王安豐常從婦飲酒, 阮醉, 便眠其婦側. 夫始殊疑之, 伺察, 終無他意.[85]

The anecdote quoted above shows how Ruan Ji interacted with people outside of his family in an unconventional but ultimately principled and sincere manner. When it came to his own family members, his behavior was similarly unconventional. When his mother passed away, Ruan did not initially behave as one was expected to at a funeral; instead, he feasted on pork and drank wine. Yet, as he was gorging himself, he suddenly cried out loudly and expressed his sorrow, lamenting to the point of vomiting blood. There are many such stories surrounding Ruan, and even if some of them may not have actually happened, they do speak to perceptions of his character. It is not certain which specific stories Yan Yanzhi was thinking of when writing his poem, but this couplet captures the most salient characteristics of Ruan: unconventional, eccentric, straightforward, and sincere.

The first three couplets of Yan's poems contain descriptions of Ruan's maverick disposition. In the last couplet, Yan lays out his understanding of Ruan's personality: someone who preferred not to delve into problems or to be involved in any political activities. Many scholars during Ruan's lifetime, including his friends, were executed or otherwise died from unnatural causes. The *Jinshu*'s comment on Ruan indicates the psychological state of typical literati during the Wei–Jin era:

Ruan Ji did harbor lofty ambitions to help society, but he lived in a very turbulent world of the Wei–Jin era where few well-known intellectuals survived intact. So he left the affairs of the world behind and began to drink habitually from day to day.[86]

籍本有濟世志, 屬魏晉之際, 天下多故, 名士少有全者, 籍由是不與世事, 遂酣飲爲常.[87]

In order to survive, neither Ruan nor Yan could comment openly on contemporary issues. Instead, literary writings became a means through which Yan could vent his strong feelings more indirectly. By commenting on Ruan's unconventional behavior, his sincere spirit, and his ability to express himself indirectly, Yan was able to console himself and to express veiled criticism towards his own contemporary society.

Two factors account for Yan Yanzhi's appreciation for Ruan Ji's insight and writing. First, Ruan had been a governor of Shi'an 始安, where Yan was transferred following his demotion. Their shared experience seemed to remind the poet of Ruan's story. Second, Ruan adopted ambiguous images and rhetorical devices to compose "Yonghuai." The ambiguous nature of these poems allowed later generations—including Yan himself—to interpret these poems in different ways. Familiar with Ruan's writings and poetic style, Yan felt he was Ruan's acquaintance across the ages, capable of understanding Ruan's pain and plight, living in a similarly treacherous society.

Zhao Wangqin 趙望秦 and Zhang Huanling 張煥玲 point to the innovation represented by Yan Yanzhi's *yongshi shi*:

> Yan Yanzhi's "Poems on the Five Lords" achieved new heights of artistry, as they were different from traditional biographical poems on history. Yan no longer focused on narrating the lives of historical figures in their totality; instead they emphasized refining the details that best reflected their spirit and elegant demeanor.
>
> 顏延之《五君詠》在藝術成就上達到一個新的高度，與傳統意義上的傳體詠史已有所不同. 詩人不再專注於歷史人物的完整敘述，而是側重於提煉最能凸顯所詠歷史人物風采神貌的細節.⁸⁸

Yan Yanzhi developed the *yongshi shi* subgenre by focusing on the inner qualities of the historical figures—that is, their refusal to engage in politics in favor of their literary expression. In doing so, Yan follows the literary mode outlined by Sima Qian:

> All of these men [such as King Wen of Zhou, Confucius, and Qu Yuan] had something eating away at their hearts; they could not carry through their ideas of the Way, so they gave an account of what had happened before while thinking of what was to come. In cases like Zuo Qiuming's sightlessness or Sunzi's amputated feet, these men could never be employed; they withdrew and put their ruminations into writing in order to give full expression to their outrage, intending to reveal themselves purely through writing that would last into the future.⁸⁹

此人皆意有所鬱結，不得通其道，故述往事，思來者。及如左丘明無目，孫子斷足，終不可用，退論書策以舒其憤，思垂空文以自見。[90]

Sima Qian's *fafen* 發憤 theory of literary production, in which writing gives full expression to otherwise suppressed outrage, carries with it the implication that the most admirable historical figures were not always the ones who were politically successful, but rather those whose good intentions are revealed through their literary production. Yan Yanzhi's poems further suggest that one can be included within cultural memory just for one's inner virtues and writing rather than any substantive accomplishments made in the realm of politics. The three poems discussed above, written by Wang Can, Cao Zhi, and Yan Yanzhi, are not the only poems that use accounts of lore as supporting commentary. Other poets represented in the "Yongshi" section of *Wen xuan* also adopted this approach to disseminate their historical perspective through poetry.[91]

Accounts of Lore as Simple Allusions

The two approaches to integrating accounts of lore into *yongshi shi* that we have discussed so far, paraphrasing historical records and articulating the poet's own opinions by commenting on historical figures, both require substantial engagement with the lore narrated or commented upon in a poem. By way of contrast, the third approach, brief allusion to accounts of lore in service of the poet's own views, has a far weaker connection to the historical figure him- or herself.

Early medieval Chinese poets made frequent use of allusion.[92] Allusions demonstrated poets' talents, attracted the attention of patrons, placed poets in a historical lineage, and, perhaps most immediately important, allowed poets to sidestep the dangers of making sociopolitical statements too directly. Early medieval China was an era of such rapid change that many scholars and poets lived through two or three short-lived dynasties. Poets therefore often worried about becoming the target of political jealousy or being caught between struggling political factions. Historical allusions provided a less direct way to express one's frustrations while maintaining plausible deniability. Various encyclopedias of historical allusions were compiled to cater to the needs of literati, who in turn facilitated more frequent use of allusions. Because of the often brief length of classical Chinese poetic forms, poets often chose a salient aspect of certain historical figures that fit the emotions they wanted to express. Bao Zhao's "Yongshi" is a good example of a poet telescoping the import of accounts of lore into a short allusion to a distinctive personal characteristic, then using that allusion to express his emotions.⁹³

	五都矜財雄，	The five capitals were haughty with wealth and grandeur.
	三川養聲利。	The three rivers nourished reputation and benefit.
	百金不市死，	People with a hundred pieces of gold did not die in a market.
4	明經有高位。	People who mastered the Classics obtained high positions.
	京城十二衢，	The capital had twelve thoroughfares,
	飛甍各鱗次。	Flying eaves overlapping like fish scales.
	仕子彯華纓，	The magnificent cap strings of officials fluttered in the wind,
8	遊客竦輕轡。	While travelers gave free rein to their nimble horses.
	明星晨未稀，	With bright stars not yet sparse in the early morning,
	軒蓋已雲至。	Covered carriages already gathered like clouds.
	賓御紛颯沓，	Guests and drivers in a jostling jumble,
12	鞍馬光照地。	Gleaming horses and saddles shone on the ground.
	寒暑在一時，	Winter turned to summer in the space of a single season,
	繁華及春媚。	A profusion of blossoms arrived with enchantments of spring.
	君平獨寂漠，	Only Junping was tranquil and aloof,
16	身世兩相棄。	He and the world abandoned each other.

The pivotal character in Bao Zhao's poem is Yan Junping 嚴君平 (86 BCE–10 CE), who is portrayed as being above and apart from the worldly pursuits of the people of the capital.⁹⁴ The accounts we have about Yan Junping before Bao Zhao's time, such as those found in *Hanshu*, *Treatise on Manifold Subjects* (*Bowu zhi* 博物志), *Biographies of the Lofty Figures* (*Gaoshi zhuan* 高士傳), and *Records of the States South of Mount Hua* (*Huayang guozhi* 華陽國志), describe him as a recluse who rejected officialdom out of principle but remained active in teaching Confucian values to his disciples. When Bao wrote this poem, he was clearly concerned only with the renunciation aspect of the Yan Junping story.

Had the poet not mentioned Yan Junping in the final couplet, it would have been difficult for readers to pinpoint the historical moment of the poem. The poet selected an important characteristic of Yan Junping, and compressed it into a historical allusion that served to express his own lofty ideals. Yan abandoning the world is mentioned in *Hanshu*, which states that he made a living by performing divinations in the city of Chengdu. After earning enough money, he stopped practicing divination and taught his disciples the *Laozi*, a canonical text of Daoist philosophy. Yan did not serve at court, but as a practitioner of divination, he was actively involved in educating people about filial piety, loyalty, and deference. According to *Hanshu*, Yan proclaimed,

> When there is a query about something perverse and unjust, then I address its advantages and harm according to divination with milfoil and tortoise. What I say to sons concerns filiality, to brothers I speak of deference, and to servitors loyalty. Each according to his particular circumstances, I direct them toward goodness, and more than half have followed my words.[95]

> 有邪惡非正之問, 則依蓍龜爲言利害.與人子言依於孝, 與人弟言依于順, 與人臣言依於忠, 各因勢導之以善, 從吾言者, 已過半矣。[96]

Yan Junping did not abandon his social responsibilities. On the contrary, he performed them in the public space of the market rather than at the closed court. This Confucian aspect of Yan's life is not mentioned by Bao in his poem.

Furthermore, although Yan Junping lived a reclusive life and abandoned officialdom, he had many disciples who sang his praises, and Yan was consequently well known and respected among officials. One disciple, Yang Xiong 揚雄 (53 BCE–18 CE), would later become an illustrious official in the capital, and his esteem for Yan ensured that the latter was held in high regard by his contemporaries.[97] For instance, the magistrate of Shu once wanted to invite Yan to become an official. Yang warned the magistrate that he should not pressure Yan to accept the position, but instead treat him with courtesy and respect. After receiving Yang's warning, the magistrate did not dare ask Yan to take a public position and took the extraordinary step of visiting him in person.[98] Such an act testifies to how well respected Yan was. Moreover, in early medieval culture, performing the role of "recluse" did not mean you were completely isolated, and Yan was indeed quite social according to historical accounts.

Bao Zhao clearly selected and adapted from records of Yan to express his own concerns. Bao seemed to portray himself as a person who did not seek fame and reputation, but instead wanted to maintain his moral integrity, even if it meant destitution and isolation. Therefore, his allusion to Yan emphasized the historical figure's detachment. Bao Zhao's attraction to the life of the recluse was likely due to his numerous failed attempts to fulfill his political ambitions. Bao probably felt that the stranglehold of influential families over court politics obstructed his pursuit of his ideals. By using Yan Junping as a literary touchstone, Bao seemed to seek to establish his moral worth through literature instead of politics.

The image of Yan Junping as a lofty hermit presented in Bao Zhao's poem became more widespread than the image of Junping as an eclectic scholar found in previous accounts.[99] For instance, Li Bai (701–762), influenced by Bao Zhao's comments on Yan Junping, opens his thirteenth "Ancient Air" ("Gu feng" 古風) with a couplet identical in meaning to Bao's: "Since Junping abandoned the world, / The world abandoned him as well." 君平既棄世, 世亦棄君平.[100] Li Bai's near quotation shaped later literati's understanding of this cultural icon.

Another example of concise allusions, but to a different historical figure, can be found in Zuo Si's "Yongshi" II in *Wen xuan*, which makes oblique references to the life of the historical figure Feng Tang:[101]

> Luxuriant pines at the bottom of a ravine.
> Lush sprouts on the top of a mountain.
> With their one-inch-diameter stems,
> They overshadow those hundred-foot-long pine branches.
> The descendants of nobility ascend to high positions,
> While the talented sink to lower offices.
> The differing terrain made it so;
> Not the result of a single day.
> The Jin and Zhang relied on the legacy of their ancestors.
> Seven generations wore the sables of Han.
> How could Sir Feng not be great?
> Even in old age, he was not summoned by the emperor.

The main historical figure, Feng Tang, does not appear until the final couplet, while the rest of the poem does not provide any clues specifying the historical context. In this poem, Zuo first demonstrates the unfairness of nature through the image of tall pine trees at the bottom of the ravine overshadowed by short sprouts on the top of the mountain. This natural contrast reflects Zuo's feelings about the strict social hierarchy of his era, the Western Jin, in which noble lineages controlled politics and occupied important positions, while the talented poor sunk to the bottom of society. The last line of the poem has two possible readings: "Even in old age, he was not summoned by the emperor" or "He was not summoned until his hair turned white." The first is a consistent expansion on the theme of the natural metaphor that expresses the poet's opinion clearly and powerfully; that is, it is a statement about an unfair society where scions of noble families, like Jin and Zhang, ascended to high positions effortlessly, while the talented poor, like Feng Tang, were not given opportunities even in old age. The second reading softens Zuo Si's social criticism by suggesting that Feng Tang's talents were ultimately, if belatedly, recognized. Both readings, however, advance the premise that Feng Tang was a great man who did not receive the appreciation he merited throughout most of his life. Records such as those found in *Shiji*, Wang Fu's 王符 (ca. 85–ca. 163) *Comments of a Recluse* (*Qian fu lun* 潛夫論), Ban Gu's *Hanshu*, and Yang Xiong's *Exemplary Words* (*Fayan* 法言) align with the depiction found in Zuo's final couplet. For instance, *Shiji* and *Hanshu* describe Feng Tang as a great man who had a reputation for filial piety in his youth. Because of his reputation, he was made the chief of the Bureau of Palace Attendants, serving Emperor Wen.[102] But Feng remained in that relatively low-ranking position for most of his career. In that respect, Feng was, as Zuo Si suggests, underappreciated.

However, this is only part of the Feng Tang story. Feng Tang's fortunes changed dramatically later in his life.[103] Emperor Wen so approved of a proposal made by Feng that he immediately promoted him, and Emperor Wen's successors continued to treat him with respect.[104] The biography of Feng Tang in *Shiji* praises both Feng Tang, as a loyal subject who advanced policies with the best interests of the state in mind, and the emperors, for being generous and open-minded rulers who recognized Feng's talent. At the end of his biography on Feng Tang and Zhang Shizhi, Sima Qian comments, "When Jizhi [Shizhi] spoke about superior persons he guarded the law and did not curry favor with [the emperor], and when Master Feng discussed generals and leaders it had real savor, real savor indeed!"[105] 張季之言長者, 守法不阿意; 馮公之論將率, 有味哉! 有味哉![106] This excerpt suggests that Sima's purpose for compiling this biography was to provide an example of the ideal harmonious relationship between an emperor and his subjects. It also complicates Zuo's portrayal of Feng as an unappreciated talent.

Zuo Si was surely familiar with the historical accounts of Feng's life, since he taught *Hanshu* to the director of the palace library, Jia Mi 賈謐 (d. 300).[107] Zuo's deliberate omission therefore suggests that the poet intended to express his own feelings of being unappreciated and lacking opportunities. Through his comments on Feng Tang, Zuo Si expressed veiled criticism of the hereditary aristocracy of his own time, implying that Feng's story reflected Zuo's own life. These resentments were not Zuo's alone; they were common to many talented men from obscure backgrounds in the Western Jin.

Zuo Si alludes only to the salient aspects of the Feng Tang story most relevant to the themes of his poem, focusing on how he was underappreciated rather than on the virtues of the Han emperors who continued to employ him. Zuo's depiction differs from the historical accounts found in *Shiji* and *Hanshu*, which tell a more complex story, praising Feng Tang's boldness and sincerity, Emperor Wen's open mind, Emperor Jing's generosity, and Emperor Wu's eagerness to employ talented men. The precedent for Zuo Si's limited portrayal of Feng Tang in his poem might be Xun Yue's 荀悅 (148–209) *Annals of the Former Han* (*Qian Han ji* 前漢紀), which was composed at the end of the Han dynasty as an explication of *Hanshu*. Xun writes, with diction that Zuo's final couplet resembles, "White haired, Feng Tang stooped to occupy a low office" 馮唐白首, 屈於郎署.[108] But both Zuo and Xun's portrayal of Feng Tang are outliers among the early accounts.

Later portrayals of Feng Tang adopted the image, established by Zuo and Xun, of Feng Tang as the epitome of unrecognized talent. For example, Wang Bo 王勃 (ca. 649–ca. 676) in his "Preface to the Prince of Teng's Pavilion" ("Tengwang ge xu" 滕王閣序) comments on Feng Tang, "Alas! Fortune is unevenly distributed, and one suffers many setbacks in life. Feng Tang rapidly grew old, and Li Guang found it difficult to achieve the rank of marquis" 嗟乎! 時運不齊, 命途多舛.馮唐易老, 李廣難封.[109] In his poem "Hanging White Hair" ("Chui bai" 垂白), also known as "White-Headed" ("Bai shou" 白首), Du Fu 杜甫 (712–770) writes, "White hair hanging down, Feng Tang became old; / In crisp autumn, Song Yu mourned" 垂白馮唐老, 清秋宋玉悲.[110] This poetic image of Feng Tang appealed to Tang literati who were themselves frustrated with how difficult political advancement was. In the Tang period, although the civil service examination allowed some scholars to advance to official positions from the lower classes, there was still much inequality. Through Feng Tang, Tang poets could lament their own lack of recognition.

The type of *yongshi shi* represented by Zuo Si's "Yongshi" II has a loose connection with historical accounts. These poets played down the specific historical context of the poems and allowed historical figures and events to become the conduits through which they could express their emotions. Without looking at the title, it would be hard to guess that these are *yongshi shi*—they almost become *yonghuai shi*.[111]

Later generations appreciated this mode of composing *yongshi*. For instance, the Qing dynasty literatus Shen Deqian 沈德潛 (1673–1769) makes the following comments on the literary style and status of Zuo's "Yongshi":

> Taichong's [Zuo Si] poems on history do not exclusively sing of a particular person or event; they sing of the ancient people, yet his own nature and emotions are fully apparent. His poetry was the pinnacle of poetic perfection for a thousand years. Later, only Mingyuan [Bao Zhao] and Taibai [Li Bai, 701–762] were capable of this."[112]

> 太沖詠史, 不必專詠一人, 專詠一事, 詠古人而已之性情俱見, 此千秋絕唱也. 後惟明遠, 太白能之.[113]

Shen Deqian put Zuo Si in the same league as the great poets Bao Zhao and Li Bai. In the hands of a poet with the skill and motivation of Zuo Si, historical figures in *yongshi shi* become a powerful means of individualized self-expression. In this sense, Zuo's "Yongshi" represent a major development of this subgenre in the pre-Tang era. Although Zuo was not the first to write *yongshi*, he developed an influential style by providing his personal reading of history—relating historical figures to his own situation rather than simply celebrating them. His poems exemplified a style that relied on substance and direct expression.

Conclusion

This chapter categorizes the "Yongshi" section in *Wen xuan* into three types based on the distance between past figures in *yongshi shi* and various accounts of lore before poets: poems that closely cite accounts of lore, poems that use historical accounts as supporting commentary, and poems that make loose allusions to lore. The boundaries between the categories are not absolute, and poems occasionally combine more than one approach, but each type represents a significantly different approach toward lore. In the first case, poets hew very closely to accounts of lore, and the intertextual links are the strongest, with poems and these accounts sharing details, diction, and interpretations. In the second type, the poems adopt certain passages and scenes from narratives of lore as supporting commentary for articulating the poets' emotions. In the third type, the relationship between poems and narration of lore is the most attenuated. If the allusion were removed, the meaning of the poem would not change, but the allusion strengthens the message of the poem. The first and second approaches both make use of narrative details and the poet's individual commentary. The second approach, however, has far fewer narrative details, and substitutes commentary from the poet for quotes from lore, thus expressing the poet's feelings and opinions more directly than in the first approach. In the second and third types, in order to get their own message across, poets sometimes exaggerate or ironize the accounts of lore, subverting the traditional understanding of the historical figures to which they allude. These depictions of historical figures can be far more profound and influential than the images conveyed in previous accounts. Examining these approaches allows us to better understand the dissemination of lore through poetry and the delicate relationships between poetry and lore, revealing the intricacies of *yongshi shi*.

Conclusion

From inscriptions on steles and monuments to rituals at ancestral temples, from quoting canonical poems in diplomatic exchanges to citing anecdotes from the past to admonish emperors, these manifestations of cultural memory demonstrate the respect of Chinese literati for their profound history. Two important vehicles for transmitting that cultural memory are historical accounts and poetry. The distinction between historical and poetic discourse was addressed explicitly in the classical era of Europe as far back as Aristotle (384–322 BCE), who drew a clear distinction between the roles of the historian and the poet:

> For the distinction between the historian and the poet is not whether they give their accounts in verse or prose. . . . The [real] difference is this: that the one [i.e., the historian] tells what happened, the other [i.e., the poet] [tells] the sort of things that *can* happen. That's why in fact poetry is a more speculative and more "serious" business than history: for poetry deals more with universals, history with particulars.[1]

According to Aristotle, while historians claim to narrate what actually happened, or the "factual" aspects of events, poets depict what *could have* happened, or what *should have* happened, focusing in their works on more general and universal values, such as the lofty ideals and moral principles that events and people represent. A similar division of labor seems relevant to the Chinese case as well.[2]

This book aims to illuminate the subgenre of *yongshi shi* as a poetic "re-presentation" of history in early medieval China. Focusing on works by poets across this era, such as Cao Zhi, Wang Can, Zuo Si, Zhang Xie, Lu Chen, Tao Yuanming, Xie Zhan, Xie Lingyun, and Yan Yanzhi, this book explores how history is disseminated and interpreted through literary writing, as well as how and why certain historical figures are repeatedly commemorated in Chinese poetry over others. It primarily relies on the framework of cultural memory, but also integrates other methodologies, such as close reading, intertextuality, and reception studies.

This book's contribution is to clarify the definition and scope of the term *yongshi shi* in early medieval China, to uncover the complexity of its circulation and reception, to explore the dissemination of history within Chinese poetry, and to challenge the traditional reception of early medieval Chinese poetry. This book also contributes to research into the larger cultural context of the development of *yongshi shi*, by exploring the cultural factors that shaped a poet's understanding of the past. This study will ideally allow us to better understand how poets, critics, readers, and anthologists critically engaged with the Chinese literary tradition. Furthermore, analyzing *yongshi shi* from the perspective of cultural memory reveals similarities and discrepancies in the literary appropriation of diction, imagery, figures of speech, and styles from the past. Examining different approaches to cultural memory through intertextual analysis enables us to comprehend how history is disseminated through poetry, and reveals the intricacies and complexities of *yongshi shi*.

With respect to the function of cultural memory in a written culture, Jan Assmann writes, "In the context of written culture and textual continuity, cultural memory organizes itself around these texts, interpreting, imitating, learning, and/or criticizing them."[3] Historical figures and their stories are recorded in poems, but poets are selective about which parts of the stories ought to appear, and their choices reflect both their own agendas and the contemporary reception of historical figures and events. The traces of the past collected and employed by poets in early medieval China for fashioning poetry to make sense of the past are reminders that, while the "glory days" are long gone, a speaking past yet remains in these poems as a reflection of the poets' imagination of the past. Moreover, the contemplation and imagination of the past in these poems played a vital role in shaping the construction and narration of history that followed them. Composing *yongshi shi* was an intellectually engaging activity—the product of emotions elicited from reading history, meditating on historical events, and visiting historical relics—but it was also a formative force in ensuing representations of the past in all genres of writing.

The cultural memory of a deceased person can be divided into retrospective memory and prospective memory.[4] This book examines both kinds of memories in *yongshi shi* to demonstrate how poets used cultural memory of historical figures to shape later reception of their images and works. Retrospective memory and prospective memory work in tandem in *yongshi shi*. In Zuo Si's poems, he adeptly cites different historical figures who correspond to each stage in his own biographical arc from youthful idealism to mature pragmatism. Zuo selected the historical figures and those elements of their biographies that he wanted to highlight; by drawing implicit analogies between their lives and his own, Zuo placed himself in this respected and honored lineage. His idealization was made more explicit by selectively employing the first-person pronoun and adopting an autobiographical style in his poems to underline the connection between himself and these historical figures as a means to catalyze a crucial process: establishing his reputation for posterity after failing to make a mark in the political world of his own era.

An analysis of *yongshi shi* in early medieval China through the lenses of retrospective and prospective memory reveals the complexity of how poems use and disseminate cultural memory, which in turn facilitates our critical understanding of poetic representations of history. This book explores three levels of the literary and cultural factors that influenced the reception of Zuo Si's poems in the early medieval period: intertextual links with other poems, literary criticism, and narratives in collections of anecdotes or standard histories that help to reveal how the educated elite used these poems in social life. As Hans Robert Jauss commented in his speech "Literary History as a Challenge to Literary Theory," "The historical life of a literary work is unthinkable without the active participation of its addressees."[5] The early medieval literati did not passively accept the prima facie meaning of a literary work, but rather enriched and complicated the meaning of the poem with their interpretations. Examining the use of prospective memory in Zuo's poems also sheds light on essential interdisciplinary questions, such as why and how poets use history, and the distinctions between conveying historical events and figures through poetry and standard historiography. The retrospective memory employed by Zuo Si of outstanding historical figures and their moral values and abilities foreshadows the positive reception of Zuo's own life story and poetry by later literati, who in turn commemorated him as a historical figure worthy of emulation. This circle of remembrance connects poets with the past and shapes their future reception, forging a lineage of influence that gradually shapes the cultural identity of the literati in general.

In engaging with cultural memory, poets such as Tao Yuanming adopt a particular perspective on life, putting their own perspective in conversation with the collective memory of widely known historical figures and events, producing texts that become part of the cultural memory of future generations. Tao, unlike other poets who limited themselves to drawing a kind of passive consolation from historical examples, claimed to actually practice the principles he gleaned from historical figures, using them to guide his life and educate his family members. Tao made these experiences personal and concrete by internalizing them. He also highlighted figures who had been mostly forgotten, such as the impoverished scholars Huang Zilian, Liu Gong, and Zhang Zhongwei. Without his praise, they would likely have disappeared from history, as we have little or no information about them outside of Tao's poems. Tao's *yongshi shi* therefore not only possess literary value, but are also of significant value to the historical record of otherwise obscure figures. Cultural memory as a collective force shaped literati's understanding of the past, and Tao's personal understanding of the past became a key element in that cultural memory.

Some *yongshi shi* were not composed about reading historical accounts directly, but rather through the medium of visiting historical sites. In these cases, cultural memory was a vehicle not only for expressing nostalgia, trying to make sense of historical circumstances and conditions, and contemplating the lessons learned from the past, but also for performing a significant sociopolitical function. The poems composed by Xie Zhan, Zheng Xianzhi, and Fan Tai on visiting sites of historical significance during Liu Yu's northern expedition, for example, demonstrate how cultural memory was used to legitimate Liu Yu's governance and leadership, build confidence among the literati in his rule, and motivate the officials surrounding him. Figures from the Han dynasty such as Liu Bang and Zhang Liang were effective vehicles for legitimating Liu Yu's ambitions. At the same time, the poets concealed within their praise of Liu Yu more nuanced emotions with respect to dynastic transition and the declining power of aristocratic families.

Towards the end of the early medieval era, the editors of the *Wen xuan* established the "Yongshi" section. The poets in this section adopted these three approaches of citing accounts of lore closely, abbreviating them to serve as supporting commentary, and condensing them into simple allusions in order to comment on the past. In their poetic imaginations, the past becomes present again. These poets selected and highlighted historical figures and events in their poems based on their own feelings and the impressions they wanted their readers to receive. They did not simply transmit historical records as a means of maintaining and preserving them, but related history to contemporary social issues and their own personal experience. Through *yongshi shi*, these poets transmuted historical records into remembered history via an expressive mode of poetry, which laid a foundation for the formation and development of later cultural memory regarding the chosen historical figures.

Finally, this book seeks to subvert the sweeping generalization of early medieval Chinese poetry as consisting mainly of superficial, exuberant images and an overwrought, ornamental style, which was an exaggerated characterization opined by later historians and literary critics who focused their judgments on the poetic subgenre known as "palace-style poetry" (*gongti shi* 宮體詩). This book shows that *yongshi shi*, with its restrained imagery and plain language, represents an important alternative style, one that transformed historical figures into icons, was a powerful vehicle through which to understand and convey cultural memory, and allowed poets to prospectively stake their own claims to fame within the literary tradition by strategically associating themselves retrospectively with select historical figures. This book discusses how literati inscribed themselves into history by expressing moral values and ideals through their poetry, which provided models of behavior for later literati. The poets drew upon and shaped a vast body of cultural memory, including written accounts and orally transmitted tales, to create a literary space in which the past still felt relevant and alive. These poems both conveyed the intimate relationship of these poets with history and sought to secure the place of the poets themselves—as men of sensitivity, talent, and moral worth—in that same historical tradition.

Notes

Introduction

1. For a detailed treatment of poetic competence in Chinese narratives, see Graham Sanders, *Words Well Put: Visions of Poetic Competence in the Chinese Tradition* (Cambridge, MA: Harvard University Asia Center, 2006).

2. For the purposes of this book, the early medieval period refers to the Six Dynasties 六朝 (220–589) or the Wei, Jin, and Northern and Southern Dynasties 魏晉南北朝. It was a long period of disunity in Chinese history, the longest period of disunity to follow the Warring States period (475–221 BCE).

3. In writing this book, for example, I used the databases maintained by the Institute of History and Philology of the Scripta Sinica in Taipei and the CHANT (Chinese Ancient Texts) databases curated by the Chinese University of Hong Kong.

4. Wendy Swartz and Robert F. Campany, *Memory in Medieval China: Text, Ritual, and Community* (Leiden: Brill, 2018), 2–5. For public and ancient memory, see K. E. Brashier, *Ancestral Memory in Early China* (Cambridge, MA: Harvard University Press, 2011), and *Public Memory in Early China* (Cambridge, MA: Harvard University Press, 2014). For religion-related memory study, see Robert Ford Campany, *Making Transcendents: Ascetics and Social Memory in Early Medieval China* (Honolulu: University of Hawai'i Press, 2009). For historical writing and memory, see David Schaberg, *A Patterned Past: Form and Thought in Early Chinese Historiography* (Cambridge, MA: Harvard University Asia Center, 2001), and Wai-yee Li, *The Readability of the Past in Early Chinese Historiography* (Cambridge, MA: Harvard University Asia Center, 2007). For cultural memory and early Chinese civilization, see Ke Mading 柯馬丁 (Martin Kern), "Chutu wenxian yu wenhua jiyi: *Shijing* zaoqi lishi yanjiu" 出土文獻與文化記憶:《詩經》早期歷史研究, *Zhongguo zhexue* 中國哲學, no. 25 (2004): 111–58, and "Zuowei jiyi de shi: *Shi* ji qi zaoqi quanshi" 作爲記憶的詩:《詩》及其早期詮釋. *Guoxue yanjiu* 國學研究, no. 16 (2005): 329–41.

5. Jan Assmann is a scholar of ancient Egyptology. His most famous work is *Das kulturelle Gedächtnis: Schrift, Erinnerung und politische Identität in frühen Hochkulturen* (Munich: C. H. Beck, 2007), translated—by Assmann himself—into

English as *Cultural Memory and Early Civilization: Writing, Remembrance, and Political Imagination* (Cambridge: Cambridge University Press, 2011). Aleida Assmann is a cultural anthropologist, focusing on modern memory and remembrance, particularly of the Second World War, in Germany and Europe, and the role that memory plays in the construction of national ideology and identity. Her most notable contribution to memory studies is *Der lange Schatten der Vergangenheit. Erinnerungskultur und Geschichtspolitik* (Munich: C. H. Beck, 2006), translated into English by Sarah Clift as *Shadows of Trauma: Memory and Politics of Postwar Identity* (New York: Fordham University Press, 2016).

6. Jan Assmann, *Cultural Memory and Early Civilization*, xi.
7. Jan Assmann, 5.
8. Jan Assmann, 5–6.
9. Jan Assmann, 5.
10. Jan Assmann, 6.
11. Jan Assmann, 36.
12. Jan Assmann, 42.
13. Jan Assmann, 42.
14. Jan Assmann, 45–46.
15. Jan Assmann, 46.
16. Although retrospective memory and prospective memory are two different categories, they relate with and occasionally influence one another.
17. For studies on applying reception studies to research premodern Chinese literature, see Yue Zhang, "Wanjin Beimei Hanxue yanjiu fangfa yu wenxueshi bianzhuan guankui" 晚近北美漢學研究方法與文學史編撰管窺, *Guoji Hanxue* 國際漢學 20, no. 3 (2019): 185–91.
18. Jan Assmann, *Cultural Memory and Early Civilization*, 85.
19. Hans H. Frankel, *Flowering Plum and the Palace Lady: Interpretations of Chinese Poetry* (New Haven, CT: Yale University Press, 1976), 104–27.
20. Stephen Owen, *Remembrances: The Experience of Past in Classical Chinese Literature* (Cambridge, MA: Harvard University Press, 1986).
21. See, for example, Li Xiaoming 李曉明, *Tangdai lishi guannian yanjiu* 唐代歷史觀念研究 (Beijing: Renmin chubanshe, 2009); Zhang Runjing 張潤靜, *Tangdai yongshi huaigu shi yanjiu* 唐代詠史懷古詩研究 (Shanghai: Shanghai Sanlian shudian, 2009); Chen Jianhua 陳建華, *Tangdai yongshi huaigu shi lungao* 唐代詠史懷古詩論稿 (Wuhan: Huazhong keji daxue chubanshe, 2008); Zhao Wangqin 趙望秦 and Pan Xiaoling 潘曉玲, *Hu Zeng "Yongshi shi" yanjiu* 胡曾《詠史詩》研究 (Beijing: Zhongguo shehui kexue chubanshe, 2008); Lai Yushu 賴玉樹, *Wan Tang Wudai yongshi shi zhi meixue yishi* 晚唐五代詠史詩之美學意識 (Taibei: Xiuwei zixun chubanshe, 2005); and Zhao Wangqin, *Tangdai yongshi shi zushi kaolun* 唐代詠史詩組詩考論 (Xi'an: San Qin chubanshe, 2003).
22. Robert Joe Cutter, "On Reading Cao Zhi's 'Three Good Men': *Yong shi shi* or *Deng lin shi*?" *Chinese Literature: Essays, Articles, Reviews* 11 (1989): 1–11.

23. J. Michael Farmer, "Zuo Si," in *Classical Chinese Writers of the Pre-Tang Period*, ed. Curtis Dean Smith (Detroit, MI: Bruccoli Clark Layman / Gale, 2011), 328.

24. For scholarship on Zuo Si, see David R. Knechtges and Taiping Chang, eds., *Ancient and Early Medieval Chinese Literature: A Reference Guide* (Leiden: Brill, 2014), 3:2380–93; Kōzen Hiroshi 興膳宏, "Sashi to Eishi shi" 左思と詠史詩, *Chūgoku bungaku hō* 中國文學報 21, (1966): 1–56; Xu Chuanwu 徐傳武, *Zuo Si Zuo Fen yanjiu* 左思左棻研究 (Beijing: Zhongguo wenlian chubanshe, 1999); Yue Zhang, "Zuo Si ji," in *Early Medieval Chinese Texts*, eds. Cynthia L. Chennault, Keith N. Knapp, Alan J. Berkowitz, and Albert E. Dien (Berkeley: University of California Press, 2016), 514–18; Yue Zhang, "A Selective Bibliography of Mainland Chinese Books (2002–2010) on Early Medieval Chinese Literature (220–589)," *Early Medieval China* 18 (2012): 76.

25. For a survey of modern research into Tao Yuanming in China, see Wu Yun 吳雲, *Ershi shiji zhonggu wenxue yanjiu* 20 世紀中古文學研究 (Tianjin: Tianjin guji chubanshe, 2004), 205–38; Zhong Shulin 鍾書林, *Tao Yuanming yanjiu xueshu dang'an* 陶淵明研究學術檔案 (Wuhan: Wuhan daxue chubanshe, 2014).

For a discussion and review of the recent English scholarship on Tao Yuanming studies, see Tian Jinfang 田晉芳, *Zhongwai xiandai Tao Yuanming jieshou zhi yanjiu* 中外現代陶淵明接受之研究 (PhD diss., Fudan University, 2010), Wu Fusheng 吳伏生, *Yingyu shijie de Tao Yuanming yanjiu* 英語世界的陶淵明研究 (Beijing: Xueyuan chubanshe, 2013), and Yue Zhang, "Ou Mei jinqi Tao Yuanming yanjiu zongshu, fenxi yu zhanwang" 歐美近期陶淵明研究綜述、分析與展望, *Gudian wenxian yanjiu* 古典文獻研究 20, no. 2 (2017): 289–304.

Three English-language monographs are representative of the newer approaches: Tian Xiaofei, *Tao Yuanming & Manuscript Culture: The Record of a Dusty Table* (Seattle: University of Washington Press, 2005); Wendy Swartz, *Reading Tao Yuanming: Shifting Paradigms of Historical Reception (427–1900)* (Cambridge, MA: Harvard University Asia Center, 2008); and Robert Ashmore, *The Transport of Reading: Text and Understanding in the World of Tao Qian (365–427)* (Cambridge, MA: Harvard University Asia Center, 2010).

26. Tao's *yongshi shi* discussed in this book do not include doubtful or uncertain works, such as "The Five Filial Biographies" ("Wuxiao zhuan" 五孝傳) and "Collective Record of Group Adjuncts to Sages" ("Ji shengxian qunfu lu" 集聖賢群輔錄). Modern scholars Yuan Xingpei and Zhong Shulin believe that though these works are suspicious, they are not necessarily fake. Another scholar Cai Danjun 蔡丹君 identifies these works as spurious, but argues that it is nonetheless meaningful to compare them with Tao's other *yongshi shi*. See Yuan Xingpei 袁行霈, ed., *Tao Yuanming ji jianzhu* 陶淵明集箋注 (Beijing: Zhonghua shuju, 2003), 571–600; Zhong, *Tao Yuanming yanjiu xueshu dang'an*, 345; and Cai Danjun, "Liuchao zashi, zazhuan yu yongshi shi xue de fazhan—cong Yang Xiuzhi *Tao Yuanming ji* suoshou 'Ji shengxian qunfu lu' shuoqi" 六朝雜史、雜傳與詠史詩學的發展—從陽

休之《陶淵明集》所收《集聖賢群輔錄》說起, *Beijing Daxue xubao (Zhexue shehui kexue ban)* 北京大學學報 (哲學社會科學版) 56, no. 2 (2019): 89–90. If some of these works were indeed written by Tao Yuanming, the number of his *yongshi shi* would be much higher and the genre would represent an even greater proportion of his literary output. Even when counting Tao's *yongshi* poems conservatively, they still form a substantial part of his collected works.

27. This chapter is a modified version of a previously published article, see Yue Zhang, "Tao Yuanming's Perspectives on Life as Reflected in His Poems on History," *Journal of Chinese Humanities* 6 (2020): 235–58.

28. Andrew Chittick, *The Jiankang Empire in Chinese and World History: Ethnic Identity and Political Culture* (Oxford: Oxford University Press, 2020), 127.

29. Chittick, 127–28.

30. Cynthia L. Chennault, "Lofty Gates or Solitary Impoverishment? Xie Family Members of the Southern Dynasties," *T'oung Pao* 85, no. 4/5 (1999): 249–327.

31. Chennault, 324.

32. Stephen Owen, *The Late Tang: Chinese Poetry of the Mid-Ninth Century (827–860)* (Cambridge, MA: Harvard University Asia Center, 2006). For studies of Owen's methodologies and perspectives on researching poems on historical themes, see Yue Zhang, "Lun Yuwen Suoan yongshi huaigu shi yanjiu de fangfa yu shijiao" 論宇文所安詠史懷古詩研究的方法與視角, *Changjiang xueshu* 長江學術 67, no. 3 (2020): 50–58.

33. Stephen Owen, *The Making of Early Chinese Classical Poetry* (Cambridge, MA: Harvard University Asia Center, 2006), 73.

Chapter 1

1. Burton Watson, trans., *The Analects of Confucius* (New York: Columbia University Press, 2007), 88.

2. Yang Bojun 楊伯峻, *Lunyu yizhu* 論語譯註 (Beijing: Zhonghua shuju, 2006), 13.150.

3. Some sections of this chapter have been adapted from a previously published article; see Yue Zhang, review of *Song qian yongshi shi shi* 宋前詠史詩史, by Wei Chunxi 韋春喜, *China Review International* 18, no. 1 (2011): 113–16.

4. Other labels have occasionally been used to refer to poems on historical themes. "Surveying the Ancient" (*langu* 覽古) poems are composed after reading historical accounts or visiting historical relics. "Poems on Antiquity" (*yonggu* 詠古) is a term rarely seen in poem titles, but often appears in literary criticism. In the Song dynasty (960–1279), writers used other synonyms, such as "Stirred by the Ancient" (*gangu* 感古), "Comments on History" (*pingshi* 評史), or "Surveying History" (*lanshi* 覽史). For details, see Ji Minghua 季明華, *Nan Song yongshi shi yanjiu* 南宋詠史詩研究 (Taibei: Wenjin chubanshe, 1997), 11–20.

5. Zhang Runjing, *Tangdai yongshi huaigu shi yanjiu*, 3.

6. Wei Chunxi 韋春喜, *Song qian yongshi shi shi* 宋前詠史詩史 (Beijing: Zhongguo shehui kexue chubanshe, 2010), 1. In the first chapter, Wei elaborates upon this definition by comparing *yongshi shi* with *huaigu shi* and the "Songs of My Heart" (*yonghuai* 詠懷) subgenres, as well as historicized myth and folklore, historical allusions, epics, and poetic history. This chapter also investigates the origin and scope of *yongshi shi* in the tradition of Chinese poetry (see Wei, 13–34).

7. Wei, 13.

8. See, for example, Chen Jianhua, *Tangdai yongshi huaigu shi lungao*, 10–13; Zhao Wangqin 趙望秦 and Zhang Huanling 張煥玲, *Gudai yongshi shi tonglun* 古代詠史詩通論 (Beijing: Zhongguo shehui kexue chubanshe, 2010), 3–7.

9. See, for example, Ji, *Nan Song yongshi shi yanjiu*, 11–20; Li Yiya 李宜涯, *Wan Tang yongshi shi yu pinghua yanyi zhi guanxi* 晚唐詠史詩與平話演義之關係 (Taibei: Wenshizhe chubanshe, 2002), 33–39; Li Han 李翰, *Han Wei Sheng Tang yongshi shi yanjiu—yanzhi zhi shixue chuantong ji shiren sixiang de kaocha* 漢魏盛唐詠史詩研究—言志之詩學傳統及士人思想的考察 (Guilin: Guangxi shifan daxue chubanshe, 2006), 18–41.

10. Stephen Owen, *Readings in Chinese Literary Thought* (Cambridge, MA: Harvard University Asia Center, 1992), 26.

11. Owen, 29.

12. Owen, 26.

13. Fan Ziye 范子燁, *Zhonggu wenren shenghuo yanjiu* 中古文人生活研究 (Jinan: Shandong jiaoyu chubanshe, 2001), 166.

14. Richard B. Mather, *Shih-shuo Hsin-yü: A New Account of Tales of the World*, 2nd ed. (Ann Arbor: Center for Chinese Studies, University of Michigan, 2002), 233.

15. Yu Jiaxi 余嘉錫, annot., *Shishuo xinyu jianshu* 世說新語箋疏 (Beijing: Zhonghua shuju, 2007), 8.513.

16. For more discussion on *qingtan*, see Yuet Keung Lo, "*Qingtan* and *Xuanxue*," in *The Cambridge History of China: Volume 2, The Six Dynasties, 220–589*, ed. Albert E. Dien and Keith N. Knapp (Cambridge: Cambridge University Press, 2019), 511–30.

17. Wang Xiaoyi 王曉毅, *Zhiren zhe zhi: Renwu zhi jiedu* 知人者智：人物志解讀 (Beijing: Zhonghua shuju, 2008), 3.

18. Sheldon Hsiao-peng Lu, *From Historicity to Functionality: The Chinese Poetics of Narrative* (Stanford: Stanford University Press, 1994), 39.

19. Wai-yee Li, "The Idea of Authority in the *Shih chi* (Records of the Historian)," *Harvard Journal of Asiatic Studies* 54, no. 2 (1994): 346.

20. On-cho Ng and Q. Edward Wang, *Mirroring the Past: The Writing and Use of History in Imperial China* (Honolulu: University of Hawai'i Press, 2005), 99. A similar view is shared by Stephen Durrant, "From 'Scribe' to 'History': The Keyword *shi* 史," in *Keywords in Chinese Culture: Thought and Literature*, eds. Wai-

yee Li and Yuri Pines (Hong Kong: The Chinese University of Hong Kong Press, 2020), 85–122.

21. Ng and Wang, *Mirroring the Past*, xi, 16, 56.

22. Albert E. Dien, "Historiography of the Six Dynasties Period (220–581)" in *The Oxford History of Historical Writing, Volume 1: Beginnings to AD 600*, ed. Andrew Feider and Gran Hardy (Oxford: Oxford University Press, 2011), 511.

23. *Suishu* 隋書 (Beijing: Zhonghua shuju, 1973), 33.953.

24. *Suishu*, 33.957.

25. Zhang Yajun 張亞軍, *Nanchao sishi yu Nanchao wenxue yanjiu* 南朝四史與南朝文學研究 (Beijing: Zhongguo shehui kexue chubanshe, 2007), 13. See also *Suishu*, 33.959.

26. *Suishu*, 33.958.

27. The English translation of the title follows Graham Sanders, "A New Note on *Shishuo xinyu*," *Early Medieval China* 20 (2014): 9–22, which departs from Mather's translation of it as *A New Account of Tales of the World*.

28. Dien, "Historiography of the Six Dynasties Period," 514.

29. Kenneth J. Dewoskin and J. I. Crump, trans., *In Search of the Supernatural: The Written Record* (Stanford: Stanford University Press, 1996), xxvi–xxvii.

30. Gan Bao 干寶, *Soushen ji* 搜神記, ed. Wang Shaoying 汪紹楹 (Beijing: Zhonghua shuju, 1979), 2.

31. Although this preface was attributed to Gan Bao, modern scholars Kenneth J. Dewoskin and J. I. Crump doubt the accuracy of this attribution, claiming "it is kin to several other *zhiguai* prefaces supposed to date from the early Six Dynasties; such attributions are in every case uncertain since there are no redundant versions or references to them." See Dewoskin and Crump, *In Search of the Supernatural*, xxvi.

32. Richard E. Strassberg, ed., *A Chinese Bestiary: Strange Creatures from the Guideways through Mountains and Seas* (Berkeley: University of California Press, 2002), 19.

33. Strassberg, 19.

34. English translations of these book titles are based on those found in Knechtges and Chang, *Ancient and Early Medieval Chinese Literature: A Reference Guide*, 3:2084 and 1806.

35. *Suishu*, 33.962.

36. The "Jingji zhi" section also includes, for example, histories of hegemons (*ba shi* 霸史); daily records of rulers (*qiju zhu* 起居注); rules, regulations, and systems (*dianzhang zhidu* 典章制度); official titles (*zhi guan* 職官); rituals and ceremonies (*yi zhu* 儀注); laws and punishments (*xing fa* 刑法); records of geography (*dili ji* 地理記); genealogy (*pu xi* 譜系); and records and catalogues (*bulu pian* 簿錄篇).

37. Cao Xu 曹旭, *Shipin jizhu* 詩品集注 (Shanghai: Shanghai guji chubanshe, 1994), 11–12, 257.

38. Owen, *Making of Early Chinese Classical Poetry*, 255.

39. See, for example, Zhao and Zhang, *Gudai yongshi shi tonglun*, 37–39, and Li Han, *Han Wei Sheng Tang yongshi shi yanjiu*, 42–46.

40. Shi Ding 施丁, "Cong '*Suishu*·Jingji zhi' kan Han Sui jian lishi zhuanshu de fazhan" 從《隋書·經籍志》看漢隋間歷史撰述的發展, *Shixue shi yanjiu* 史學史研究, no. 2 (1980): 30.

41. Tian Xiaofei, *Beacon Fire and Shooting Star: The Literary Culture of the Liang (502–557)* (Cambridge, MA: Harvard University Asia Center, 2007), 97.

42. A detailed discussion of Zhang's and Lu's poems appears in chapter 6.

43. Sima Qian was motivated to compile *Shiji* by his own personal interest and desire to follow in the family tradition. In contrast, Ban Gu's aims in editing and writing *Hanshu* was to use past experiences to guide contemporary governance. See Ng and Wang, *Mirroring the Past*, 81. For detailed research on the reception of Sima Qian and *Shiji*, see Lü Shihao 呂世浩, *Cong Shiji dao* Hanshu: *Zhuanzhe guocheng yu lishi yiyi* 從《史記》到《漢書》：轉折過程與歷史意義 (Taibei: Guoli Taiwan daxue chuban zhongxin, 2009), and Esther S. Klein, *Reading Sima Qian from Han to Song: The Father of History in Pre-Modern China* (Leiden: Brill, 2019). For detailed research on Ban Gu and historiography, see Anthony E. Clark, *Ban Gu's History of Early China* (Amherst, NY: Cambria Press, 2008). For a detailed discussion of research into *Shiji* and *Hanshu*, see Wang Chunhong 汪春泓, *Shi Han yanjiu* 史漢研究 (Shanghai: Shanghai guji chubanshe, 2014).

44. Yuan, *Tao Yuanming ji jianzhu*, 6.512. A detailed discussion of some of Tao's "Du *Shi* shu jiuzhang" appears in chapter 4.

45. Xiao Tong's editorial team likely included Liu Xiaochuo 劉孝綽 (481–539) and He Xun 何遜 (d. 518).

46. A detailed discussion of Wang's and Cao's poems appears in chapter 6.

47. Wei, *Song qian yongshi shi shi*, 114. See also, Zhao and Zhang, *Gudai yongshi shi tonglun*, 51. A detailed discussion of Zheng's and Fan's poems appears in chapter 5.

48. For a detailed discussion of *Tang wencui*, see Anna M. Shields, "Defining the 'Finest': A Northern Song View of Tang Dynasty Literary Culture in the *Wen cui*," *Journal of Chinese Literature and Culture* 4, no. 2 (2017): 306–35.

49. Robert Joe Cutter, "Poetry from 200 B.C.E. to 600 C.E.," in *The Columbia History of Chinese Literature*, ed. Victor Mair (New York: Columbia University Press, 2001), 254–255.

50. Owen, *The Making of Early Chinese Classical Poetry*; Tian Xiaofei, *Beacon Fire and Shooting Star*; Christopher Nugent, *Manifest in Words, Written on Paper: Producing and Circulating Poetry in Tang Dynasty China* (Cambridge, MA: Harvard University Asia Center, 2010).

51. Tian Xiaofei, *Tao Yuanming & Manuscript Culture*, 97.

Chapter 2

1. This chapter follows my previous article with some modifications. See Yue Zhang, "Self-Canonization in Zuo Si's Poems on History," *Journal of Chinese Humanities* 5 (2019): 215–44.

2. For Zuo Si's biography, see *Jinshu* 晉書 (Beijing: Zhonghua shuju, 1974), 92.2375–77. Other accounts about Zuo can be found in *A New Account of Tales of the World* (*Shishuo xinyu* 世說新語). See, for example, Yu Jiaxi, *Shishuo xinyu jianshu*, 4.292–96. For an English translation of this work, see Mather, *Shih-shuo Hsin-yü*, 135–36. For recent studies of Zuo Si's biographies, see Zeb Raft, "A New Approach to Biography in Early Medieval China: The Case of Zuo Si," *Zhongguo wen zhe yanjiu jikan* 中國文哲研究集刊 55, (2019): 41–81.

3. *Suishu*, 35.1063.

4. Lu Kanru 陸侃如 and Feng Yuanjun 馮沅君, *Zhongguo shishi* 中國詩史 (Jinan: Shandong daxue chubanshe, 1985), 287.

5. Xu Gongchi 徐公持, *Wei Jin wenxue shi* 魏晉文學史 (Beijing: Renmin wenxue chubanshe, 1999), 393–94; Lü Huijuan 呂慧鵑, Liu Bo 劉波, and Lu Da 盧達, eds., *Zhongguo lidai zhuming wenxuejia pingzhuan (di yi juan)* 中國歷代著名文學家評傳 (第一卷) (Jinan: Shandong jiaoyu chubanshe, 1983), 345; Ye Riguang 葉日光, *Zuo Si shengping ji qi shi zhi xilun* 左思生平及其詩之析論 (Taibei: Wen shi zhe chubanshe, 1979), 24.

6. Mou Shijin 牟世金 and Xu Chuanwu 徐傳武, "Zuo Si wenxue yeji xinlun" 左思文學業績新論, *Wenxue yichan* 文學遺產, no. 2 (1988): 30; Qian Zhixi 錢志熙, *Wei Jin shige yishu yuanlun* 魏晉詩歌藝術原論 (Beijing: Beijing daxue chubanshe, 1993), 308–9; Ge Xiaoyin 葛曉音, *Badai shishi* 八代詩史 (Xi'an: Shanxi renmin chubanshe, 1989), 121–26.

7. Owen, *Readings in Chinese Literary Thought*, 26.

8. Owen, 40.

9. Owen, 68.

10. This idea of using literature to express one's frustrated political ambitions for posterity is discussed at length by Sima Qian in "The Letter to Ren Shaoqing" ("Bao Ren Shaoqing shu" 報任少卿書). More discussion on this can be found in chapter 4.

11. David R. Knechtges, "From the Eastern Han through the Western Jin (25–317)," in *The Cambridge History of Chinese Literature*, ed. Kang-i Sun Chang and Stephen Owen (Cambridge: Cambridge University Press, 2010), 191.

12. Xiao Tong 蕭統, ed., *Wen xuan* 文選, annot. Li Shan 李善 (Shanghai: Shanghai guji chubanshe, 1986), 21.987–88. The English translation of Zuo Si's poems is based on the commentaries of the Five Ministers 五臣 and Li Shan 李善 (630–689).

13. *Ruoguan* 弱冠 refers to the capping ceremony that Chinese men underwent around the age of twenty.

14. *Zhuoluo* 卓犖 means "outstanding."

15. "The Faults of Qin" ("Guo Qin lun" 過秦論) was written by Jia Yi 賈誼 (200–168 BCE). He discussed and summarized the errors of the Qin dynasty (221–206 BCE) and explained the reasons for its rapid decline.

16. "Rhapsody of Sir Vacuous" ("Zixu fu" 子虛賦) was written by Sima Xiangru 司馬相如 (ca. 179–118 BCE).

17. *Yuxi* 羽檄 refers to an urgent official military declaration, written on a wooden slip with a feather attached to mark its urgency.

18. "Rangju" refers to Sima Rangju 司馬穰苴 (fl. 531 BCE). His military strategies are referenced in the *Shiji*: "King Wei of Qi ordered his ministers to compile and edit the old *Sima bingfa* 司馬兵法 (*The Marshal's Arts of War*) and to append Rangju's (works) to them. The book was thus called *Sima Rangju bingfa* 司馬穰苴兵法 (*Marshal Rangju's Arts of War*)." 齊威王使大夫追論古者司馬兵法而附穰苴於其中，因號曰司馬穰苴兵法. See William H. Nienhauser, Jr., ed., *The Grand Scribe's Records*, vol. 7, *The Memoirs of Pre-Han China* (Bloomington: Indiana University Press, 1994), 33–35; *Shiji* 史記 (Beijing: Zhonghua shuju, 1959), 64.2160.

19. *Qingfeng* 清風 literally means "cool breeze." Here it refers to pure moral value.

20. Eastern Wu refers to the state of Wu 吳 (222–280). When Zuo Si wrote this poem, it is probable that the Jin had not yet conquered Wu. The Jin unified the country in 280. This line refers to Zuo's youthful ambition to contribute to the defeat of the state of Wu and the unification of the country.

21. A lead knife is a metaphor for incapable people—lead is soft and therefore not a good metal to use in the manufacture of knives. A lead knife can cut things once, but then it will become dull and will not cut well again. This metaphor is borrowed from Ban Chao's 班超 (32–102) memorandum to the emperor: "I ride the sage Han's magnificent spirit and am willing to die ten thousand deaths. I wish to serve the court as a lead knife that works best with its first cuts." 班超上疏曰：「臣乘聖漢威神，出萬死之志，冀效鉛刀一割之用。」See Wu Shuping 吳樹平, ed., *Dongguan Hanji jiaozhu* 東觀漢記校注 (Beijing: Zhonghua shuju, 2008), 16.658.

22. *Mian* 眄 and *xi* 眲 both mean "look sideways."

23. *Jinshu*, 92.2376.

24. Mather, *Shih-shuo Hsin-yü*, 135–36.

25. Yu Jiaxi, *Shishuo xinyu jianshu*, 4.292.

26. Xiao, *Wen xuan*, 21.988–89.

27. Duangan is Duangan Mu's 段干木 (ca. 475–ca. 396 BCE) family name. See David R. Knechtges, *Wen xuan or Selections of Refined Literature*, vol. 1, *Rhapsodies on Metropolises and Capitals* (Princeton, NJ: Princeton University Press, 1982), 470.

28. The story about Duangan Mu and the ruler of Wei can be found in the *Shiji*: "Marquis Wen learned the arts from Zi Xia 子夏 (507–ca. 420 BCE), and welcomed Duangan Mu as his guest. Whenever he passed Duangan's gate, he never failed to pay his respects by saluting in his carriage. Qin wanted to attack Wei, and someone said, 'The Lord of Wei treats people with respect, and people in Wei praise him as benevolent. The high and the low are in harmony, so we cannot yet make plans against Wei.'" 文侯受子夏經藝，客段干木，過其間，未嘗不軾也。秦欲伐魏，或曰：「魏君賢人是禮，國人稱仁，上下和合，未可圖也。」See *Shiji*, 44.1839.

29. The story about Lu Zhonglian 魯仲連 (ca. 305–245 BCE) and his defeat of the Qin army is in the *Shiji*: "The King of Wei sent his Foreign General Xinyuan Yan 新垣衍 (fl. 257 BCE) to have Zhao confer the title of emperor on

Qin." 魏王使客將軍新垣衍令趙帝秦. See Nienhauser, *The Grand Scribe's Records*, 7:281; *Shiji*, 83.2460. Lu Zhonglian then had a heated discussion with Xinyuan Yan, who was eventually persuaded by Lu Zhonglian and did not dare again to propose making Qin emperor. When the Qin commander heard this, he retreated fifty *li*. See *Shiji*, 83.2465.

30. *Zu* 組 refers to a silk band used to tie official seals to the waist.

31. A *gui* 珪 ("jade tablet") was conferred upon feudal princes by the emperor as a symbol of dignity and authority.

32. "Drifting clouds" is an allusion to the *Analects*: "Eating simple food, drinking water, a bended arm for a pillow—there's happiness in these things too. Wealth and eminence gained by unrightful means are to me mere drifting clouds." 子曰: "飯疏食, 飲水, 曲肱而枕之, 樂亦在其中矣! 不義而富且貴, 於我如浮雲." Watson, *Analects of Confucius*, 49–50; Zhang Yanying 張燕嬰, ed., *Lun yu* 論語 (Beijing: Zhonghua shuju, 2006), 7.92.

33. *Shiji*, 83.2465.

34. Nienhauser, *The Grand Scribe's Records*, 7:284.

35. *Shiji*, 83.2465.

36. *Jinshu*, 92.2376.

37. Although this example is from the anecdotal collection *Shishuo xinyu*, it probably reflects Zuo's efforts to promote his rhapsody.

38. Mather, *Shih-shuo Hsin-yü*, 135; Yu Jiaxi, *Shishuo xinyu jianshu*, 4.292.

39. *Jinshu*, 92.2377.

40. An idiom describing this episode, "the price of paper in Luoyang is dear" 洛陽紙貴, is still used to describe a bestselling book.

41. Xiao, *Wen xuan*, 21.988.

42. "Luxuriant pines at the bottom of a ravine" is a metaphor for those who come from humble backgrounds but have real talents and abilities.

43. "Sprouts on the top of mountain" is a metaphor for those who hold high positions but lack talent.

44. "Terrain" is a metaphor for a person's status.

45. Jin refers to the clan of Jin Midi 金日磾 (134–86 BCE), and Zhang refers to the clan of Zhang Tang 張湯 (d. 116 BCE). The Jin clan held the position of palace attendant (*nei shi* 內侍) for seven generations, from the reign of Emperor Wu of Han 漢武帝 (r. 141–87 BCE) to the reign of Emperor Ping 漢平帝 (r. 1 BCE–6 CE), and a member of the Zhang clan was appointed as either palace attendant or palace attendant-in-ordinary (*zhong chang shi* 中常侍) for seven successive generations, from the reign of Emperor Xuan of Han 漢宣帝 (r. 74–48 BCE) to the reign of Emperor Yuan 漢元帝 (r. 48–33 BCE). The stories of the Jin and Zhang families are in the *Hanshu* (Beijing: Zhonghua shuju, 1962), 68.2959–67, 59.2637–57.

46. Sir Feng refers to Feng Tang 馮唐 in the Western Han dynasty (202 BCE–8 CE). According to *Shiji*: "Feng Tang's grandfather was a native of Zhao

趙. His father had been transferred to Dai 代, and when the Han arose he was moved to Anling 安陵. [Feng] Tang was known for his filial piety and therefore became chief of the Bureau of Palace Attendants, serving Emperor Wen." 馮唐者，其大父趙人. 父徙代. 漢興徙安陵. 唐以孝著，爲中郎署長，事文帝. See William H. Nienhauser, Jr., ed., *The Grand Scribe's Records*, vol. 8, *The Memoirs of Han China, Part I* (Bloomington: Indiana University Press, 2008), 364; *Shiji*, 102.2757.

47. "Was not summoned by the emperor," i.e., he was not given an important position in the court. The English translation of this poem largely follows Yue Zhang, "Approaches to Lore in 'Poems on History' from the *Selections of Refined Literature*," *Journal of Oriental Studies* 49, no. 2 (2017): 106–7.

48. *Shiji*, 102.2757.

49. Nienhauser, *The Grand Scribe's Records*, 8:367.

50. *Shiji*, 102.2759 and 2761. According to *Hanshu* (50.2314–15), this event took place ten, not seven, years after Emperor Jing ascended to the throne.

51. For a detailed discussion on the cultural construction of Feng Tang, see Yue Zhang, "Approaches to Lore," 106–10.

52. Xiao, *Wen xuan*, 21.991.

53. "Zhufu" refers to Zhufu Yan 主父偃 (fl. 127 BCE), whose story is in the *Shiji*: "His family was very poor, and he likewise failed in all attempts to borrow money. Later he traveled north to Yan, Zhao, and the region of Zhongshan, but again was unable to find anyone who would employ him. He suffered great hardship on his travels." 家貧，假貸無所得，乃北游燕、趙、中山，皆莫能厚遇，爲客甚困. See Burton Watson, trans., *Records of the Grand Historian: Han Dynasty*, rev. ed. (New York: Columbia University Press, 1996), 2:192–93; *Shiji*, 112.2953.

54. "Maichen" refers to Zhu Maichen 朱買臣 (fl. 115 BCE), whose story is in *Hanshu*: "His family was poor, but he liked reading books. He did not manage any property, and often made his living by cutting lumber. He recited books to himself as he carried the timber on his shoulder. His wife followed him, also carrying timber, and stopped him from singing on the way to the market. Maichen sang even more loudly, and his wife was ashamed of this. She asked to leave him." 貧，好讀書，不治產業，常艾薪樵，賣以給食，擔束薪，行且誦書. 其妻亦負戴相隨，數止買臣毋歌嘔道中. 買臣愈益疾歌，妻羞之，求去. See *Hanshu*, 64.2791.

55. Chen Ping's 陳平 (fl. 178 BCE) story is in *Shiji*: "Prime Minister Chen Ping was a native of Huyou 戶牖 in Yangwu 陽武 county. In his boyhood, his family was poor. . . . He lived in a poor lane at the foot of the city wall with only some worn-out matting as a door." 陳丞相平者，陽武戶牖鄉人也. 少時家貧……家乃負郭窮巷，以弊席爲門. The English translation is based on Watson, *Records of the Grand Historian: Han Dynasty*, 2:118; *Shiji*, 56.2051–52.

56. "Changqing" refers to Sima Xiangru.

57. Sima Qian mentioned twice how poor Sima Xiangru's home was. The details are in *Shiji*: "With the death of King Xiao, he (Sima Xiangru) left Liang

and returned to his home in Chengdu, but by this time his family had grown very poor and he had no means of making a living. . . . That night Wenjun ran away from home and joined Xiangru, and the two of them galloped off to Chengdu. There they took up residence in Xiangru's house, four bare walls with nothing inside." 會梁孝王卒, 相如歸, 而家貧, 無以自業……文君夜亡奔相如, 相如乃與馳歸成都. 家居徒四壁立. See Watson, *Records of the Grand Historian: Han Dynasty*, 2:259; *Shiji*, 117.3000.

58. Before they received the golden opportunity that vaulted them into the stratosphere, these figures were all human beings who struggled to live their simple lives. Sima Xiangru 司馬相如 (ca. 179–117 BCE), for example, encountered great difficulties after he eloped with Zhuo Wenjun. "She (Zhuo Wenjun) and Xiangru accordingly went to Linqiong, where they sold their carriage and all their riding equipment and bought a wine-shop. Xiangru left Wenjun to mind the counter while he himself, dressed in a workman's loincloth, went off on errands with the other hired men or washed the wine vessels at the well in the marketplace." See Watson, *Records of the Grand Historian: Han Dynasty*, 2:261. 相如與俱之臨邛, 盡賣其車騎, 買一酒舍酤酒, 而令文君當爐. 相如身自著犢鼻褌, 與保庸雜作, 滌器於市中. See *Shiji*, 117.3000.

59. This couplet is Zuo's summary of the life experiences of these four great figures.

60. Watson, *Records of the Grand Historian: Han Dynasty*, 2:192–93.

61. *Shiji*, 112.2953.

62. Yang Xianyi 楊憲益 and Dai Naidie 戴乃迭, trans., *Selections from Records of the Historian*. (Beijing: Waiwen chubanshe, 2004), 143; *Shiji*, 56.2062–63.

63. *Shiji*, 56.2062–63.

64. Gong Kechang, *Studies on the Han Fu*, trans. David R. Knechtges (Ann Arbor, MI: American Oriental Society, 1997), 326.

65. Xiao, *Wen xuan*, 21.990.

66. The English translation of this poem largely follows Yue Zhang, "Teaching Classical Chinese Poetry through Reception Studies," *ASIANetwork Exchange: A Journal for Asian Studies in the Liberal Arts* 26, no. 1 (2019): 89–90.

67. Nienhauser, *The Grand Scribe's Records*, 7:326.

68. *Shiji*, 86.2528.

69. Nienhauser, *The Grand Scribe's Records*, 7:326.

70. *Shiji*, 86.2528.

71. *Shiji*, 86.2534.

72. *Shiji*, 86.2537.

73. For a detailed discussion on Zuo Si's adaptation of the Jing Ke lore in this poem, see Yue Zhang, "Teaching Classical Chinese Poetry," 75–95.

74. For a detailed discussion of the reception of the Jing Ke lore in China, see Yuri Pines, "A Hero Terrorist: Adoration of Jing Ke Revisited," *Asia Major*, 3rd ser., 21, no. 2 (2008): 1–34.

75. J. Michael Farmer, "On the Composition of Zhang Hua's 'Nüshi zhen,'" *Early Medieval China* 10–11, no. 1 (2004): 163–64.

76. Farmer, 163–64.

77. *Jinshu*, 92.2377.

78. *Jinshu*, 92.2375–77.

79. Xiao, *Wen xuan*, 21.989–90.

80. "Capital" refers to the capital of the Western Han dynasty, Chang'an 長安.

81. The caesura for this line could also be placed between the second and third characters, 赫赫 / 王侯居, which would read "How impressive princes' and marquises' mansions are."

82. *Guan* 冠 refers to an official cap that goes with formal dress. *Gai* 蓋 refers to a circular awning over grand carriages.

83. Xu 許 and Shi 史 refer to Xu Guanghan 許廣漢 (117–61 BCE) and Shi Gao 史高 (d. 42 BCE). They were relatives of Emperor Xuan of the Han: Xu Guanghan was the empress's father, while Shi Gao was the eldest son of the emperor's great-uncle. Xu and Shi are often used together as a metonym for prominent families.

84. *Sheng* 笙 refers to a reed pipe wind instrument. *Yu* 竽 refers to another ancient wind instrument.

85. See *Hanshu*, 88.3585: "His home was often poor, but he liked drinking wine. Few people came to visit him." 家素貧, 耆酒, 人希至其門.

86. This couplet about Yang Xiong has two possible interpretations. It could mean he physically stayed in his quiet house, teaching his understanding of the *Yijing* to select disciples: "Isolated and lonely, he remained in his empty house." Or it could be a metaphor for his mental journeys: "His mind wandered in the empty expanses of the cosmos." It could very well refer to both states at once.

87. *Mystery* refers to *The Supreme Mystery* (*Tai xuan* 太玄), the title of one of Yang's works. See *Hanshu*, 88.3583: "Yang Xiong thought no canon was more influential than the *Book of Changes*, and so, imitating the book, he wrote *The Supreme Mystery*." 以爲經莫大于《易》, 故作《太玄》. Yang Xiong was poor and taught from his works *The Supreme Mystery* and *Exemplary Words* (*Fayan* 法言) at home. See *Hanshu*, 88.3585: "Hou Pa, a native of Julu, often learned from him in Yang Xiong's empty house, where Yang taught him *The Supreme Mystery* and *Exemplary Words*." 巨鹿侯芭常從雄居, 受其《太玄》、《法言》焉.

88. *Xuanni* 宣尼 refers to Confucius. Emperor Ping of the Han dynasty conferred upon Confucius the title Xuanni. Yang Xiong, imitating the *Analects of Confucius*, wrote *Exemplary Words*. The details can be seen in *Hanshu*, 88.3583: "Yang Xiong thought no biographies were more influential than the *Analects of Confucius*; so, imitating it, he wrote *Exemplary Words*." 傳莫大於《論語》, 作《法言》.

89. Yang Xiong, imitating Sima Xiangru, wrote four rhapsodies. The details can be seen in *Hanshu*: "Previously, Shu had Sima Xiangru, who wrote rhapsodies very magnificent and gentle. Yang Xiong admired Sima Xiangru's writings, and so

every time when he wrote rhapsodies, he often imitated Sima Xiangru's style. . . . No diction was more beautiful than Sima Xiangru, and so imitating his rhapsodies, Yang Xiong wrote four rhapsodies." 先是時, 蜀有司馬相如, 作賦甚弘麗溫雅, 雄心壯之, 每作賦, 常擬之以爲式⋯⋯辭莫麗於相如, 作四賦. *Hanshu*, 88.3515, 3583.

90. The following comparison between Zuo and Yang is based on Yue Zhang, "Zuo Si 'Yongshi,'" 91–94, and Kōzen, "Sashi to Eishi shi," 28–32.

91. Gong, *Studies on the Han Fu*, 224.

92. From the preface: "'The *Songs* has six principles. The second is called *Exposition*.' Yang Xiong has said, 'The *fu* of the *Songs* poets are beautiful but maintain standards.'" 蓋詩有六義焉, 其二曰賦. 楊雄曰: "詩人之賦麗以則." See Knechtges, *Wen xuan or Selections*, 1:337; Xiao, *Wen xuan*, 4.173.

93. Lu Qinli 逯欽立, *Xian Qin Han Wei Jin Nanbei chao shi* 先秦漢魏晉南北朝詩, 3 vols. (Beijing: Zhonghua shuju, 1983), 3:2491.

94. Xiao, *Wen xuan*, 21.990.

95. The most common usage of "Purple Palace" during this period is as the name of a constellation. Here it is an allusion to the capital of Western Jin, Luoyang.

96. "Dragon-mounted guest" refers to those who try to curry favor with nobility.

97. *Changhe* 閶闔 refers to the palace gate of Luoyang.

98. "With long strides," i.e., Zuo Si would like to be far away from the snobbish and sordid world of the capital. According to folklore, Xu You was a hermit who lived during the time of Yao 堯. "Yao yielded the world to Xu You, but Xu You would not accept. Humiliated at Yao's offer, he fled into hiding." 堯讓天下於許由, 許由不受, 恥之逃隱. See Nienhauser, *The Grand Scribe's Records*, 7:1; Sima, *Shiji*, 61.2121.

99. A *ren* is a unit of measurement equivalent to about eight feet.

100. "Shaking clothes and washing feet": for example, Zuo Si wanted to get away from worldly customs.

101. David Hawkes, *Ch'u Tz'ŭ: The Songs of the South, An Ancient Chinese Anthology* (Boston: Beacon Press, 1962), 90.

102. Wang Siyuan 王泗原, *Chuci jiaoshi* 楚辭校釋 (Beijing: Renmin jiaoyu chubanshe, 1990), 295.

103. Xiao, *Wen xuan*, 21.387.

104. Xiao, *Wen xuan*, 21.990.

105. Xiao, *Wen xuan*, 21.991–92.

106. *Zhi* 枳 refers to *Citrus trifoliata*, trifoliate orange trees. *Ji* 棘 refers to *Ziziphus jujuba var. spinosa*, sour jujube trees.

107. Su Qin's 蘇秦 (d. 284 BCE) story is in the *Shiji*: "Su Qin was a native of East Zhou's Luoyang. . . . (He said), 'I hope, Great King, that you might join in alliance with Zhao. When the world is as one, the state of Yan is sure to have no fears.' Marquis Wen said, 'Your advice is acceptable, sir, but my state is small. To the west we are near mighty Zhao, to the south we are close to Qi. Qi and

Zhao are mighty states. If you are set on forming an alliance to secure the safety of Yan, we ask permission to follow with our state.'" 蘇秦者，東周雒陽人也……願大王與趙從親，天下爲一，則燕國必無患矣。文侯曰："子言則可，然吾國小，西迫彊趙，南近齊，齊、趙彊國也。子必欲合從以安燕，寡人請以國從。" See Nienhauser, *The Grand Scribe's Records*, 7:97, 99; *Shiji*, 69.2241, 2244.

108. Li Si's 李斯 (284–208 BCE) story is in the *Shiji*: "Li Si was a native of Shangcai in Chu. . . . The clansmen of the House of Qin and the great vassals all said to the King of Qin: 'Most of the men of the feudal lords who come to serve Qin seek to advise or spy on Qin for their rulers. We ask that you expel all foreigners.' Li Si was also proposed as one of those to be expelled. (Li) Si thus submitted a memorial to refute this idea. . . . The King of Qin then revoked the decree expelling foreigners, restored Li Si's position, and eventually adopted his schemes. (His) position reached Commandant of Justice." 李斯者，楚上蔡人也……秦宗室大臣皆言秦王曰："諸侯人來事秦者，大抵爲其主游閒於秦耳，請一切逐客。" 李斯議亦在逐中。斯乃上書……秦王乃除逐客之令，復李斯官，卒用其計謀。官至廷尉。See Nienhauser, *The Grand Scribe's Records*, 7:335, 340; *Shiji*, 87.2539, 2541, 2546.

109. This is a reference to a parable from *Zhuangzi* 莊子: "When the tailorbird builds her nest in the deep wood, she uses no more than one branch. When the mole drinks at the river, he takes no more than a bellyful. Go home and forget the matter, my lord. I have no use for the rulership of the world!" 鷦鷯巢於深林，不過一枝；偃鼠飲河，不過滿腹。歸休乎君，予无所用天下爲。See Burton Watson, trans., *The Complete Works of Zhuangzi* (New York: Columbia University Press, 2013), 3–4; Chen Guying 陳鼓應, *Zhuangzi jinzhu jinyi* 莊子今註今譯 (Beijing: Zhonghua shuju, 1983), 1.18.

110. Nienhauser, *The Grand Scribe's Records*, 7:355–57.

111. *Shiji*, 87.2562–63.

112. *Jinshu*, 92.2377.

113. *Jinshu*, 92.2377.

114. Irene Bloom, trans., *Mencius* (New York: Columbia University Press, 2009), 119.

115. Jiao Xun 焦循, *Mengzi zhengyi* 孟子正義 (Beijing: Zhonghua shuju, 1987), 21.725–26.

116. Young men could not yet understand the importance of family background, networks, and historical opportunities.

Chapter 3

1. This chapter follows my previous article with some modifications. See Yue Zhang, "The Reception of Zuo Si's 'Poems on History' in Early Medieval China," *Frontiers of Literary Studies in China* 14, no. 1 (2020): 48–75.

2. Xu Chuanwu, *Zuo Si Zuo Fen yanjiu*, 308–15, and Kōzen, "Sashi to Eishi shi," 47–48.

3. Xu Chuanwu, *Zuo Si Zuo Fen yanjiu*, 315–29; Kōzen, "Sashi to Eishi shi," 49–53; Dai Jianye 戴建業, "Zuo Bao yitong chutan—Bijiao fenxi Zuo Si, Bao Zhao de rensheng jingyu yu rensheng jueze" 左鮑異同初探——比較分析左思、鮑照的人生境遇與人生抉擇, *Zhonghua wenshi luncong* 中華文史論叢 92, no. 4 (2008): 349–73.

4. In Zuo's case, the first poem serves as the preface to the entire series of poems, while for Tao, the first two poems have this function. See Kōzen, "Sashi to Eishi shi," 49, and Mou and Xu, "Zuo Si wenxue yeji xinlun," 31.

5. Zuo's other works also influenced Tao's writing. For example, the authentic feeling and representation of family life in Tao's poems to his sons seem inspired in part by Zuo's poems to his daughters. Tao's embrace of Zuo's poetry was unusual among his early medieval contemporaries. See Xu Chuanwu, *Zuo Si Zuo Fen yanjiu*, 315–21.

6. Xu Chuanwu, 321.

7. Cao Xu, *Shipin jizhu*, 1.154.

8. Xu Chuanwu, *Zuo Si Zuo Fen yanjiu*, 325.

9. Xu Chuanwu, 323–24, and Kōzen, "Sashi to Eishi shi," 50–53.

10. Dai, "Zuo Bao yitong chutan," 349–73.

11. Xu Chuanwu, *Zuo Si Zuo Fen yanjiu*, 323–24, and Kōzen, "Sashi to Eishi shi," 50–53.

12. The connection between the two subjects of the poems goes even deeper: Yan Junping was Yang Xiong's teacher. For a detailed discussion of Bao's poem on Yan Junping, see Yue Zhang, "Approaches to Lore," 103–6.

13. The major connection between Zuo and Jiang is that Jiang wrote an imitation poem on Zuo's "Yongshi" poems.

14. Imitation poems refer to poems that imitate different poetic elements of available poems, such as topic, structure, diction, and rhetoric, as well as aesthetic and artistic values. The imitation poems may or may not cover the similar content as the original poems.

15. Stephen Owen believes that this series of poems was "probably written toward the end of the fifth century." See Owen, *Making of Early Chinese Classical Poetry*, 36.

16. Cao Daoheng, "Jiang Yan," in *Zhongguo lidai zhuming wenxuejia pingzhuan* 中國歷代著名文學家評傳, ed. Lü Huijuan 呂慧鵑, Liu Bo 劉波, and Lu Da 盧達 (Jinan: Shandong jiaoyu chubanshe, 1983), 1:518–20.

17. Owen, *Making of Early Chinese Classical Poetry*, 44.

18. Hu Zhiji 胡之驥, *Jiang Wentong ji huizhu* 江文通集彙註 (Shanghai: Shanghai guji chubanshe, 1984), 4.136.

19. Owen, *Making of Early Chinese Classical Poetry*, 44.

20. Hu Zhiji, *Jiang Wentong ji huizhu*, 4.136.

21. Owen, *Making of Early Chinese Classical Poetry*, 44.

22. Hu Zhiji, *Jiang Wentong ji huizhu*, 136. *Mei* 美 refers to external expressions, such as words or diction; "shan" 善 refers to the exemplary moral values and thoughts that characterize the poets' inner disposition.

23. According to Cao Daoheng, there are two major categories of imitation poems. The first is a strict imitation, using the same or similar structure, diction, and imagery of the poem on which it is modeled. The other type calls itself an imitation, but in reality is the poet only expressing his or her own emotions and concerns without explicitly referencing any previous poems. Lu Ji's 陸機 (261–303) "Imitation Poems" ("Nigu" 擬古) are an example of the former; Tao Yuanming's 陶淵明 (ca. 365–427) and Bao Zhao's 鮑照 (ca. 415–470) "Imitation Poems" are examples of the latter. See Cao Daoheng, *Nanbei chao wenxue shi* 南北朝文學史 (Beijing: Renmin wenxue chubanshe, 1991), 111–12. Some imitation poems straddle the line between these two categories. Jiang's imitation poem of Zuo's "Yongshi," for instance, both alludes to Zuo's poem directly and makes indirect references to Zuo's themes and overall style.

24. In Jiang Yan's own rhapsodies, such as "Rhapsody on Bitter Regret" ("Hen fu" 恨賦) and "Rhapsody on Parting" ("Bie fu" 別賦), he uses historical people or events to describe his own emotions, so he may have had an affinity for Zuo's approach.

25. Two scholarly works provide English translations of this poem. Nicholas Morrow Williams, *Imitations of the Self: Jiang Yan and Chinese Poetics* (Leiden: Brill, 2015), 74 and 258; John Marney, *Chiang Yen* (Boston: Twayne Publishers, 1981), 96–97.

26. "Sir Han" refers to Han Kang 韓康 (fl. 146), who was a recluse during the Eastern Han dynasty. He did not pursue worldly fame and reputation, and instead preferred hiding in the mountains, where he earned a living by selling the medical herbs he picked. Even when an official offered him a position, he tried to escape and continued to reside on a remote mountain. His story appears in Huangfu Mi's 皇甫謐 (215–82) *Gaoshi zhuan* 高士傳 (Beijing: Zhonghua shuju, 1985), 97–98.

27. "Mr. Mei" refers to Mei Fu 梅福 of the Western Han dynasty (202 BCE–8 CE). He submitted admonitory petitions to the court because lesser men, such as Wang Feng 王鳳 (d. 22 BCE), monopolized power. Mei was scolded for his impertinence for daring to comment on court governance as a low-ranking official. After Wang Mang's 王莽 (45 BCE–23 CE) usurpation, Mei resigned his position and retired to a mountain to practice Daoism. See *Hanshu*, 67.2917–18.

28. The implication is that, as with the generals Wei Qing 衛青 (d. 106 BCE) and Huo Qubing 霍去病 (140–117 BCE), one should make a great contribution to the country, rather than escaping from the realities of society by becoming a recluse. For Wei Qing and Huo Qubing's biographies, see *Shiji*, 111.2921–47.

29. Zhong Jun 終軍 (ca. 133–112 BCE) was a brave general who obtained power when he was very young but died in his twenties. See *Hanshu*, 64.2814–15.

30. Jia Yi 賈誼 (200–168 BCE) reached a high position when he was only twenty years old, but unfortunately died young. See *Shiji*, 84.2496–2504.

31. Nicholas Williams understands this couplet as a "metalepsis," a recontextualization of the historical allusions in Zuo's "Yongshi" that adds another layer of meaning onto Zuo's original allusions. See Williams, *Imitations of the Self*, 75.

32. This line refers to Lou Jing 婁敬 (fl. 202 BCE), originally a commoner in the early Western Han dynasty, who quickly rose to power and prestige because of his advice on the selection of a location for the capital for his fighting against the Xiongnu. See *Shiji*, 99.2715–17.

33. This line alludes to Tian Qianqiu 田千秋 (d. 77 BCE). He was promoted soon after he submitted a letter to defend Crown Prince Wei (128–91 BCE), who was slandered by Jiang Chong 江充 (d. 91 BCE) and unjustly executed. Tian's words enlightened Emperor Wu (r. 141–87 BCE), who promoted him to the rank of prime minister after only a few months. See *Shiji*, 20.1058–61.

34. After reviewing all the historical figures, Jiang recalls Zhang Zhongwei 張仲蔚 (fl. 266), a skilled writer who avoided politics and lived as a recluse in his remote cottage in order to maintain his moral integrity.

35. Cao Daoheng, "Jiang Yan," 521–22.

36. Xu Chuanwu, *Zuo Si Zuo Fen yanjiu*, 327.

37. Williams, *Imitations of the Self*, 75.

38. Williams, 76.

39. Xiao, *Wen xuan*, 21.988.

40. Xiao, 21.989–90. This poem draws upon a common repertoire of images; Zuo was not the first poet to use these allusions, as they also appear in Zhang Hua's 張華 (232–300) poem "Poem on Frivolous Behavior" ("Qingbo pian" 輕薄篇). However, in this context and its specifics ("marten ear-ornaments"), this image is more closely associated with Zuo.

41. Marney, *Chiang Yen*, 97.

42. Xiao, *Wen xuan*, 21.987.

43. Xiao, 21.990.

44. In order to achieve political success, family background and networks, as well as historical opportunities, were important factors that young people do not fully understand.

45. Xiao, *Wen xuan*, 21.991–92. For further analysis of this poem, see Chapter 2.

46. Xiao, 21.988.

47. For the English translation and a detailed analysis of Zhang Xie's "Yongshi," see Yue Zhang, "Approaches to Lore" 85–88.

48. Xiao, *Wen xuan*, 21.994.

49. They played an important role during Emperor Xuan's 宣 (91–49 BCE) reign in the Western Han dynasty.

50. Xiao, *Wen xuan*, 21.989–90. For further analysis of this poem, see chapter 2.

51. *Hanshu*, 87.3585.

52. Xiao, *Wen xuan*, 21.989–90. For a detailed analysis of this poem, see Yue Zhang, "Zuo Si 'Yongshi,'" 91–94.

53. For discussions of Jiang's influence on Zhong Rong, see Wang Daheng 王大恒, *Jiang Yan wenxue chuangzuo yanjiu* 江淹文學創作研究 (Beijing: Zhongguo shehui kexue chubanshe, 2013).

54. A convincing argument for Jiang's influence on Xiao can be found in Fu Gang 傅剛, *Zhaoming Wen xuan yanjiu* 昭明文選研究 (Beijing: Zhongguo shehui kexue chubanshe, 2000), 193–221.

55. "The first reader" is used in a broader sense here: not the very first person to read and comment on a literary work, but the central individual involved in the initial stage of its transmission.

56. Pauline Yu argues that this point was initially made by Wang Yao 王瑤 (1914–1989) in his paper "Zhongguo wenxue piping yu zongji" 中國文學批評與總集, in *Guanyu Zhongguo gudian wenxue wenti* 關於中國古典文學問題 (Shanghai: Gudian wenxue chubanshe, 1956), 46. She concurs with Wang's view: "To be sure, there are other more obviously 'theoretical' texts that one could consider, ranging from Liu Xie's *Wenxin diaolong* or Zhong Rong's *Shipin* to the numerous 'poetry-talks' (*shihua*) written from the eleventh century onward, which might seem more cogent and interesting (to the modern reader), but the fact remains that those works were either virtually unknown during their own time or were looked at seriously, if at all, only much later in the tradition." See Pauline Yu, "Poems in Their Place: Collections and Canons in Early Chinese Literature," *Harvard Journal of Asiatic Studies* 50, no. 1 (June 1990): 165. See also Tian Xiaofei: "It is, however, quite uncertain how much impact Liu Xie's work, or Zhong Rong's for that matter, had at the time it was written. Both Liu and Zhong were minor literary figures in their time." *Beacon Fire and Shooting Star*, 150.

57. Yuan Xingpei 袁行霈, ed., *Zhongguo wenxue shi (di er juan)* 中國文學史 (第二卷) (Beijing: Gaodeng jiaoyu chubanshe, 1999), 60–63; Liu Yuejin 劉躍進, *Zhongguo gudai wenxue tonglun: Wei Jin Nanbei chao juan* 中國古代文學通論: 魏晉南北朝卷 (Shenyang: Liaoning renmin chubanshe, 2005), 365–66; Zheng Zhenduo 鄭振鐸, *Zhongguo wenxue shi* 中國文學史 (Beijing: Xinshijie chubanshe, 2012), 120–22.

58. The English translation of this quotation is based on Yue Zhang, "*Zuo Si ji*," 516.

59. Zhou Ming 周明, *Wenxin diaolong jiaoshi yiping* 文心雕龍校釋譯評 (Nanjing: Nanjing daxue chubanshe, 2007), 47.436.

60. John Wixted dates the composition of *Shipin* to between 513 and 518. He states, "The *Shi pin* was written in the second decade of the sixth century. Since it treats only deceased poets, the latest being Shen Yue (d. 513), and Zhong Rong died in 518, the work was written (or completed) between 513 and 518." John Timothy Wixted, "*Shi pin*," in *Early Medieval Chinese Texts*, ed. Cynthia L. Chennault et al. (Berkeley: University of California Press, 2016), 283.

61. Although Liu Xie and Zhong Rong were contemporaries, Zhong may not have known of the existence of Liu's *Wenxin diaolong*, because he does not mention this work in his *Shipin*. See Stephen Owen, "Zhong Rong's Preface to *Grades of the Poets*," in *Early Medieval China: A Sourcebook*, ed. Wendy Swartz et al. (New York: Columbia University Press, 2014), 288.

62. This translation largely follows the one provided by Siu-kit Wong, ed. and trans., *Early Chinese Literary Criticism* (Hong Kong: Joint Publishing Co., 1983), 100.

63. Cao Xu, *Shipin jizhu*, 347.
64. Owen, *Readings in Chinese Literary Thought*, 49.
65. Owen, 48.
66. The discussion in this paragraph is based on Xu Chuanwu, *Zuo Si Zuo Fen yanjiu*, 343–44.
67. This translation largely follows the one provided by Yue Zhang, "*Zuo Si ji*," 516.
68. *Qingqie* 清切 in this sentence is written as *jingqie* 精切 ("refined and precise") in other editions. See Cao Xu, *Shipin jizhu*, 154.
69. Cao Xu, 157; Yang Ming 楊明, *Wenfu Shipin yizhu* 文賦詩品譯註 (Shanghai: Shanghai guji chubanshe, 1999), 56; and Wang Shumin 王叔岷, *Zhong Rong Shipin jianzheng gao* 鍾嶸詩品箋證稿 (Beijing: Zhonghua shuju, 2007), 191.
70. Cao Xu, 157.
71. Ma Qiangcai 馬強才, *Zhongguo gudai shige yongshi guannian yanjiu* 中國古代詩歌用事觀念研究 (Beijing: Zhongguo shehui kexue chubanshe, 2014), 22–28.
72. Knechtges, *Wen xuan or Selections*, 1:13.
73. D. C. Lau, trans., *Confucius: The Analects* (New York: Penguin, 1979), 174–75. This translation adopts Lau's translation with some modifications.
74. Owen, "Zhong Rong's Preface to *Grades of the Poets*," 294.
75. Cao Xu, 47.
76. Owen, "Zhong Rong's Preface to *Grades of the Poets*," 295–96.
77. Cao Xu, 174.
78. Owen, "Zhong Rong's Preface to *Grades of the Poets*," 295.
79. Cao Xu, 174.
80. Owen, "Zhong Rong's Preface to *Grades of the Poets*," 291.
81. Yeh Chia-ying and Jan W. Walls, "Theory, Standards, and Practice of Criticizing Poetry in Chung Hung's *Shih P'in*," in *Studies in Chinese Poetry and Poetics*, Vol. 1, ed. Ronald Miao (San Francisco: Chinese Materials Center, 1978), 57.
82. Gu Nong 顧農, "Shuo 'Zuo Si fengli' ji qi beijing" 說 "左思風力" 及其背景, *Shandong shida xuebao* 山東師大學報, no. 3 (1999): 8–9.
83. Cao Xu, *Shipin jizhu*, 260.
84. *Beishi* 北史 (Beijing: Zhonghua shuju, 1974), 36.1344–45.
85. Wang Liqun 王立群, *Wen xuan chengshu yanjiu* 《文選》成書研究 (Zhengzhou: Daxiang chubanshe, 2015), 208–9.
86. Xiao, *Wen xuan*, 21.988.
87. Farmer, "Zuo Si," 328.
88. The major Southern Dynasties anthology *New Songs from the Jade Terrace* (*Yutai xinyong* 玉臺新詠) did not include any of Zuo's "Yongshi" because of the nature of the anthology: most of the selections are "palace style" poems dealing with erotic topics.

89. The English translation largely follows the one provided in Wong, *Early Chinese Literary Criticism*, 43.

90. Liu Yunhao 劉運好, ed., *Lu Shiheng wenji jiaozhu* 陸士衡文集校注 (Nanjing: Fenghuang chubanshe, 2007), 22. According to Yuan Xingpei 袁行霈, during the Western Jin, "The poetry world, represented by Lu Ji and Pan Yue, was devoted to poetic form and complex descriptions; their diction was very flowery, and their poetic style overelaborate." 西晉詩壇以陸機、潘岳爲代表, 講究形式, 描寫繁複, 辭采華麗, 詩風繁縟. See Yuan, *Zhongguo wenxue shi*, 2:51.

91. Kōzen, "Sashi to Eishi shi," 1–2.

92. Chris Connery, "Tso Ssu," in *The Indiana Companion to Traditional Chinese Literature*, Vol. 1, ed. William H. Nienhauser, Jr. (Bloomington: Indiana University Press, 1986), 806.

Chapter 4

1. Before the Tang dynasty, four biographies were compiled and written on Tao's life, including Xiao Tong's *The Collection of Tao Yuanming's Writings* (*Tao Yuanming ji* 陶淵明集), and those found in three standard histories: *The History of the Song Dynasty* (*Songshu* 宋書), *The History of the Jin Dynasty* (*Jinshu* 晉書), and *The History of the Southern Dynasties* (*Nanshi* 南史).

2. For recent studies on *Xuanxue*, see David Chai, ed., *Dao Companion to Xuanxue* 玄學 *(Neo-Daoism)* (Cham: Springer, 2020). For the relationship between *xuanxue* and Tao Yuanming's perspective on life, see Luo Zongqiang 羅宗強, *Xuanxue yu Wei Jin shiren xintai* 玄學與魏晉士人心態 (Hangzhou: Zhejiang renmin chubanshe, 1991), 342–58; Tao Xinmin 陶新民, *Tao Yuanming: Xuanxue rensheng guan de zhongjie yu xuanyan shi de chaoyue* 陶淵明: 玄學人生觀的終結與玄言詩的超越, *Anhui daxue xuebao* 安徽大學學報 24, no. 1 (2000): 40–46; Li Yaonan 李耀南, "Xuanxue shiye zhong de Tao Yuanming rensheng guan he shenmei rensheng jingjie" 玄學視野中的陶淵明人生觀和審美人生境界, *Huazhong keji daxue xuebao (Renwen shehui kexue ban)* 華中科技大學學報 (人文社會科學版), no. 6 (2002): 23–28.

3. Wei Chunxi, *Song qian yongshi shi shi*, 94.

4. For example, previous research into Tao's use of the theme of the unappreciated scholar has placed it in the larger context of Chinese literature and culture, not in the context of Tao's other thematic preoccupations. See Hellmut Wilhelm, "The Scholar's Frustration: Notes on a Type of *Fu*," in *Chinese Thought and Institutions*, ed. John K. Fairbank (Chicago: University of Chicago Press, 1957), 310–19; David W. Pankenier, "'The Scholar's Frustration' Reconsidered: Melancholia or Credo?" *Journal of the American Oriental Society* 110, no. 3 (1990): 434–59; Liu Zhoutang 劉周堂, "Lun wenshi buyu" 論文士不遇, *Zhongguo wenxue yanjiu* 中國文學研究, no. 1 (1997): 7–12.

5. Ashmore, *Transport of Reading*, 3–4.

6. Tian Xiaofei 田曉菲, "Tao Yuanming de shujia he Xiao Gang de yixue yanguang: Zhonggu de yuedu yu yuedu zhonggu" 陶淵明的書架和蕭綱的醫學眼光: 中古的閱讀與閱讀中古, *Guoxue yanjiu* 國學研究 37, no. 1 (2016): 124–25.

7. Tian Xiaofei, 125.

8. Qi Yishou 齊益壽, *Huangju dongli yao gujin: Tao Yuanming qiren qishi sanlun* 黃菊東籬耀古今: 陶淵明其人其詩散論 (Taibei: Guoli Taiwan daxue chubanshe, 2016), 7.

9. Zhong Shulin 鍾書林, *Yinshi de shendu: Tao Yuanming xintan* 隱士的深度: 陶淵明新探 (Beijing: Zhongguo shehui kexue chubanshe, 2015), 337–39.

10. *Songshu* 宋書 (Beijing: Zhonghua shuju, 1974), 93.2287.

11. I adopt the English translation of the title from A. R. Davis, *T'ao Yüan-ming (AD 365–427): His Works and Their Meaning* (Cambridge: Cambridge University Press, 2009), 1:xii.

12. Aat Vervoorn, *Men of the Cliffs and Caves: The Development of the Chinese Eremitic Tradition to the End of the Han Dynasty* (Hong Kong: The Chinese University of Hong Kong Press, 1990), 40–87.

13. For the English translation of Tao's writing on "the lack of appreciation for scholars," see James Robert Hightower, "The *Fu* of T'ao Ch'ien," *Harvard Journal of Asiatic Studies* 17, nos. 1/2 (1954): 169–230.

14. Gong Kechang 龔克昌 et al., *Quan Han fu pingzhu* 全漢賦評註 (Shijiazhuang: Huashan wenyi chubanshe, 2003), 210.

15. Yuan, *Tao Yuanming ji jianzhu*, 5.431.

16. Yuan, 5.432.

17. Yuan, 5.432.

18. Yuan, 6.520. Qu Yuan was a legendary scholar-official in the state of Chu during the Warring States period (475–221 BCE). He was slandered and exiled to the south, where he eventually drowned himself in the Miluo River 汨羅江. Jia Yi was a scholar official in the Western Han dynasty (202 BCE–8 CE). He sought to institute reforms and reduce the power of local lords, but he was slandered by officials opposed to him and died young at the age of 33.

19. The first couplet also appears in the biography that Tao wrote for Meng Jia, Tao's maternal grandfather.

20. Ji and Xie were virtuous and capable officials during the reign of the mythical emperor Shun. See *Shiji*, 1.38.

21. "The two virtuous scholars" refers to Qu Yuan and Jia Yi.

22. This line refers to an episode in which Qu Yuan asked Zheng Zhanyin 鄭詹尹 (ca. fourth–third centuries BCE) to perform a divination to resolve his questions and doubts. "Divination on Dwelling" ("Buju" 卜居), traditionally attributed to Qu Yuan, records their dialogue.

23. This line refers to an incident in which Jia Yi saw an owl entering his house, an omen of a shortened life span. In lamentation, he composed "Rhapsody on an Owl" ("Funiao fu" 鵩鳥賦).

24. Yuan, *Tao Yuanming ji jianzhu*, 6.512. In a series of thirteen poems on "Reading *The Classic of Mountains and Seas*" ("Du *Shanhai jing*" 讀山海經), Tao is very explicit about his reading practices.

25. Swartz, *Reading Tao Yuanming*, 102.

26. Xiao, *Wen xuan*, 41.1864–65.

27. Yuan, *Tao Yuanming ji jianzhu*, 6.523.

28. This couplet alludes to a passage in the *Zhuangzi*: "The sleek-furred fox and the elegantly spotted leopard dwell in the mountain forest and crouch in the cliffside caves—such is their quietude. They go abroad by night but lurk at home by day—such is their caution. Though hunger, thirst, and hardship press them, they steal forth only one by one to seek food by the rivers and lakes—such is their forethought. And yet they can't seem to escape the disaster of nets and traps. Where is the blame? Their fur is their undoing." 夫豐狐文豹，棲於山林，伏於巖穴，靜也；夜行晝居，戒也；雖飢渴隱約，猶且胥疏於江湖之上而求食焉，定也。然且不免於罔羅機辟之患。是何罪之有哉？其皮爲之災也. The English translation follows the one provided by Watson, *Complete Works of Zhuangzi*, 157. The original Chinese is from Wang Xianqian 王先謙, Liu Wu 劉武, and Shen Xiaohuan 沈嘯寰, *Zhuangzi jijie* 莊子集解 (Beijing: Zhonghua shuju, 1987), 20.168. My translation of Tao's couplet borrows from Burton's translation of the *Zhuangzi* passage.

29. For a detailed discussion of Han Fei's "Shuinan," see *Shiji*, 63.2147–48, and Michael Hunter, "The Difficulty with 'The Difficulties of Persuasion' ('Shuinan' 說難)," in *Dao Companion to the Philosophy of Han Fei*, ed. P. R. Goldin (New York: Springer, 2013), 169–95. For the English translation of Han Fei's works, see Burton Watson, trans., *Han Fei Tzu: Basic Writings* (New York: Columbia University Press, 1964).

30. For Han Fei's story, see *Shiji*, 63.2146–48.

31. Yuan, *Tao Yuanming ji jianzhu*, 6.525.

32. There is a variant version of this line, where *dai* 代 is replaced by *da* 大. If we choose the variant, the line reads "changes largely follow the times." This variant reading shows even clearer evidence of the importance of historical moment to Tao. See Yuan, *Tao Yuanming ji jianzhu*, 6.525.

33. *Poetry* and *Documents* refer specifically to the *Classic of Poetry* and the *Book of Documents*. When the two are combined, they could also refer to classic books in general.

34. *Shiji*, 99.2722–23.

35. *Shiji*, 99.2722.

36. *Shiji*, 99.2726.

37. Yuan, *Tao Yuanming ji jianzhu*, 5.433.

38. Yuan, 3.203. This poem was written in the second year of the Yuanxing 元興 reign (403), when Tao was 52 years old.

39. This line is a direct quote from the *Analects*. See footnote 42 for details.

40. D. C. Lau, trans., *Confucius: The Analects* (New York: Penguin, 1979), 136. I have substituted "Dao" for "Way."

41. Shisanjing zhushu zhengli weiyuanhui 十三經注疏整理委員會, ed., *Lunyu zhushu* 論語注疏 (Beijing: Zhonghua shuju, 1980), 246.

42. Tian Xiaofei argues that Tao may have actually worked on the field himself, but to produce enough to support his family, he certainly had servants working alongside him. See Tian Xiaofei, *Tao Yuanming & Manuscript Culture*, 119–20.

43. Alan J. Berkowitz, *Patterns of Disengagement: The Practice and Portrayal of Reclusion in Early Medieval China* (Stanford, CA: Stanford University Press, 2000), 64.

44. Most modern scholars have dated this series of poems to Tao's later life, between 420 and 421, but Davis believes that this poem could have been written earlier, between 402 and 405. See Davis, *T'ao Yüan-ming*, 1:136.

45. Swartz, *Reading Tao Yuanming*, 24.

46. Yuan, *Tao Yuanming ji jianzhu*, 4.366.

47. Tao described other difficulties he encountered in other poems. For example, his house was destroyed by a fire ("Suffering a Fire in the Sixth Month of the Year Wuwu" 戊午歲六月中遇火), and he occasionally begged for food during famines ("Begging for Food" 乞食). The English translation of these titles follows Davis's English translation.

48. A reference to an episode in the life of Confucius, in which he and his disciples were imperiled in the state of Chen.

49. Ashmore, *Transport of Reading*, 220.

50. Ashmore, 221.

51. Yuan, *Tao Yuanming ji jianzhu*, 3.206–9.

52. Yuan, 4.368.

53. The meaning of "Shang" 商 here is somewhat unclear. It could mean the second note of the pentatonic scale, which is often associated with melancholy and depression. Davis argues, "Since T'ao appears to follow written sources so closely here, it seems best to understand it as 'The Hymns of Shang' (from the *Book of Songs*), which Yuan Xian is described as singing." See Davis, *T'ao Yüan-ming*, 1:137.

54. Chonghua refers to the mythical emperor Shun.

55. Ci refers to Duanmu Ci 端木賜 (ca. 520–446 BCE), a disciple of Confucius known for his eloquence. He had a successful career as an official, which was rare among Confucius's disciples.

56. Davis, *T'ao Yüan-ming*, 2:90.

57. Yuan, *Tao Yuanming ji jianzhu*, 4.369.

58. Lau, *Confucius: The Analects*, 72.

59. Shisanjing zhushu zhengli weiyuanhui, *Lunyu zhushu*, 4.52.

60. The translation is based on that of Alan J. Berkowitz, "Biographies of Recluses: Huangfu Mi's Accounts of High-Minded Men," in *Early Medieval China: A Sourcebook*, ed. Wendy Swartz et al. (New York: Columbia University Press, 2014), 342.

61. *Shiji*, 67.2208

62. Ashmore, *Transport of Reading*, 207–8.
63. Yuan, *Tao Yuanming ji jianzhu*, 4.375.
64. The translation is based on Davis, *T'ao Yüan-ming*, 1:139.
65. Yuan, *Tao Yuanming ji jianzhu*, 4.376.
66. Lau, *Confucius: The Analects*, 88.
67. Shisanjing zhushu zhengli weiyuanhui, *Lunyu zhushu*, 7.100.
68. Tao Yuanming claimed that music could help people realize *anpin ledao*. For a discussion of Tao's understanding of the educational function of music, see Fan Ziye 范子燁, *Youran wang Nanshan—wenhua shiyu zhong de Tao Yuanming* 悠然望南山—文化視域中的陶淵明 (Shanghai: Dongfang chuban zhongxin, 2010), 40–45.
69. James Robert Hightower, *The Poetry of T'ao Ch'ien* (Oxford: Oxford University Press, 1970), 213.
70. Yuan, *Tao Yuanming ji jianzhu*, 3.271. Tian Xiaofei, *Tao Yuanming & Manuscript Culture*, 194–95.
71. For a detailed analysis of the four major biographies of Tao Yuanming from the Six Dynasties, see Tian Xiaofei, *Tao Yuanming & Manuscript Culture*, 67–94, and Swartz, *Reading Tao Yuanming*, 27–47.
72. Swartz, *Reading Tao Yuanming*, 140.
73. Swartz, 128.
74. D. C. Lau, trans., *Tao Te Ching* (Hong Kong: The Chinese University of Hong Kong Press, 1989), 2.4–5.
75. This Dao (from Daoism) is different from the Dao of Confucianism that Tao Yuanming was alluding to earlier. The latter is following a "way" of human morality, while the former is following the "way" of nature.
76. Lau, *Tao Te Ching*, 12–13.
77. Yuan, *Tao Yuanming ji jianzhu*, 4.379–80. The two Shus refer to Shu Guang 疏廣 (d. 45 BCE) and Shu Shou 疏受 (d. 48 BCE), tutors of Emperor Xuan 宣 (r. 74–48 BCE). Their combined biography appears in *Hanshu*, 71.3040.
78. *Daxiang* 大象 refers to the origin of things. This term appears in the *Dao de jing*. For example, in chapter 35, it states, "Have in your hold the great image / And the empire will come to you." 執大象，天下往. See Lau, *Tao Te Ching*, 51–52.
79. Zhang Xie's "Yongshi" can be found in Xiao Tong 蕭統, ed., *Liuchen zhu Wen xuan* 六臣注文選, annot. Li Shan 李善 et al. (Beijing: Zhonghua shuju, 1987), 21.390. For a discussion of Zhang's "Yongshi" and other *yongshi shi* in *Wen xuan*, see Yue Zhang, "Approaches to Lore," 83–112.
80. Yuan, *Tao Yuanming ji jianzhu*, 4.383.
81. The "ferry in all directions" (*tongjin* 通津) is a conventional trope for embarking on an official career.
82. The English translation is adopted, with some modifications, from Ming Dong Gu, *Chinese Theories of Reading and Writing: A Route to Hermeneutics and Open Poetics* (Albany: State University of New York Press, 2005), 168.

83. Ming Dong Gu, 168.
84. Cutter, "On Reading," 1.
85. Cutter, 1.
86. This poem was written for his eldest son, Tao Yan 陶儼, during the fourteenth year of the Taiyuan 太元 reign (389), when Tao Yan was three years old. See Yuan, *Tao Yuanming ji jianzhu*, 1.44. Between 386 and 397, Tao Yuanming resided at home, and several of his sons were born during this period: his second son Si 俟 was born in 388, his twin sons Fen 份 and Yi 佚 were born in 389, and his youngest child Tong 佟 was born in 394. See Yuan, 845–67.
87. Tao Kan's posthumous title was Huan 桓, which when reduplicated means "mighty and powerful." He was granted the title Commandery Duke of Changsha (*Changsha jungong* 長沙郡公) in recognition of his military merits.
88. Yuan, *Tao Yuanming ji jianzhu*, 1.41.

Chapter 5

1. For Xie Zhan's biography, see *Songshu*, 55.1557–58. For studies of him, see Li Shi'e 李世萼, "Lun Jinmo Songchu shiren Xie Zhan" 論晉末宋初詩人謝瞻, *Shandong daxue xuebao (Zhexue shehui kexue ban)* 山東大學學報 (哲學社會科學版), no. 2 (1992): 30–37.
2. Xiao, *Wen xuan*, 21.998.
3. He Zhuo 何焯, *Yimen dushu ji* 義門讀書記 (Beijing: Zhonghua shuju, 1987), 46.894.
4. Fang Dongshu 方東樹, *Zhaomei zhanyan* 昭昧詹言 (Beijing: Renmin wenxue chubanshe, 1961), 1.38.
5. Xiao, *Wen xuan*, 21.998.
6. For studies of "Wei Songgong xiu Zhang Liang miao jiao," see Tong Ling 童嶺, "Yixi nianjian Liu Yu beifa de tianming yu wenxue—yi Fu Liang 'Wei Songgong xiu Zhang Liang miao jiao,' 'Wei Songgong xiu Chu Yuanwang mu jiao' wei zhongxin'" 義熙年間劉裕北伐的天命與文學—以傅亮《爲宋公修張良廟教》、《爲宋公修楚元王墓教》爲中心, *Zhonghua wenshi luncong* 中華文史論叢 135, no. 3 (2019): 303–35; Cheng Zhangcan 程章燦, "Zhongmu: Zuowei Liu Song de wenhua changyu" 冢墓：作爲劉宋的文化場域, *Zhongguo wenhua* 中國文化 53, no. 1 (2021): 28–35.
7. For discussion on Zhang Liang's influence in Chinese culture, see Lydia Thompson, "Confucian Paragon or Popular Deity? Legendary Heroes in a Late-Eastern Han Tomb," *Asia Major*, 3rd ser., 12, no. 2 (1999): 15–16; Mark Bender, "A Description of 'Jiangjing' (Telling Scriptures) Services in Jingjiang, China," *Asian Folklore Studies* 60, no. 1 (2001): 101–33; John W. Killigrew, "The Role of the Moushi 謀士 in the Jin Shu and Wei Shu during the Northern Kingdoms Period, 309–450 AD," *Journal of Asian History* 47, no. 2 (2013): 151–96.

8. Xiao, *Wen xuan*, 21.998–1002. This translation and several of the explanations of the allusions draw on Li Shan's 李善 (630–689) commentary.

9. This line quotes from the "Great Preface" to the *Shijing*, which states, "The tones of a ruined state are filled with lament and brooding" 亡國之音哀以思. Owen, *Readings in Chinese Literary Thought*, 43.

10. He Zhuo notes that this line is a garbled reference to the *Book of Shang* (*Shangshu* 商書). The original passage has the conjunction *yu* 與 instead of *xing* 興, "to rise" versus "to prosper": "If one follows the same path as disorder and chaos, one cannot but perish." 與亂同道罔不亡. See *Yimen dushu ji*, 46.894. If Xie intended to use the character 與, the line should be rendered as "joining with disorder, they could not but perish." However, no extant edition of this poem uses 與, so I will preserve Xie's use of 興.

11. The nine tripods were large bronze vessels possessed by the Zhou court, which represented the nine states of the Zhou dynasty, and therefore symbolized paramount imperial authority. See *Shiji*, 5.218.

12. This line describes the excessive severity of Qin laws and punishments. According to Li Shan, "demise of three generations" 三殤 is a reference to this story from *The Book of Rites* (*Liji* 禮記): "In passing by the side of Mount Tai, Confucius came on a woman who was wailing bitterly by a grave. The Master bowed forward to the cross-bar and listened to her; and then sent Zigong to question her. 'Your wailing,' said he, 'is altogether like that of one who has suffered sorrow upon sorrow.' She replied, 'It is so. Formerly, my husband's father was killed here by a tiger. My husband was also killed (by another), and now my son has died in the same way.' The Master said, 'Why do you not leave the place?' The answer was, 'There is no oppressive government here.' The Master then said (to the disciples), 'Remember this, my little children. Oppressive government is more terrible than tigers.'" See James Legge, *Li Chi: Book of Rites: An Encyclopedia of Ancient Ceremonial Usages, Religious Creeds, and Social Institutions* (New York: University Books, 1967), 1:190–91. 孔子過泰山側，婦人哭於墓者而哀，夫子式而聽之，使子貢問之曰："子之哭也，一似重有憂者。" 而曰："然。昔者吾舅死於虎，吾夫又死焉，今吾子又死焉。" 夫子曰："何不去也?" 曰："無苛政。" 夫子曰："小子識之，苛政猛於虎也。" See Xiao, *Wen xuan*, 21.999.

13. This line describes the popular support the Han had for replacing the oppressive Qin.

14. *Lingjian* 靈鑒 means "numinous insight." *Zhuguang* 朱光 literally means "vermillion light." It alludes to Liu Bang, the founding emperor of the Han dynasty, who possessed the virtue of fire in the Chinese Five Elements (*Wuxing* 五行) system. See *Shiji*, 8.342.

15. After defeating Xiang Yu, Liu Bang enfeoffed his major adviser Zhang Liang, who humbled himself before Liu: "When I first began an uprising at Xiapei [Xiapi], I met Your Majesty at Liu. It was as though Heaven had sent me to serve you. You listened to my suggestions, and fortunately they turned out to be apt for

the times." See Watson, *Records of the Grand Historian: Han Dynasty*, 1:107. 始臣起下邳，與上會留，此天以臣授陛下。陛下用臣計，幸而時中。See *Shiji*, 55.2042.

16. *Boshi* 薄蝕 refers to an eclipse. In *The Annals of Lü Buwei* (*Lüshi chunqiu* 呂氏春秋), it states, "The Moon: There are occasions when it is eclipsed, when vapors surround it like a halo or dangle from its side like earrings, when it partially disappears." 其月有薄蝕，有暈珥，有偏盲。See John Knoblock and Jeffrey Riegel, *The Annals of Lü Buwei: A Complete Translation and Study* (Stanford, CA: Stanford University Press, 2000), 168–69. This line is a reference to an encounter between Liu Bang and his rival, Xiang Yu, ruler of Chu, at the "Grand Gate" 鴻門, east of present-day Lintong 臨潼 Prefecture in Shaanxi 陝西 Province. Zhang Liang helped Liu Bang avoid danger, and his escape was a turning point in the contention between Chu and Han. See *Shiji*, 7.311–15.

17. The Chanqiang 欃槍 comet was often associated with warfare and disaster. Here, it alludes to Xiang Yu, who was defeated at Gaixia, in the southeastern part of present-day Lingbi 靈壁 Prefecture in Anhui 安徽 Province. See *Shiji*, 7.331–33.

18. "Ennobling the enemy" is a reference to Zhang Liang's proposal that Liu Bang demonstrate his impartiality by enfeoffing Yong Chi, whom Liu did not like, as marquis of Shifang. Zhang Liang also recommended that Liu Bang appoint Xiao He 蕭何 (257–193 BCE) as prime minister. See *Shiji*, 55.2042.

19. Zhang Liang suggested that Liu Bang make Chang'an his capital. See *Shiji*, 55.2044.

20. Zhang Liang assisted Empress Lü in opposing Liu Bang's plan to depose the crown prince, by coming up with the plan to invite to the court the Four Old Men of Mount Shang (Shangshan sihao 商山四皓). See *Shiji*, 55.2045.

21. This line is a reference to the legend of Zhang Liang acquiring a book of military strategy from an immortal, which he then used to advise Liu Bang. As the story appears in the *Shiji*, "Zhang Liang was once strolling idly along an embankment in Xiapei [Xiapi] when an old man wearing a coarse gown appeared. . . . [He dropped his shoes and asked Zhang Liang to put them back on his feet, which Zhang Liang did.] When the old man had gone some distance, he turned and came back. 'You could be taught, young man,' he said, 'Meet me here at dawn five days from now!' . . . Producing a book, he said, 'If you read this you may become the teacher of kings. Ten years from now your fortune will rise.'" Watson, *Records of the Grand Historian: Han Dynasty*, 1:100. 良嘗閒從容步遊下邳圯上，有一老父，衣褐，至良……父去里所，復還，曰："孺子可教矣。後五日平明，與我會此。"……出一編書，曰："讀此則爲王者師矣。後十年興。" *Shiji*, 55.2034–35.

22. This line directly refers to the later legend that Zhang Liang eventually left the court to become a recluse and achieved immortality. It may also be an allusion to *Zhuangzi*: "After a thousand years, should he weary of the world, he will leave it and ascend to the immortals, riding on those white clouds all the way up to the village of God." Watson, *Complete Works of Zhuangzi*, 88. 千歲厭世，去而上僊，乘彼白雲，至於帝鄉。Wang, Liu, and Shen, *Zhuangzi jijie*, 3.103.

23. Xie Zhan is praising Zhang Liang's noble character. This couplet marks the end of the section that focuses on Zhang Liang.

24. "The divine warrior" is a reference to Liu Yu, the future emperor of the Song dynasty. "Aligned the three realms" means that Liu created harmony between heaven, the earth, and the people.

25. "The eight lands" refers to the whole kingdom.

26. "Double brightness" (*mingliang* 明兩) and "auspicious clouds" (*qingxiao* 慶霄) are images from the *Book of Changes* (*Yijing* 易經) used to describe how Liu Yu's merits extend over the whole kingdom. "THE IMAGE / That which is bright rises twice: / The image of FIRE. / Thus, the great man, by perpetuating this brightness, / Illumines the four quarters of the world." Richard Wilhelm and Cary F. Baynes, trans., *The I Ching or Book of Changes* (Princeton, NJ: Princeton University Press, 1977), 294. 《象》曰: 明兩作, 離. 大人以繼明照于四方. Guo Yu 郭彧, annot., *Zhouyi* 周易 (Beijing: Zhonghua shuju, 2006), 33.158.

27. This line describes Liu Yu's army ("flags of carriages") passing Zhang Liang's temple ("collapsed chamber"), which was in ruins at the end of the Eastern Jin dynasty. To demonstrate his admiration for Zhang, Liu Yu asked his officials to repair the collapsed temple and made a sacrifice to the deified official.

28. "The deceased" refers to Zhang Liang.

29. *Kui* 揆 means to "surmise." *Zi* 子 refers to Zhang Liang. This line refers to the procession of officials under the command of Liu Yu.

30. By using the reduplicative words *jiji* 濟濟 ("many") and *cancan* 粲粲 ("brilliant"), Xie Zhan emphasizes that the multitude of talented military commanders and civilian officials Liu Yu was able to assemble would even make the ancients envious.

31. "This blind man" is the poet making a self-deprecating reference to himself.

32. Zheng Xianzhi supported Liu Yu over his nephew Liu Yi 劉毅 (d. 412). See Shen Yue, *Songshu*, 64.1696–98; *Nanshi*, 33.861–62.

33. *Songshu*, 64.1696.

34. Lu Qinli, *Xian Qin Han Wei Jin Nanbeichao shi*, 2:1143.

35. "The Dao" here may refer to the Mandate of Heaven. The tripod (*ding* 鼎) symbolizes the power and sovereignty of the state.

36. The "great storm" (*changfeng* 長風) was an allusion to social chaos.

37. The Si 泗 is a major branch of the Huai River, running through what is now Shandong, Anhui, and Jiangsu Provinces. The "hidden dragon" (*qianlong* 潛龍) refers to Liu Bang, the founder of the Han dynasty, who grew up in the Si River region and was appointed the county governor of Sishui 泗水亭長. In Chinese culture, dragons are traditionally a symbol of the emperor and of supreme power.

38. "Purple smoke" (*ziyan* 紫煙) is an auspicious sign. It may refer to the appearance of Zhang Liang, who became key to Liu Bang's success in establishing the Han dynasty. *Qiu* 虯, a small dragon without horns, symbolizes the young Liu Bang.

39. The "divine sorceress" (*ling'ao* 靈媼) is the mother of the "White Emperor," a snake killed by the Red Emperor, Liu Bang. This is an allusion to an episode recounted in Sima Qian's biography of Liu Bang. When he was the county governor of Sishui 泗水, some prisoners in his custody escaped, and as this meant certain death for Liu under the laws of Qin, he was forced to rebel. As he fled into the wilderness, he drunkenly killed a white snake that was then mourned by its mother. See *Shiji*, 8.347.

40. According to Lu Qinli 逯欽立, this poem appears in *juan* 38 of the *Collection of Literature Arranged by Subject* (*Yiwen leiju* 藝文類聚), a Tang dynasty encyclopedia, and *juan* 53 of the *Annals of Classical Poems* (*Shiji* 詩紀), a Ming dynasty literary collection of pre-Tang poems. This poem appears to be a fragment. The extant version only describes the beginning of the Liu Bang rebellion, and does not go into detail about Zhang Liang or the ceremony that Liu Yu organized. See Lu Qinli, *Xian Qin Han Wei Jin Nanbeichao shi*, 2:1143.

41. I have adopted Burton Watson's translation, with slight modifications. See Burton Watson, trans., *Records of the Grand Historian of China: Translated from the Shih Chi of Ssu-ma Ch'ien* (New York: Columbia University Press, 1961), 1:150.

42. *Shiji*, 55.2048.

43. *Shiji*, 55.2035.

44. *Songshu*, 54.1531–32.

45. Ding Fulin 丁福林, "Cong gangzao fuqi dao chugui yiquan—Tan Dong Jin shanshui shiren Xie Zhan" 從剛躁負氣到處貴遺權—談東晉山水詩人謝瞻, *Gudian wenxue zhishi* 古典文學知識, no. 5 (2003): 76–81; see also Chen Qun 陳群, "'Lineng zhi shi' yu 'wenyi zhi shi': Songchu de wenren zhi zheng" "吏能之士" 與"文義之士": 宋初的文人之爭, *Qinghua daxue xuebao* 清華大學學報, 2nd suppl., no. 24 (2009): 11–12.

46. Wang Xiaomeng 王曉萌, "Dong Jin monian zhengju de dongdang yu wenfeng de zhuanbian" 東晉末年政局的動盪與文風的轉變, *Zhongguo dianji yu wenhua* 中國典籍與文化, no. 1 (2010): 109–14.

47. *Songshu*, 2.43–44.

48. *Songshu*, 2.41.

49. *Songshu*, 2.41–42.

50. *Songshu*, 2.44–45.

51. Jan Assmann, *Cultural Memory and Early Civilization*, 38.

52. Chittick, *Jiankang Empire*, 120.

53. *Songshu*, 42.1300–11.

54. Lu Qinli, *Xian Qin Han Wei Jin Nanbeichao shi*, 2:1143–44.

55. The "Five Sacred Peaks" (*Wuyue* 五岳) refers to the five sacred mountains of China: Mount Tai 泰山 in the east, Mount Hua 華山 in the west, Mount Heng 衡山 in the south, Mount Heng 恒山 in the north, and Mount Song 嵩山 in the center.

56. "Double pupils" (*chongtong* 重瞳) is a metonym for Xiang Yu, Liu Bang's main rival after the fall of the Qin, who, according to legend, had double pupils.

Double pupils were associated with miraculous power. Other mythical and historical figures who supposedly had double pupils were Cangjie 倉頡 (fl. ca. 2650 BCE), Shun (ca. 2287–ca. 2067 BCE), and Chong'er 重耳 (671–628 BCE).

57. This line is adapted from "His power can topple a mountain and his spirit covers the world" 力拔山兮氣蓋世, a song attributed to Xiang Yu, who supposedly composed it when surrounded by Liu Bang's army at Gaixia 垓下. See *Shiji*, 7.333.

58. According to the conventional historical narrative, Xiang Yu relied on his strength and courage, but lacked Liu Bang's intelligence and wisdom, and so was doomed to be defeated by Liu. See *Shiji*, 7.295–339.

59. The Dao in this context means the way of things, encompassing the Mandate of Heaven, the will of the people, and many other factors.

60. *Songshu*, 2.42.

61. *Songshu*, 3.52.

62. Watson, *Records of the Grand Historian: Han Dynasty*, 1:76.

63. *Shiji*, 8.381.

64. *Shiji*, 7.311–15.

65. *Shiji*, 7.332–33.

66. *Shiji*, 55.2043–45.

67. The English translation largely follows the one provided by Watson, *Records of the Grand Historian: Han Dynasty*, 1:107–08.

68. *Shiji*, 55.2043.

69. *Shiji*, 55.2044.

70. The English translation largely follows the one provided by Watson, *Records of the Grand Historian: Han Dynasty*, 1:109–10.

71. *Shiji*, 55.2045.

72. *Shiji*, 55.2045. For a more in-depth discussion of the Four Old Men of Mount Shang, see Ping Wang, *The Age of Courtly Writing: Wen xuan Compiler Xiao Tong (501–531) and His Circle* (Leiden: Brill, 2012), 258.

73. Ping Wang, "The Art of Poetry Writing: Liu Xiaochuo's 'Becoming the Number-One Person for the Number-One Position,'" in *Early Medieval China: A Sourcebook*, ed. Wendy Swartz et al. (New York: Columbia University Press, 2014), 245. See also Luo Zongqiang 羅宗強, *Wei Jin Nanbeichao wenxue sixiang shi* 魏晉南北朝文學思想史 (Beijing: Zhonghua shuju, 2006), 134.

74. Yan Buke 閻步克, *Bofeng yu bogu: Qin Han Wei Jin Nanbeichao de zhengzhi wenming* 波峰與波谷：秦漢魏晉南北朝的政治文明 (Beijing: Beijing daxue chubanshe, 2009), 325.

75. This image later became a stock phrase used to express deference to a superior.

76. Ye Miaona 葉妙娜, "Dong Jin Nanchao qiaoxing gaomen zhi shihuan—Chenjun Xieshi ge'an yanjiu" 東晉南朝僑姓高門之仕宦：陳郡謝氏個案研究, *Zhongshan daxue xuebao (Shehui kexue ban)* 中山大學學報 (社會科學版), no. 3 (1986): 43–51.

77. As Andrew Chittick has pointed out, Liu Yu's recruitment policies were relatively meritocratic: "He [Liu Yu] also initiated several important new policies: he

promoted men of low birth who demonstrated achievement, especially in military matters, in order to dilute the influence of privileged court clans." *Patronage and Community in Medieval China: The Xiangyang Garrison, 400–600 CE* (Albany: State University of New York, 2009), 20.

78. *Nanshi*, 19.522.

79. *Songshu*, 42.1305.

80. Watson, *Records of the Grand Historian: Han Dynasty*, 1:99.

81. *Shiji*, 55.2034.

82. By way of contrast, the assassination attempt is mentioned in later poetic tributes to Zhang Liang, such as Li Bai's 李白 (701–762) "Passing the Bridge at Xiapi, I Think of Zhang Zifang" 經下邳圯橋懷張子房 and Hu Zeng's 胡曾 (fl. ca. 840) "Historical Poem on Bolangsha" 詠史詩·博浪沙.

83. *Nanshi*, 19.541.

84. This line alludes to Zhang Liang's attempts to seek revenge against the Qin after it annexed his native state of Han. See *Shiji*, 55.2034.

85. This line refers to Lu Zhonglian successfully persuading Xinyuan Yan to abandon the idea of asking the state of Zhao to surrender territory to the Qin by pointing out Qin's greedy and cruel nature.

86. *Jianghai ren* 江海人 refers to someone who wanders around without a fixed destination.

87. *Nanshi*, 19.541.

88. As the conventional depiction of the Wei–Jin transition, for example, reads: "Throughout the realm there were many dire affairs, and few were the men of renown who remained unscathed." See Alan Berkowitz, "Social and Cultural Dimensions of Reclusion in Early Medieval China," in *Philosophy and Religion in Early Medieval China*, ed. Alan K. L. Chan and Yuet-Keung Lo (Albany: State University of New York, 2010), 294.

89. This is the context provided by Li Shan, who quotes *The History of Qi* (*Qi shu* 齊書) and *Songshu* in support. See Xiao, *Wen xuan*, 30.956.

90. Xiao, *Wen xuan*, 30.956–57.

91. The English translation of this poem largely follows the one provided by Wu Fusheng, *Written at Imperial Command: Panegyric Poetry in Early Medieval China* (Albany: State University of New York, 2009), 77.

92. *Songshu*, 1531–32.

93. After Liu Yu rose to power, the power of the Xie clan gradually declined. However, different Xie clan members dealt with this new political situation in different ways. Xie Zhan's general outlook and attitude towards politics were different from those of most Xie clan members. Ma Xiaokun 馬曉坤 divides the political strategies of members of the Xie clan into three categories: active participation 積極有爲, reticence and caution 謹慎因循, and unconventional behavior 狂狷型. These different responses were a product of the interaction between their personal

character traits and the cultural tradition of their family as they sought to adjust to a rapidly changing political and historical milieu. See Ma Xiaokun 馬曉坤, "Dong Jin Nanchao Chenjun Xieshi zhengzhi xingwei tanxi" 東晉南朝陳郡謝氏政治行爲探析, *Xueshu yanjiu* 學術研究, no. 6 (2009): 148–53.

94. *Songshu*, 56.1557–58.
95. Chennault, "Lofty Gates," 278.
96. *Nanshi*, 19.526.
97. Xiao, *Wen xuan*, 25.1191–92. I adopt J. D. Frodsham's translation with slight modifications. See *The Murmuring Stream: The Life and Works of the Chinese Nature Poet Hsieh Ling-yün (385–433), Duke of K'ang-Lo*, Volume One (Kuala Lumpur: University of Malaya Press, 1967), 189.
98. For a detailed analysis of "Response to Lingyun at Ancheng," see Chennault, "Lofty Gates," 276–77.
99. Ding Hongqi 丁紅旗 investigated the history of illness in the Xie clan and the strategies Xie clan members adopted to cope with these congenital maladies: devotion to Daoism 歸誠道門, experimenting with medical herbs 重視草藥療效, and finding solace in the natural landscape 縱情丘壑. See "Dong Jin Nanchao Xieshi jiazu bingshi yu Daojiao xinyang" 東晉南朝謝氏家族病史與道教信仰, *Zongjiao xue yanjiu* 宗教學研究 no. 3 (2006): 172–76.
100. *Nanshi*, 19.526.
101. *Songshu*, 56.1348.
102. Tian Yuqing 田余慶, *Dong Jin menfa zhengzhi* 東晉門閥政治 (Beijing: Beijing daxue chubanshe, 1996), 230–31.
103. For the first few decades of the Eastern Jin dynasty, until Xie An 謝安 (320–385) walked onto the political stage, the Xie clan was not a powerful or influential aristocratic family. The rise of this family was largely due to its track record for producing eminent scholars, marriage alliances made with powerful aristocratic families, and most important, Xie An's long-lasting political dominance within the Eastern Jin court. See Zhou Changmei 周昌梅 and Zhang Ying 張鶯, "Houjin · qiangsheng · shuaibai—Liuchao Chenjun Xieshi jiazu de lishi guiji" 後進 · 強盛 · 衰敗—六朝陳郡謝氏家族的歷史軌跡, *Shixue jikan* 史學集刊, no. 6 (2007): 3–8.
104. Jan Assmann, *Cultural Memory and Early Civilization*, 35.

Chapter 6

1. Knechtges, *Wen xuan or Selections*, 1:1.
2. Knechtges, 1:1.
3. *Wen xuan* was compiled and edited under the auspices of Xiao Tong 蕭統 (501–531), the Liang Prince Zhaoming 昭明. For a comprehensive review of the study of *Wen xuan*, see "Introduction: *Wen xuan* Scholarship and Editions" in

Knechtges, *Wen xuan or Selections*, 1:52–72. Meanwhile, Knechtges updated recent studies on this important anthology in a bibliographical article. See David Knechtges, "*Wen xuan* Studies," *Early Medieval China* 10 (2004): 1–22. For studies of Xiao Tong, see Ping Wang, *The Age of Courtly Writing: Wen xuan Compiler Xiao Tong (501–531) and His Circle* (Leiden: Brill, 2012). For studies of commentaries on *Wen xuan*, see Wang Xibo 汪習波, *Sui Tang Wen xuan xue* 隋唐文選學 (Shanghai: Shanghai guji chubanshe, 2005).

4. Jan Assmann, *Cultural Memory and Early Civilization*, 37–38.

5. This chapter follows my previous article with modifications. See Yue Zhang, "Approaches to Lore in 'Poems on History' from the *Selections of Refined Literature*," *Journal of Oriental Studies* 49, no. 2 (2017): 83–112.

6. "Cool breezes" is a metaphor for Shu Guang and Shu Shou's moral influence.

7. Xiao, *Wen xuan*, 21.994–95.

8. Michael Loewe, *A Biographical Dictionary of the Qin, Han and Xin Dynasties* (Leiden: Brill, 2000), 481.

9. Burton Watson, trans., *Courtier and Commoner in Ancient China: Selections from the History of the Former Han* (New York: Columbia University Press, 1974), 164.

10. *Hanshu*, 71.3040.

11. Watson, *Courtier and Commoner in Ancient China*, 164.

12. *Hanshu*, 71.3040.

13. Watson, *Courtier and Commoner in Ancient China*, 164.

14. *Hanshu*, 71.3040.

15. *Jinshu*, 55.1518–24.

16. Pauline Lin, "Zhang Xie," in *Classical Chinese Writers of the Pre-Tang Period*, ed. Curtis Dean Smith (Detroit: Bruccoli Clark Layman / Gale, 2011), 320.

17. Lu Chen (courtesy name Ziliang 子諒) was a native of Fanyang (in present-day Hebei). He was born into a reputable family and enjoyed prominence when he was young. When the Western Jin collapsed, Lu Chen spent his lifetime in the conquered north, which caused him to feel ashamed. He was well versed in the Daoist canon and annotated *Zhuangzi*. See *Jinshu*, 44.1259. Lu Chen had several exchanges with Liu Kun 劉琨 (271–318) through poems which were later included in *Wen xuan*. Lu Chen was often paired with Liu Kun in literary history.

18. *Shiji*, 82.2439–51.

19. Another way of translating the second line is, "Xiangru deflected his pretext," as the word *duan* 端 also means pretext. The king of Qin wanted to provoke a war by insulting Zhao, but Lin bravely outwitted him. See the account given in *Shiji*: "The king of Qin drank until he was intoxicated, 'We have heard that the king of Zhao is fond of music. Might you play the zither?' The king of Zhao strummed the zither. . . . Lin Xiangru came forward. 'The king of Zhao has heard that the king of Qin is skilled at playing Qin tunes. We ask permission to present a clay pot drum to the king of Qin for our mutual pleasure.' " Nienhauser, *The Grand Scribe's Records*, 7:266. 秦王飲酒酣, 曰: "寡人竊聞趙王好音, 請奏瑟." 趙王鼓瑟……藺相如前曰: "趙王竊聞秦王善爲秦聲, 請奏盆瓵秦王, 以相娛樂." *Shiji*, 81.2442.

20. A *fou* 缶 is an earthen jar with a large body and a small mouth, sometimes played as a percussion instrument.

21. A *se* 瑟 is a zither-like instrument with 25 strings.

22. "Zhang Terrace" was the name of the imperial palace of Qin.

23. Xiao, *Wen xuan*, 21.995–97.

24. Nienhauser, *The Grand Scribe's Records*, 7:263.

25. *Shiji*, 81.2439.

26. Nienhauser, *The Grand Scribe's Records*, 7:263.

27. *Shiji*, 81.2439–40.

28. Nienhauser, *The Grand Scribe's Records*, 7:272.

29. *Shiji*, 81.2451.

30. Nienhauser, *The Grand Scribe's Records*, 7:272.

31. *Shiji*, 81.2452.

32. The two deeds refer to Lin protecting the jade and returning it intact to Zhao, and successfully negotiating with the king of Qin at Mianchi.

33. The famous writer Sima Xiangru 司馬相如 (ca. 179–117 BCE) adopted Lin's personal name out of respect for his accomplishments. According to *Shiji*, "Sima Xiangru was a native of Chengdu in the province of Shu. His polite name was Sima Changqing. When he was young, he loved to read books. He also studied swordsmanship, and for this reason his parents gave him the name 'Dog Boy.' In the course of his studies, however, he developed a great admiration for the famous statesman of antiquity, Lin Xiangru, and accordingly changed his name to Xiangru." Watson, *Records of the Grand Historian of China*, 1:259. 司馬相如者，蜀郡成都人也，字長卿。少時好讀書，學擊劍，故其親名之曰犬子。相如既學，慕藺相如之爲人，更名相如。*Shiji*, 117.2999.

34. David R. Knechtges, "Liu Kun, Lu Chen, and Their Writings in the Transition to the Eastern Jin," *Chinese Literature: Essays, Articles, Reviews* 28 (2006): 1–66.

35. Knechtges, 52.

36. In these correspondences, Liu Kun is often compared with Bian He 卞和, who discovered the precious jade, and the jade itself is often compared to Lu Chen. For example, in a poem to Liu Kun, Lu Chen states, "I received from you favor commensurate with a Bian He, but my worth is not that of the stone from Jing. The high regard I received from you was like that of You and Liang, but I lacked the quality of strong chargers." 承侔卞和。質非荊璞。眷同尤良。用乏驥駼。This translation and quotation is from Knechtges, 50.

37. For the dating of these poems, see Knechtges, 25–27; Dong Huixiu 董慧秀, "Liu Kun, Lu Chen zengda shi shimo tuilun" 劉琨、盧諶贈答詩始末推論, *Wei Jin Nanbeichao Sui Tang shi ziliao* 魏晉南北朝隋唐史資料 20 (2003): 19–29; Liu Wenzhong 劉文忠, "Lu Chen, Liu Kun zengda shi kaobian" 盧諶、劉琨贈答詩考辨, *Wen shi zhe* 文史哲, no. 2 (1988): 89–90; Lu Kanru 陸侃如 and Fang Buhe 方步和, "Heyi bai liangang, huawei raozhi rou?—lun Liu Kun 'Chongzeng Lu Chen' shi ji qita" 何意百煉鋼，化爲繞指柔？—論劉琨《重贈盧諶》詩及其他, *Shanxi daxue xuebao* 山西大學學報, no. 1 (1985): 89–93.

38. It is uncertain whether Lu voluntarily joined Duan's administration, and competing accounts are discussed by Knechtges. The *Jinshu* compiled in the Tang does not answer this question, only mentioning that Duan Pidi appointed Lu Chen as his mounted escort 取諶爲別駕. *Jinshu*, 44.1259. The *Jinshu* compiled by Wang Yin 王隱 (fl. 317) states that Lu Chen asked Duan Pidi for this position. See Knechtges, "Liu Kun, Lu Chen, and Their Writings," 26–27. Another possibility is discussed by Dong Huixiu, who contends that Liu Kun sent Lu Chen to Duan Pidi in order to strengthen their alliance. See "Liu Kun, Lu Chen zengda shi shimo tuilun," 19–29. Dong states that Liu Kun believed that Duan Pidi was loyal to the Jin, and therefore forming an alliance with him could extend his reach in the north. With these considerations in mind, he recommended that the initially reluctant Lu Chen join Duan Pidi. According to Dong, Lu believed Liu Kun was making a miscalculation, and that even though Liu Kun and his forces were weak, he still had Bingzhou 并州 as his base. After allying himself with Duan Pidi, however, Liu was forced to completely rely on him. See "Liu Kun, Lu Chen zengda shi shimo tuilun," 23.

39. Lu Chen valued Liu Kun's esteem: "You [Liu Kun] have treated me with great favor, and your sincere regard has been increasingly dear." Knechtges, "Liu Kun, Lu Chen, and Their Writings," 46.

40. Knechtges, 1–66.

41. Dong, "Liu Kun, Lu Chen zengda shi shimo tuilun," 24.

42. Several poems in the "Yong shi" section of *Wen xuan* adopt this associative approach. Examples include Xie Zhan's 謝瞻 (385–421) "Poem on Zhang Zifang" ("Zhang Zifang shi" 張子房詩), Yan Yanzhi's 顏延之 (384–456) "Poem on Qiu Hu" ("Qiu Hu shi" 秋胡詩), and Yu Xi's 虞羲 (fl. 510) "Poem on General Huo's Northern Expedition" ("Yong Huo jiangjun beifa shi" 詠霍將軍北伐詩).

43. Lu Hongsheng 魯洪生, ed., *Shijing jijiao jizhu jiping* 詩經集校集注集評, 15 vols. (Beijing: Xiandai chubanshe, Zhonghua shuju, 2015), 5:2841.

44. Lu Hongsheng, 2841; Cutter, "On Reading," 2.

45. Martin Kern accepts the connection drawn by the preface, stating, "In Han times, this song was related to an event of 621 BC, narrated in the *Zuo Tradition*, when three brothers and 174 others were sacrificed to follow Lord Mu of Qin into the grave; accordingly, the song was attributed to 'the people of Qin' (Zheng Xuan) who deplored the fate of their 'Three Good Men.'" See "Early Chinese Literature, Beginnings through Western Han," in *The Cambridge History of Chinese Literature*, ed. Kang-i Sun Chang and Stephen Owen (Cambridge: Cambridge University Press, 2010), 33.

46. Stephen Durrant, Wai-yee Li, and David Schaberg, trans., *Zuo Tradition / Zuozhuan: Commentary on the "Spring and Autumn Annals"* (Seattle: University of Washington Press, 2016), 1:491, 493.

47. Durrant, Li, and Schaberg, 1:490, 492.

48. Ming Dong Gu, *Chinese Theories of Reading and Writing*, 168–69.

49. The story of the three good men is the only topic covered by two different poets in the "Yongshi" section of *Wen xuan*.

50. Cutter, "On Reading," 1–11.

51. During the Jian'an period, Wang Can, Cao Zhi, and other men of letters wrote frequently about their experience of traveling on military campaigns and visiting historical sites. For a detailed discussion of this phenomenon, see Qiulei Hu, "Following the Troops, Carrying along Our Brushes: Jian'an (196–220 AD) *Fu* and *Shi* Written for Military Campaigns," *Asia Major*, 3rd ser., 33, no. 2 (2020): 61–91; Ding Han 丁涵, "Jixing fu zai Jian'an shidai de bianzou ji qi chengyin tanwei" 紀行賦在建安時代的變奏及其成因探微, *Zhejiang daxue xuebao (Renwen shehui kexue ban)* 浙江大學學報 (人文社會科學版) 48, no. 4 (2018): 204–15.

52. Cutter, "On Reading," 1–11. Another possibility is that these poems were inspired by the *Shijing*, *Shiji*, or a similar account of the three good men. In any case, both poets composed these poems in response to the story of the three good men, and it seems possible that they did so on the same occasion, because the structure of the poems are similar: first, they comment on Lord Mu's behavior, then they narrate the story, and eventually they cite the "Huangniao" poem.

53. Chen Hongtian 陳宏天, Zhao Fuhai 趙福海, and Chen Fuxing 陳復興, eds., *Zhaoming Wen xuan yizhu (Di er juan)* 昭明文選譯注 (第二卷) (Changchun: Jilin wenshi chubanshe, 2007), 412.

54. Although this poem is about the three good men, the title "Poem on History" is rather general, and so some scholars speculate that the title was added by later editors. See Cutter, "On Reading," 2.

55. *Xun* 殉 means to "bury people alive with the dead."

56. *Daren* 達人 refers to an open-minded and optimistic person, a learned person.

57. A Chinese man of this period would traditionally bind up his hair in a coming-of-age ritual, so the implication is that the three men came to serve Lord Mu when they were very young. This line switches the focus of the poem from the poet's comments to a retrospective narration of the historical event.

58. *Buzi* 不訾 means "without measure."

59. *Mo* 殁 means "to die." *Zhi* 之 refers to the three good men.

60. Compare with the description in the *Shijing*: "When he came to the grave, He looked terrified and trembled. Thou azure Heaven there! Thou art destroying our good men." James Legge, trans., *The Chinese Classics*, vol. 4, *The She King* (Hong Kong: Hong Kong University Press, 1960), 198. 臨其穴、惴惴其慄。彼蒼者天、殲我良人. Lu Hongsheng, *Shijing jijiao jizhu jiping (di wu juan)*, 2841.

61. *Geng* 綆 refers to a rope for drawing water. *Mi* 縻 refers to a halter for an ox. In classical Chinese poetry, the subject in one line or couplet can be ignored or changed without any indication, and readers are expected to infer the subject of a given line based on the context. This convention poses a challenge for the translation and interpretation of an already concise poem. Because this couplet lacks a subject,

we are uncertain whether it refers to the three good men or the poet, Wang Can. If it were the three good men, the focus of the couplet is their response to their ruler's order and their immediate tragedy. If the subject of this couplet were the poet, it would demonstrate that Wang visited the three good men's tomb and was touched by their deeds. This ambiguity already exists in the *Shijing* poem, where it seems that the anonymous persona blames heaven for sacrificing the three good men.

62. "A purpose" here refers to their loyalty and duties to Lord Mu.

63. *Zhuangshi* 壯士 means heroic man or vigorous man.

64. This line can also be understood as "yellow birds make sorrowful songs."

65. Xiao, *Wen xuan*, 21.985–86.

66. A detailed discussion of human sacrifices in the state of Qin can be found in Wang Zhiyou 王志友 and Liu Chunhua 劉春華, "Qin Wugong 'chu yiren congsi' de kaogu xue guancha" 秦武公"初以人從死"的考古學觀察, *Qin wenhua luncong* 秦文化論叢 (2008): 348–69.

67. *Shiji*, 5.183.

68. Lord Mu was one of the famous "Five Hegemons in the Spring and Autumn Period" ("Chunqiu wuba" 春秋五霸), and renowned for his employment of the talented, including the well-known strategist Baili Xi 百里奚 (d. 621 BCE). See *Shiji*, 5.173–222.

69. Bloom, *Mencius*, 127.

70. Jiao, *Mengzi zhengyi*, 11.783.

71. Xiao, *Wen xuan*, 21.986.

72. Another possible understanding of this couplet is that it is direct speech from the three good men themselves. In that case, the second line would be translated as "loyalty and righteousness are what satisfies us." See Cutter, "On Reading," 3.

73. Cao Zhi seemed to believe that the three good men had a prior agreement with Lord Mu. Cao may have been influenced by Ying Shao's 應劭 (ca. 153–196) comments on their story in *Hanshu*: "Lord Mu of Qin drank with a group of officials. When intoxicated, Lord Mu said, 'In life, we share this happiness; in death, we will be mourned for together.' Yan Xi and others agreed. When Lord Mu died, all of them died along with him." 秦穆與羣臣飲酒, 酒酣, 公曰: 生共此樂, 死共此哀." 奄息等許諾. 及公薨, 皆從死. Xiao, *Wen xuan*, 21.986.

74. *Huangniao* 黃鳥 could refer to the "Huangniao" poem in the *Shijing*. If this is the case, this line could be rendered as "'Huangniao' is written to lament the Three Good Men."

75. Qian Nanxiu, *Spirit and Self in Medieval China: The Shih-shuo hsin-yü and Its Legacy* (Honolulu: University of Hawai'i Press, 2001), 137.

76. Qian Nanxiu, 137.

77. *Songshu*, 73.1891–1904. See also *Nanshi*, 34.877–81.

78. This translation is a modified version of the one provided by Tina Marie Harding, "Echoes of the Past: Yan Yanzhi's (384–456) Lyric *Shi*" (PhD diss., University of Colorado at Boulder, 2007), 48.

79. *Songshu*, 73.1893.
80. Xiao, *Wen xuan*, 21.1007–8.
81. The English translation of *bubing* as "commandant of infantry" in the title follows Mather, *Shih-shuo Hsin-yü*, 649.
82. Mather, *Shih-shuo Hsin-yü*, 401.
83. Yu Jiaxi, *Shishuo xinyu jianshu*, 23.858.
84. The English translation largely follows Mather, *Shih-shuo Hsin-yü*, 402.
85. Yu Jiaxi, *Shishuo xinyu jianshu*, 23.859.
86. The English translation is based on Wu Fusheng 吳伏生, modern Chinese trans., *Ruan Ji shixuan* 阮籍詩選, English trans. Wu Fusheng and Graham Hartill (Beijing: Zhonghua shuju, 2006), 171.
87. *Jinshu*, 49.1360.
88. Zhao and Zhang, *Gudai yongshi shi tonglun*, 51.
89. This English translation is based on Stephen Owen, *An Anthology of Chinese Literature* (New York: W. W. Norton & Company, 1996), 141.
90. *Hanshu*, 62.2735.
91. Other poems in the "Yong shi" section of the *Wen xuan* that I would place in this category include Zuo Si's "Yongshi" III and IV, along with Yan Yanzhi's other "Wujun yong" on Ji Kang 嵇康 (ca. 224–ca. 263), Liu Ling 劉伶 (ca. 221–300), Ruan Xian 阮咸 (fl. third century), and Xiang Xiu 向秀 (ca. 227–272); Zuo's poems III and IV comment on Duangan Mu, Lu Zhonglian, and Yang Xiong.
92. During early medieval China, scholars often disputed matters of literary style—whether writing should be ornate and elaborate with many allusions, as in Yan Yanzhi's poems, or whether it should be simple and easy to understand, as Shen Yue advocated. Although the practice was not universally embraced, heavy use of allusion was favored by most poets during this period. For details, see Tian Xiaofei, "From the Eastern Jin through the Early Tang (317–649)," 246–47.
93. Xiao, *Wen xuan*, 21.1012.
94. Junping, family name Yan, was also known as Zhuang Zun 莊尊.
95. Berkowitz, *Patterns of Disengagement*, 93.
96. *Hanshu*, 72.3056.
97. Yang Xiong's own comments on his successes are quoted in *Hanshu*: "During the reign of the Filial Emperor Cheng, there was an [imperial] retainer who recommended my compositions as resembling the style of [Sima] Xiangru. The emperor was about to perform the suburban sacrifices at the Grand Altar in Sweet Springs and to the Sovereign Earth at Fenyin, in order to seek an heir to succeed him. He summoned me as Candidate for Appointment in the courtyard of the Hall of Received Brilliance." David R. Knechtges, *The Han shu Biography of Yang Xiong (53 B.C.–A.D. 18)* (Tempe: Center for Asian Studies, Arizona State University, 1982), 17. 孝成帝時，客有薦雄文似相如者，上方郊祠甘泉泰畤、汾陰后土，以求繼嗣，召雄待詔承明之庭。正月，從上甘泉，還奏《甘泉賦》以風。*Hanshu*, 87.3522.
98. *Hanshu*, 72.3056–57.

99. Allan Berkowitz argues that "Zhuang Zun (Yan Junping) . . . epitomizes a perfect blend of laudatory Confucian as well as Taoist characteristics, actualized into a private life disengaged from the world of public affairs." *Patterns of Disengagement*, 94.

100. Qu Tuiyuan 瞿蛻園 et al., eds. *Li Bai ji jiaozhu* 李白集校注 (Shanghai: Shanghai guji chubanshe, 1980), 2.116.

101. Xiao, *Wen xuan*, 21.988. A detailed discussion of this poem appears in chapter 2.

102. Nienhauser, *The Grand Scribe's Records*, 8:364; *Shiji*, 102.2757; *Hanshu*, 50.2312.

103. Nienhauser, *The Grand Scribe's Records*, 8:367; *Shiji*, 102.2759; *Hanshu*, 50.2314.

104. Nienhauser, *The Grand Scribe's Records*, 8:367; *Shiji*, 102.2761; *Hanshu*, 50.2315. According to *Hanshu*, this event took place ten, not seven, years after Emperor Jing ascended to the throne.

105. Nienhauser, *The Grand Scribe's Records*, 8:368.

106. *Shiji*, 102.2761.

107. *Jinshu*, 92.2375–77.

108. Xiao, *Wen xuan*, 21.988.

109. Jiang Qingyi 蔣清翊, ed., *Wang Zi'an ji zhu* 王子安集注 (Shanghai: Shanghai guji chubanshe, 1995), 8.233.

110. Qiu Zhaoao 仇兆鰲, ed., *Dushi xiangzhu* 杜詩詳注 (Beijing: Zhonghua shuju, 1979), 13.1462.

111. Several of the other Zuo Si "Yongshi" collected in *Wen xuan* adopt the same approach as "Yongshi" II. Poem I uses brief allusions to Sima Rangju 司馬穰苴 and Sima Xiangru 司馬相如 (ca. 179–ca. 118 BCE) to portray Zuo's youthful political ambitions; poem V uses an allusion to Xu You 許由 to discuss Zuo's failures in the capital; poem VII compares the lack of appreciation Zuo received to the cases of Zhufu Yan 主父偃 (fl. 127 BCE), Zhu Maichen 朱買臣 (fl. 115 BCE), Chen Ping 陳平 (fl. 178 BCE), and Sima Xiangru; poem VIII uses allusions to Su Qin 蘇秦 (d. 284 BCE) and Li Si 李斯 (ca. 284–208 BCE) to make the case for Daoist detachment. The main focus of these poems is on Zuo's own emotions and personal reflections rather than on the historical figures.

112. Yue Zhang, "*Zuo Si ji*," 516.

113. Shen Deqian 沈德潛, ed., *Gushi yuan* 古詩源 (Beijing: Huaxia chubanshe, 1998), 14.305.

Conclusion

1. John Baxter and Patrick Atherton, eds., *Aristotle's Poetics*, trans. George Whalley (Montreal: McGill-Queen's University Press, 1997), 81.

2. For studies of the relationship between history and poetry in premodern China, see Yue Zhang and Yinchi Chen 陳引馳, eds., *Zhonggu wenxue zhong de shi yu shi* 中古文學中的詩與史 (Shanghai: Fudan daxue chubanshe, 2020).

3. Jan Assmann, *Cultural Memory and Early Civilization*, 86.

4. Jan Assmann, 45–46.

5. Hans Robert Jauss, *Toward an Aesthetic of Reception*, trans. Timothy Bahti (Minneapolis: University of Minnesota Press, 1982), 19.

Bibliography

Ashmore, Robert. *The Transport of Reading: Text and Understanding in the World of Tao Qian (365–427)*. Cambridge, MA: Harvard University Asia Center, 2010.
Assmann, Aleida. *Der lange Schatten der Vergangenheit: Erinnerungskultur und Geschichtspolitik*. München: Verlag C. H. Beck, 2006.
———. *Shadows of Trauma: Memory and Politics of Postwar Identity*. Translated by Sarah Clift. New York: Fordham University Press, 2016.
Assmann, Jan. *Cultural Memory and Early Civilization: Writing, Remembrance, and Political Imagination*. Cambridge: Cambridge University Press, 2011.
———. *Das kulturelle Gedächtnis: Schrift, Erinnerung und politische Identität in frühen Hochkulturen*. München: Verlag C. H. Beck, 2007.
Baxter, John, and Patrick Atherton, eds. *Aristotle's Poetics*. Translated by George Whalley. Montreal: McGill-Queen's University Press, 1997.
Beishi 北史. 10 vols. Beijing: Zhonghua shuju, 1974.
Bender, Mark. "A Description of 'Jiangjing' (Telling Scriptures) Services in Jingjiang, China." *Asian Folklore Studies* 60, no. 1 (2001): 101–33.
Berkowitz, Alan J. "Biographies of Recluses: Huangfu Mi's Accounts of High-Minded Men." In *Early Medieval China: A Sourcebook*, edited by Wendy Swartz, Robert Ford Campany, Yang Lu, and Jessey J. C. Choo, 333–49. New York: Columbia University Press, 2014.
———. *Patterns of Disengagement: The Practice and Portrayal of Reclusion in Early Medieval China*. Stanford, CA: Stanford University Press, 2000.
———. "Social and Cultural Dimensions of Reclusion in Early Medieval China." In *Philosophy and Religion in Early Medieval China*, edited by Alan K. L. Chan and Yuet-Keung Lo, 291–318. Albany: State University of New York, 2010.
Bloom, Irene, trans. *Mencius*. New York: Columbia University Press, 2009.
Brashier, K. E. *Ancestral Memory in Early China*. Cambridge, MA: Harvard University Press, 2011.
———. *Public Memory in Early China*. Cambridge, MA: Harvard University Press, 2014.

Cai Danjun 蔡丹君. "Liuchao zashi, zazhuan yu yongshi shi xue de fazhan—cong Yang Xiuzhi *Tao Yuanming ji* suoshou 'Ji shengxian qunfu lu' shuoqi" 六朝雜史、雜傳與詠史詩學的發展——從陽休之《陶淵明集》所收《集聖賢群輔錄》說起. *Beijing daxue xuebao (Zhexue shehui kexue ban)* 北京大學學報 (哲學社會科學版) 56, no. 2 (2019): 89–98.

Campany, Robert Ford. *Making Transcendents: Ascetics and Social Memory in Early Medieval China*. Honolulu: University of Hawai'i Press, 2009.

Cao Daoheng 曹道衡. "Jiang Yan." In *Zhongguo lidai zhuming wenxuejia pingzhuan* 中國歷代著名文學家評傳, edited by Lü Huijuan 呂慧鵑, Liu Bo 劉波, and Lu Da 盧達, 1:503–26. Jinan: Shandong jiaoyu chubanshe, 1983.

———. *Nanbei chao wenxue shi* 南北朝文學史. Beijing: Renmin wenxue chubanshe, 1991.

Cao Xu 曹旭. *Shipin jizhu* 詩品集注. Shanghai: Shanghai guji chubanshe, 1994.

Chai, David, ed. *Dao Companion to Xuanxue* 玄學 *(Neo-Daoism)*. Cham: Springer, 2020.

Chen Guying 陳鼓應. *Zhuangzi jinzhu jinyi* 莊子今註今譯. 3 vols. Beijing: Zhonghua shuju, 1983.

Chen Hongtian 陳宏天, Zhao Fuhai 趙福海, and Chen Fuxing 陳復興, eds. *Zhaoming Wen xuan yizhu (Di er juan)* 昭明文選譯注 (第二卷). Changchun: Jilin wenshi chubanshe, 2007.

Chen Jianhua 陳建華. *Tangdai yongshi huaigu shi lungao* 唐代詠史懷古詩論稿. Wuhan: Huazhong keji daxue chubanshe, 2008.

Chen Qun 陳群. " 'Lineng zhi shi' yu 'wenyi zhi shi': Songchu de wenren zhi zheng" "吏能之士"與"文義之士": 宋初的文人之爭. *Qinghua daxue xuebao* 清華大學學報, 2nd suppl., no. 24 (2009): 5–16.

Cheng Zhangcan 程章燦. "Zhongmu: Zuowei Liu Song de wenhua changyu" 冢墓: 作爲劉宋的文化場域. *Zhongguo wenhua* 中國文化 53, no. 1 (2021): 28–35.

Chennault, Cynthia L. "Lofty Gates or Solitary Impoverishment? Xie Family Members of the Southern Dynasties," *T'oung Pao* 85, no. 4/5 (1999): 249–327.

Chittick, Andrew. *The Jiankang Empire in Chinese and World History: Ethnic Identity and Political Culture*. Oxford: Oxford University Press, 2020.

———. *Patronage and Community in Medieval China: The Xiangyang Garrison, 400–600 CE*. Albany: State University of New York, 2009.Clark, Anthony E. *Ban Gu's History of Early China*. Amherst, NY: Cambria Press, 2008.

Connery, Chris. "Tso Ssu." In *The Indiana Companion to Traditional Chinese Literature*, Vol. 1, edited by William H. Nienhauser, Jr., 806. Bloomington: Indiana University Press, 1986.

Cutter, Robert Joe. "On Reading Cao Zhi's 'Three Good Men': *Yong shi shi* or *Deng lin shi*?" *Chinese Literature: Essays, Articles, Reviews* 11 (1989): 1–11.

———. "Poetry from 200 B.C.E. to 600 C.E." In *The Columbia History of Chinese Literature*, edited by Victor Mair, 248–73. New York: Columbia University Press, 2001.

Dai Jianye 戴建業. "Zuo Bao yitong chutan—Bijiao fenxi Zuo Si, Bao Zhao de rensheng jingyu yu rensheng jueze" 左鮑異同初探——比較分析左思、鮑照的人生境遇與人生抉擇. *Zhonghua wenshi luncong* 中華文史論叢 92, no. 4 (2008): 349–73.

Davis, A. R. *T'ao Yüan-ming (AD 365–427): His Works and Their Meaning*, 2 vols. Cambridge: Cambridge University Press, 2009.

Dewoskin, Kenneth J., and J. I. Crump, trans. *In Search of the Supernatural: The Written Record*. Stanford, CA: Stanford University Press, 1996.

Dien, Albert E. "Historiography of the Six Dynasties Period (220–581)." In *The Oxford History of Historical Writing, Volume 1: Beginnings to AD 600*, edited by Andrew Feider and Gran Hardy, 509–34. Oxford: Oxford University Press, 2011.

Ding Fulin 丁福林. "Cong gangzao fuqi dao chugui yiquan—Tan Dong Jin shanshui shiren Xie Zhan" 從剛躁負氣到處貴遺權——談東晉山水詩人謝瞻. *Gudian wenxue zhishi* 古典文學知識, no. 5 (2003): 76–81.

Ding Han 丁涵. "Jixing fu zai Jian'an shidai de bianzou ji qi chengyin tanwei" 紀行賦在建安時代的變奏及其成因探微. *Zhejiang daxue xuebao (Renwen shehui kexue ban)* 浙江大學學報 (人文社會科學版) 48, no. 4 (2018): 204–15.

Ding Hongqi 丁紅旗. "Dong Jin Nanchao Xieshi jiazu bingshi yu Daojiao xinyang" 東晉南朝謝氏家族病史與道教信仰. *Zongjiao xue yanjiu* 宗教學研究, no. 3 (2006): 172–76.

Dong Huixiu 董慧秀. "Liu Kun, Lu Chen zengda shi shimo tuilun" 劉琨、盧諶贈答詩始末推論. *Wei Jin Nanbeichao Sui Tang shi ziliao* 魏晉南北朝隋唐史資料 20 (2003): 19–29.

Durrant, Stephen. "From 'Scribe' to 'History': The Keyword *shi* 史." In *Keywords in Chinese Culture: Thought and Literature*, edited by Wai-yee Li and Yuri Pines, 85–122. Hong Kong: The Chinese University of Hong Kong Press, 2020.

Durrant, Stephen, Wai-yee Li, and David Schaberg, trans. *Zuo Tradition / Zuozhuan: Commentary on the "Spring and Autumn Annals."* 3 vols. Seattle: University of Washington Press, 2016.

Fan Ziye 范子燁. *Youran wang Nanshan—wenhua shiyu zhong de Tao Yuanming* 悠然望南山——文化視域中的陶淵明. Shanghai: Dongfang chuban zhongxin, 2010.

———. *Zhonggu wenren shenghuo yanjiu* 中古文人生活研究. Jinan: Shandong jiaoyu chubanshe, 2001.

Fang Dongshu 方東樹. *Zhaomei zhanyan* 昭昧詹言. Beijing: Renmin wenxue chubanshe, 1961.

Fang Xuanling 房玄齡. *Jinshu* 晉書. 10 vols. Beijing: Zhonghua shuju, 1974.

Farmer, Michael J. "On the Composition of Zhang Hua's 'Nüshi zhen.'" *Early Medieval China* 10–11, no. 1 (2004): 151–75.

———. "Zuo Si." In *Classical Chinese Writers of the Pre-Tang Period*, edited by Curtis Dean Smith, 327–32. Detroit: Bruccoli Clark Layman / Gale, 2011.

Frankel, Hans H. *The Flowering Plum and the Palace Lady: Interpretations of Chinese Poetry*. New Haven, CT: Yale University Press, 1976.
Frodsham, J. D. *The Murmuring Stream: The Life and Works of the Chinese Nature Poet Hsieh Ling-yün (385–433), Duke of K'ang-Lo*. Vol. 1. Kuala Lumpur: University of Malaya Press, 1967.
Fu Gang 傅剛. *Zhaoming Wen xuan yanjiu* 昭明文選研究. Beijing: Zhongguo shehui kexue chubanshe, 2000.
Gan Bao 干寶. *Soushen ji* 搜神記. Edited by Wang Shaoying 汪紹楹. Beijing: Zhonghua shuju, 1979.
Ge Xiaoyin 葛曉音. *Badai shishi* 八代詩史. Xi'an: Shanxi renmin chubanshe, 1989.
Gong Kechang 龔克昌. *Studies on the Han Fu*. Translated by David R. Knechtges. Ann Arbor, MI: American Oriental Society, 1997.
Gong Kechang et al. *Quan Han fu pingzhu* 全漢賦評註. Shijiazhuang: Huashan wenyi chubanshe, 2003.
Gu, Ming Dong. *Chinese Theories of Reading and Writing: A Route to Hermeneutics and Open Poetics*. Albany: State University of New York Press, 2005.
Gu Nong 顧農. "Shuo 'Zuo Si fengli' ji qi beijing" 說"左思風力"及其背景. *Shandong shida xuebao* 山東師大學報, no. 3 (1999): 4–10.
Guo Yu 郭彧, annot. *Zhouyi* 周易. Beijing: Zhonghua shuju, 2006.
Hanshu 漢書. 12 vols. Beijing: Zhonghua shuju, 1962.
Harding, Tina Marie. "Echoes of the Past: Yan Yanzhi's (384–456) Lyric *Shi*." PhD diss., University of Colorado at Boulder, 2007.
Hawkes, David. *Ch'u Tz'ŭ: The Songs of the South, An Ancient Chinese Anthology*. Boston: Beacon Press, 1962.
He Zhuo 何焯. *Yimen dushu ji* 義門讀書記. Beijing: Zhonghua shuju, 1987.
Hightower, James Robert. "The *Fu* of T'ao Ch'ien." *Harvard Journal of Asiatic Studies* 17, nos. 1/2 (1954): 169–230.
———. *The Poetry of T'ao Ch'ien*. Oxford: Oxford University Press, 1970.
Hu, Qiulei. "Following the Troops, Carrying along Our Brushes: Jian'an (196–220 AD) *Fu* and *Shi* Written for Military Campaigns." *Asia Major*, 3rd ser., 33, no. 2 (2020): 61–91.
Hu Zhiji 胡之驥. *Jiang Wentong ji huizhu* 江文通集彙註. Shanghai: Shanghai guji chubanshe, 1984.
Huangfu Mi 皇甫謐. *Gaoshi zhuan* 高士傳. Beijing: Zhonghua shuju, 1985.
Hucker, Charles O. *A Dictionary of Official Titles in Imperial China*. Stanford, CA: Stanford University Press, 1985.
Hunter, Michael. "The Difficulty with 'The Difficulties of Persuasion' ('Shuinan' 說難)." In *Dao Companion to the Philosophy of Han Fei*, edited by P. R. Goldin, 169–95. New York: Springer, 2013.
Jauss, Hans Robert. *Toward an Aesthetic of Reception*. Translated by Timothy Bahti. Minneapolis: University of Minnesota Press, 1982.

Ji Minghua 季明華. *Nan Song yongshi shi yanjiu* 南宋詠史詩研究. Taibei: Wenjin chubanshe, 1997.

Jiang Qingyi 蔣清翊, ed. *Wang Zi'an ji zhu* 王子安集注. Shanghai: Shanghai guji chubanshe, 1995.

Jiao Xun 焦循. *Mengzi zhengyi* 孟子正義. Beijing: Zhonghua shuju, 1987.

Ke Mading 柯馬丁 (Kern, Martin). "Chutu wenxian yu wenhua jiyi: *Shijing* zaoqi lishi yanjiu" 出土文獻與文化記憶:《詩經》早期歷史研究. *Zhongguo zhexue* 中國哲學, no. 25 (2004): 111–58.

———. "Zuowei jiyi de shi: *Shi* ji qi zaoqi quanshi" 作爲記憶的詩:《詩》及其早期詮釋. *Guoxue yanjiu* 國學研究, no. 16 (2005): 329–41.

Kern, Martin. "Early Chinese Literature, Beginnings through Western Han." In *The Cambridge History of Chinese Literature*, edited by Kang-i Sun Chang and Stephen Owen, 1–115. Cambridge: Cambridge University Press, 2010.

Killigrew, John W. "The Role of the Moushi 謀士 in the Jin Shu and Wei Shu during the Northern Kingdoms Period, 309–450 AD." *Journal of Asian History* 47, no. 2 (2013): 151–96.

Klein, Esther S. *Reading Sima Qian from Han to Song: The Father of History in Pre-Modern China*. Leiden: Brill, 2019.

Knechtges, David R. "From the Eastern Han through the Western Jin (25–317)." In *The Cambridge History of Chinese Literature*, edited by Kang-i Sun Chang and Stephen Owen, 116–98. Cambridge: Cambridge University Press, 2010.

———. *The Han shu Biography of Yang Xiong (53 B.C.–A.D. 18)*. Tempe: Center for Asian Studies, Arizona State University, 1982.

———. "Liu Kun, Lu Chen, and Their Writings in the Transition to the Eastern Jin." *Chinese Literature: Essays, Articles, Reviews* 28 (2006): 1–66.

———, trans. *Wen xuan or Selections of Refined Literature*. Vol. 1, *Rhapsodies on Metropolises and Capitals*. Princeton, NJ: Princeton University Press, 1982.

———. "*Wen xuan* Studies." *Early Medieval China* 10 (2004): 1–22.

Knechtges, David R., and Taiping Chang, eds. *Ancient and Early Medieval Chinese Literature: A Reference Guide*. 4 vols. Leiden: Brill, 2010, 2014.

Knoblock, John, and Jeffrey Riegel. *The Annals of Lü Buwei: A Complete Translation and Study*. Stanford, CA: Stanford University Press, 2000.

Kōzen Hiroshi 興膳宏. "Sashi to Eishi shi" 左思と詠史詩. *Chūgoku bungaku hō* 中國文學報 21 (1966): 1–56.

Kroll, Paul W. *A Student's Dictionary of Classical and Medieval Chinese*. Leiden: Brill, 2017.

Lai Yushu 賴玉樹. *Wan Tang Wudai yongshi shi zhi meixue yishi* 晚唐五代詠史詩之美學意識. Taibei: Xiuwei zixun chubanshe, 2005.

Lau, D. C., trans. *Confucius: The Analects*. New York: Penguin, 1979.

———, trans. *Tao Te Ching*. Hong Kong: The Chinese University of Hong Kong, 1989.

Legge, James, trans. *The Chinese Classics*. Vol. 4, *The She King*. Hong Kong: Hong Kong University Press, 1960.

———, trans. *Li Chi: Book of Rites: An Encyclopedia of Ancient Ceremonial Usages, Religious Creeds, and Social Institutions*. Vol. 1. Edited by Ch'u Chai and Winberg Chai. New York: University Books, 1967.

Li Han 李翰. *Han Wei Sheng Tang yongshi shi yanjiu—yanzhi zhi shixue chuantong ji shiren sixiang de kaocha* 漢魏盛唐詠史詩研究——言志之詩學傳統及士人思想的考察. Guilin: Guangxi shifan daxue chubanshe, 2006.

Li Shi'e 李世萼. "Lun Jinmo Songchu shiren Xie Zhan" 論晉末宋初詩人謝瞻. *Shandong daxue xuebao (Zhexue shehui kexue ban)* 山東大學學報 (哲學社會科學版), no. 2 (1992): 30–37.

Li Wai-yee. "The Idea of Authority in the *Shih chi* (Records of the Historian)." *Harvard Journal of Asiatic Studies* 54, no. 2 (1994): 345–405.

———. *The Readability of the Past in Early Chinese Historiography*. Cambridge, MA: Harvard University Asia Center, 2007.

Li Xiaoming 李曉明. *Tangdai lishi guannian yanjiu* 唐代歷史觀念研究. Beijing: Renmin chubanshe, 2009.

Li Yaonan 李耀南. "Xuanxue shiye zhong de Tao Yuanming rensheng guan he shenmei rensheng jingjie" 玄學視野中的陶淵明人生觀和審美人生境界. *Huazhong keji daxue xuebao (Renwen shehui kexue ban)* 華中科技大學學報 (人文社會科學版), no. 6 (2002): 23–28.

Li Yiya 李宜涯. *Wan Tang yongshi shi yu pinghua yanyi zhi guanxi* 晚唐詠史詩與平話演義之關係. Taibei: Wenshizhe chubanshe, 2002.

Lin, Pauline. "Zhang Xie." In *Classical Chinese Writers of the Pre-Tang Period*, edited by Curtis Dean Smith, 318–22. Detroit: Bruccoli Clark Layman / Gale, 2011.

Liu Wenzhong 劉文忠. "Lu Chen, Liu Kun zengda shi kaobian" 盧諶、劉琨贈答詩考辨. *Wen shi zhe* 文史哲, no. 2 (1988): 89–90.

Liu Yuejin 劉躍進. *Zhongguo gudai wenxue tonglun: Wei Jin Nanbei chao juan* 中國古代文學通論：魏晉南北朝卷. Shenyang: Liaoning renmin chubanshe, 2005.

Liu Yunhao 劉運好. *Lu Shiheng wenji jiaozhu* 陸士衡文集校注. Nanjing: Fenghuang chubanshe, 2007.

Liu Zhoutang 劉周堂. "Lun wenshi buyu" 論文士不遇. *Zhongguo wenxue yanjiu* 中國文學研究, no. 1 (1997): 7–12.

Lo, Yuet Keung. "*Qingtan* and *Xuanxue*." In *The Cambridge History of China*, Volume 2, *The Six Dynasties, 220–589*, edited by Albert E. Dien and Keith N. Knapp, 511–30. Cambridge: Cambridge University Press, 2019.

Loewe, Michael. *A Biographical Dictionary of the Qin, Han and Xin Dynasties*. Leiden: Brill, 2000.

Lu Hongsheng 魯洪生, ed. *Shijing jijiao jizhu jiping* 詩經集校集注集評. 15 vols. Beijing: Xiandai chubanshe, Zhonghua shuju, 2015.

Lü Huijuan 呂慧鵑, Liu Bo 劉波, and Lu Da 盧達, eds. *Zhongguo lidai zhuming wenxuejia pingzhuan (di yi juan)* 中國歷代著名文學家評傳（第一卷）. Jinan: Shandong jiaoyu chubanshe, 1983.

Lu Kanru 陸侃如 and Fang Buhe 方步和. "Heyi bai liangang, huawei raozhi rou—lun Liu Kun 'Chongzeng Lu Chen' shi ji qita" 何意百煉鋼, 化爲繞指柔?——論劉琨《重贈盧諶》詩及其他. *Shanxi daxue xuebao* 山西大學學報, no. 1 (1985): 89–93.

Lu Kanru 陸侃如 and Feng Yuanjun 馮沅君. *Zhongguo shishi* 中國詩史. Jinan: Shandong daxue chubanshe, 1985.

Lu Qinli 逯欽立. *Xian Qin Han Wei Jin Nanbei chao shi* 先秦漢魏晉南北朝詩. 3 vols. Beijing: Zhonghua shuju, 1983.

Lu, Sheldon Hsiao-peng. *From Historicity to Functionality: The Chinese Poetics of Narrative*. Stanford, CA: Stanford University Press, 1994.

Lü Shihao 呂世浩. *Cong Shiji dao Hanshu: Zhuanzhe guocheng yu lishi yiyi* 從《史記》到《漢書》: 轉折過程與歷史意義. Taibei: Guoli Taiwan daxue chuban zhongxin, 2009.

Luo Zongqiang 羅宗強. *Wei Jin Nanbeichao wenxue sixiang shi* 魏晉南北朝文學思想史. Beijing: Zhonghua shuju, 2006.

———. *Xuanxue yu Wei Jin shiren xintai* 玄學與魏晉士人心態. Hangzhou: Zhejiang renmin chubanshe, 1991.

Ma Qiangcai 馬強才. *Zhongguo gudai shige yongshi guannian yanjiu* 中國古代詩歌用事觀念研究. Beijing: Zhongguo shehui kexue chubanshe, 2014.

Ma Xiaokun 馬曉坤. "Dong Jin Nanchao Chenjun Xieshi zhengzhi xingwei tanxi" 東晉南朝陳郡謝氏政治行爲探析. *Xueshu yanjiu* 學術研究, no. 6 (2009): 148–53.

Marney, John. *Chiang Yen*. Boston: Twayne Publishers, 1981.

Mather, Richard B. *Shih-shuo Hsin-yü: A New Account of Tales of the World*. 2nd ed. Ann Arbor: Center for Chinese Studies, University of Michigan, 2002.

Mou Shijin 牟世金 and Xu Chuanwu 徐傳武. "Zuo Si wenxue yeji xinlun" 左思文學業績新論. *Wenxue yichan* 文學遺產, no. 2 (1988): 30–38.

Nanshi 南史. 6 vols. Beijing: Zhonghua shuju, 1975.

Ng, On-cho and Q. Edward Wang. *Mirroring the Past: The Writing and Use of History in Imperial China*. Honolulu: University of Hawai'i Press, 2005.

Nienhauser, William H., Jr., ed. *The Grand Scribe's Records*. Vol. 7, *The Memoirs of Pre-Han China*. Bloomington: Indiana University Press, 1994.

———, ed. *The Grand Scribe's Records*. Vol. 8, *The Memoirs of Han China, Part I*. Bloomington: Indiana University Press, 2008.

Nugent, Christopher. *Manifest in Words, Written on Paper: Producing and Circulating Poetry in Tang Dynasty China*. Cambridge, MA: Harvard University Asia Center, 2010.

Owen, Stephen. *An Anthology of Chinese Literature*. New York: W. W. Norton, 1996.

———. *The Late Tang: Chinese Poetry of the Mid-Ninth Century (827–860)*. Cambridge, MA: Harvard University Asia Center, 2006.

———. *The Making of Early Chinese Classical Poetry*. Cambridge, MA: Harvard University Asia Center, 2006.

———. *Readings in Chinese Literary Thought*. Cambridge, MA: Harvard University Asia Center, 1992.

———. *Remembrances: The Experience of Past in Classical Chinese Literature*. Cambridge, MA: Harvard University Press, 1986.

———. "Zhong Rong's Preface to *Grades of the Poets*." In *Early Medieval China: A Sourcebook*, edited by Wendy Swartz, Robert Ford Campany, Yang Lu, and Jessey J. C. Choo, 287–306. New York: Columbia University Press, 2014.

Pankenier, David W. "'The Scholar's Frustration' Reconsidered: Melancholia or Credo?" *Journal of the American Oriental Society* 110, no. 3 (1990): 434–59.

Pines, Yuri. "A Hero Terrorist: Adoration of Jing Ke Revisited." *Asia Major*, 3rd ser., 21, no. 2 (2008): 1–34.

Qi Yishou 齊益壽, *Huangju dongli yao gujin: Tao Yuanming qiren qishi sanlun* 黃菊東籬耀古今: 陶淵明其人其詩散論. Taibei: Guoli Taiwan daxue chubanshe, 2016.

Qian, Nanxiu. *Spirit and Self in Medieval China: The Shih-shuo hsin-yü and Its Legacy*. Honolulu: University of Hawai'i Press, 2001.

Qian Zhixi 錢志熙. *Wei Jin shige yishu yuanlun* 魏晉詩歌藝術原論. Beijing: Beijing daxue chubanshe, 1993.

Qiu Zhaoao 仇兆鰲, ed. *Dushi xiangzhu* 杜詩詳注. 5 vols. Beijing: Zhonghua shuju, 1979.

Qu Tuiyuan 瞿蛻園 et al., eds. *Li Bai ji jiaozhu* 李白集校注. Shanghai: Shanghai guji chubanshe, 1980.

Raft, Zeb. "A New Approach to Biography in Early Medieval China: The Case of Zuo Si." *Zhongguo wen zhe yanjiu jikan* 中國文哲研究集刊 55 (2019): 41–81.

Sanders, Graham. "A New Note on *Shishuo xinyu*." *Early Medieval China* 20 (2014): 9–22.

———. *Words Well Put: Visions of Poetic Competence in the Chinese Tradition*. Cambridge, MA: Harvard University Asia Center, 2006.

Schaberg, David. *A Patterned Past: Form and Thought in Early Chinese Historiography*. Cambridge, MA: Harvard University Asia Center, 2001.

Shen Deqian 沈德潛, ed. *Gushi yuan* 古詩源. Beijing: Huaxia chubanshe, 1998.

Shen Yue 沈約. *Songshu* 宋書. 8 vols. Beijing: Zhonghua shuju, 1974.

Shi Ding 施丁. "Cong '*Suishu*·Jingji zhi' kan Han Sui jian lishi zhuanshu de fazhan" 從《隋書·經籍志》看漢隋間歷史撰述的發展. *Shixue shi yanjiu* 史學史研究, no. 2 (1980): 25–31.

Shields, Anna M. "Defining the 'Finest': A Northern Song View of Tang Dynasty Literary Culture in the *Wen cui*." *Journal of Chinese Literature and Culture* 4, no. 2 (2017): 306–35.

Shiji 史記. 10 vols. Beijing: Zhonghua shuju, 1959.

Shisanjing zhushu zhengli weiyuanhui 十三經注疏整理委員會, ed. *Lunyu zhushu* 論語注疏. Beijing: Zhonghua shuju, 1980.

Strassberg, Richard E., ed. *A Chinese Bestiary: Strange Creatures from the Guideways through Mountains and Seas*. Berkeley: University of California Press, 2002.

Suishu 隋書. 6 vols. Beijing: Zhonghua shuju, 1973.

Swartz, Wendy. *Reading Tao Yuanming: Shifting Paradigms of Historical Reception (427–1900)*. Cambridge, MA: Harvard University Asia Center, 2008.

Swartz, Wendy, and Robert F. Campany. *Memory in Medieval China: Text, Ritual, and Community* Leiden: Brill, 2018.

Tao Xinmin 陶新民. *Tao Yuanming: Xuanxue rensheng guan de zhongjie yu xuanyan shi de chaoyue* 陶淵明: 玄學人生觀的終結與玄言詩的超越. *Anhui daxue xuebao* 安徽大學學報 24, no. 1 (2000): 40–46.

Thompson, Lydia. "Confucian Paragon or Popular Deity? Legendary Heroes in a Late-Eastern Han Tomb." *Asia Major*, 3rd ser., 12, no. 2 (1999): 1–38.

Tian Jinfang 田晉芳. "Zhongwai xiandai Tao Yuanming jieshou zhi yanjiu" 中外現代陶淵明接受之研究. PhD diss., Fudan University, 2010.

Tian Xiaofei 田曉菲. *Beacon Fire and Shooting Star: The Literary Culture of the Liang (502–557)*. Cambridge, MA: Harvard University Asia Center, 2007.

———. "From the Eastern Jin through the Early Tang (317–649)." In *The Cambridge History of Chinese Literature*, edited by Kang-i Sun Chang and Stephen Owen, 199–285. Cambridge: Cambridge University Press, 2010.

———. *Tao Yuanming & Manuscript Culture: The Record of a Dusty Table*. Seattle: University of Washington Press, 2005.

———. "Tao Yuanming de shujia he Xiao Gang de yixue yanguang: Zhonggu de yuedu yu yuedu zhonggu" 陶淵明的書架和蕭綱的醫學眼光: 中古的閱讀與閱讀中古. *Guoxue yanjiu* 國學研究 37, no. 1 (2016): 119–44.

Tian Yuqing 田余慶. *Dong Jin menfa zhengzhi* 東晉門閥政治. Beijing: Beijing daxue chubanshe, 1996.

Tong Ling 童嶺. "Yixi nianjian Liu Yu beifa de tianming yu wenxue—yi Fu Liang 'Wei Songgong xiu Zhang Liang miao jiao,' 'Wei Songgong xiu Chu Yuanwang mu jiao' wei zhongxin'" 義熙年間劉裕北伐的天命與文學——以傅亮《爲宋公修張良廟教》、《爲宋公修楚元王墓教》爲中心. *Zhonghua wenshi luncong* 中華文史論叢 135, no. 3 (2019): 303–35.

Vervoorn, Aat. *Men of the Cliffs and Caves: The Development of the Chinese Eremitic Tradition to the End of the Han Dynasty*. Hong Kong: The Chinese University of Hong Kong Press, 1990.

Wang Chunhong 汪春泓. *Shi Han yanjiu* 史漢研究. Shanghai: Shanghai guji chubanshe, 2014.

Wang Daheng 王大恒. *Jiang Yan wenxue chuangzuo yanjiu* 江淹文學創作研究. Beijing: Zhongguo shehui kexue chubanshe, 2013.

Wang Liqun 王立群. *Wen xuan chengshu yanjiu* 《文選》成書研究. Zhengzhou: Daxiang chubanshe, 2015.

Wang, Ping. *The Age of Courtly Writing: Wen xuan Compiler Xiao Tong (501–531) and His Circle*. Leiden: Brill, 2012.

———. "The Art of Poetry Writing: Liu Xiaochuo's 'Becoming the Number-One Person for the Number-One Position.'" In *Early Medieval China: A Sourcebook*, edited by Wendy Swartz, Robert Ford Campany, Yang Lu, and Jessey J. C. Choo, 245–55. New York: Columbia University Press, 2014.

Wang Shumin 王叔岷. *Zhong Rong Shipin jianzheng gao* 鍾嶸詩品箋證稿. Beijing: Zhonghua shuju, 2007.

Wang Siyuan 王泗原. *Chuci jiaoshi* 楚辭校釋. Beijing: Renmin jiaoyu chubanshe, 1990.

Wang Xianqian 王先謙, Liu Wu 劉武, and Shen Xiaohuan 沈嘯寰. *Zhuangzi jijie* 莊子集解. Beijing: Zhonghua shuju, 1987.

Wang Xiaomeng 王曉萌. "Dong Jin monian zhengju de dongdang yu wenfeng de zhuanbian" 東晉末年政局的動盪與文風的轉變. *Zhongguo dianji yu wenhua* 中國典籍與文化, no. 1 (2010): 109–14.

Wang Xiaoyi 王曉毅. *Zhiren zhe zhi: Renwu zhi jiedu* 知人者智：人物志解讀. Beijing: Zhonghua shuju, 2008.

Wang Xibo 汪習波. *Sui Tang Wen xuan xue* 隋唐文選學. Shanghai: Shanghai guji chubanshe, 2005.

Wang Yao 王瑤. *Guanyu Zhongguo gudian wenxue wenti* 關於中國古典文學問題. Shanghai: Gudian wenxue chubanshe, 1956.

Wang Zhiyou 王志友 and Liu Chunhua 劉春華. "Qin Wugong 'chu yiren congsi' de kaogu xue guancha" 秦武公"初以人從死"的考古學觀察. *Qin wenhua luncong* 秦文化論叢 (2008): 348–69.

Watson, Burton, trans. *The Analects of Confucius*. New York: Columbia University Press, 2007.

———, trans. *The Complete Works of Zhuangzi*. New York: Columbia University Press, 2013.

———, trans. *Courtier and Commoner in Ancient China: Selections from the History of the Former Han*. New York: Columbia University Press, 1974.

———, trans. *Han Fei Tzu: Basic Writings*. New York: Columbia University Press, 1964.

———, trans. *Records of the Grand Historian of China*. New York: Columbia University Press, 1971.

———, trans. *Records of the Grand Historian: Han Dynasty*. Rev. ed., 2 vols. New York: Columbia University Press, 1993, 1996.

———, trans. *Records of the Grand Historian of China: Translated from the Shih Chi of Ssu-ma Ch'ien*. 2 vols. New York: Columbia University Press, 1961.

Wei Chunxi 韋春喜. *Song qian yongshi shi shi* 宋前詠史詩史. Beijing: Zhongguo shehui kexue chubanshe, 2010.

Wilhelm, Hellmut. "The Scholar's Frustration: Notes on a Type of *Fu*." In *Chinese Thought and Institutions*, edited by John K. Fairbank, 310–19. Chicago: University of Chicago Press, 1957.

Wilhelm, Richard, and Cary F. Baynes, trans. *The I Ching or Book of Changes*. Princeton, NJ: Princeton University Press, 1977.

Wilkinson, Endymion. *Chinese History: A Manual*. 2nd ed. Cambridge, MA: Harvard University Asia Center, 2000.

Williams, Nicholas Morrow. *Imitations of the Self: Jiang Yan and Chinese Poetics*. Leiden: Brill, 2015.

Wixted, John Timothy. "*Shi pin*." In *Early Medieval Chinese Texts*, edited by Cynthia L. Chennault, Keith N. Knapp, Alan J. Berkowitz, and Albert E. Dien, 275–88. Berkeley: University of California Press, 2016.

Wong, Siu-kit, ed. and trans. *Early Chinese Literary Criticism*. Hong Kong: Joint Publishing Co., 1983.
Wu, Fusheng 吳伏生, trans. [modern Chinese]. *Ruan Ji shixuan* 阮籍詩選. Translated into English by Wu Fusheng and Graham Hartill. Beijing: Zhonghua shuju, 2006.
———. *Written at Imperial Command: Panegyric Poetry in Early Medieval China*. Albany: State University of New York, 2009.
———. *Yingyu shijie de Tao Yuanming yanjiu* 英語世界的陶淵明研究. Beijing: Xueyuan chubanshe, 2013.
Wu Shuping 吳樹平, ed. *Dongguan Hanji jiaozhu* 東觀漢記校注. Beijing: Zhonghua shuju, 2008.
Wu Yun 吳雲. *Ershi shiji zhonggu wenxue yanjiu* 20世紀中古文學研究. Tianjin: Tianjin guji chubanshe, 2004.
Xiao Tong 蕭統, ed. *Liuchen zhu Wen xuan* 六臣注文選. 3 vols. Annotated by Li Shan 李善, Lü Yanji 呂延濟, Liu Liang 劉良, Zhang Xian 張銑, Lü Xiang 呂向, and Li Zhouhan 李周翰. Beijing: Zhonghua shuju, 1987.
———, ed. *Wen xuan* 文選. Annotated by Li Shan 李善. 6 vols. Shanghai: Shanghai guji chubanshe, 1986.
Xu Chuanwu 徐傳武. *Zuo Si Zuo Fen yanjiu* 左思左棻研究. Beijing: Zhongguo wenlian chubanshe, 1999.
Xu Gongchi 徐公持. *Wei Jin wenxue shi* 魏晉文學史. Beijing: Renmin wenxue chubanshe, 1999.
Yan Buke 閻步克. *Bofeng yu bogu: Qin Han Wei Jin Nanbeichao de zhengzhi wenming* 波峰與波谷：秦漢魏晉南北朝的政治文明. Beijing: Beijing daxue chubanshe, 2009.
Yang Bojun 楊伯峻. *Lunyu yizhu* 論語譯註. Beijing: Zhonghua shuju, 2006.
Yang Ming 楊明. *Wenfu Shipin yizhu* 文賦詩品譯註. Shanghai: Shanghai guji chubanshe, 1999.
Yang Xianyi 楊憲益 and Dai Naidie 戴乃迭, trans. *Selections from Records of the Historian*. Beijing: Waiwen chubanshe, 2004.
Ye Miaona 葉妙娜. "Dong Jin Nanchao qiaoxing gaomen zhi shihuan—Chenjun Xieshi ge'an yanjiu" 東晉南朝僑姓高門之仕宦——陳郡謝氏個案研究. *Zhongshan daxue xuebao (Shehui kexue ban)* 中山大學學報 (社會科學版), no. 3 (1986): 43–51.
Ye Riguang 葉日光. *Zuo Si shengping ji qi shi zhi xilun* 左思生平及其詩之析論. Taibei: Wen shi zhe chubanshe, 1979.
Yeh, Chia-ying, and Jan W. Walls. "Theory, Standards, and Practice of Criticizing Poetry in Chung Hung's *Shih P'in*." In *Studies in Chinese Poetry and Poetics*, Vol. 1, edited by Ronald Miao, 43–79. San Francisco: Chinese Materials Center, 1978.
Yu Jiaxi 余嘉錫, annot. *Shishuo xinyu jianshu* 世說新語箋疏. 3 vols. Beijing: Zhonghua shuju, 2007.
Yu, Pauline. "Poems in Their Place: Collections and Canons in Early Chinese Literature." *Harvard Journal of Asiatic Studies* 50, no. 1 (1990): 163–96.

Yuan Xingpei 袁行霈, ed. *Tao Yuanming ji jianzhu* 陶淵明集箋注. Beijing: Zhonghua shuju, 2003.

———, ed. *Zhongguo wenxue shi (di er juan)* 中國文學史 (第二卷). Beijing: Gaodeng jiaoyu chubanshe, 1999.

Zhang Runjing 張潤靜. *Tangdai yongshi huaigu shi yanjiu* 唐代詠史懷古詩研究. Shanghai: Shanghai Sanlian shudian, 2009.

Zhang Yajun 張亞軍. *Nanchao sishi yu Nanchao wenxue yanjiu* 南朝四史與南朝文學研究. Beijing: Zhongguo shehui kexue chubanshe, 2007.

Zhang Yanying 張燕嬰, ed. *Lun yu* 論語. Beijing: Zhonghua shuju, 2006.

Zhang, Yue 張月. "Approaches to Lore in 'Poems on History' from the *Selections of Refined Literature*." *Journal of Oriental Studies* 49, no. 2 (2017): 83–112.

———. "Lun Yuwen Suoan yongshi huaigu shi yanjiu de fangfa yu shijiao" 論宇文所安詠史懷古詩研究的方法與視角. *Changjiang xueshu* 長江學術 67, no. 3 (2020): 50–58.

———. "Ou Mei jinqi Tao Yuanming yanjiu zongshu, fenxi yu zhanwang" 歐美近期陶淵明研究綜述、分析與展望. *Gudian wenxian yanjiu* 古典文獻研究 20, no. 2 (2017): 289–304.

———. "The Reception of Zuo Si's 'Poems on History' in Early Medieval China." *Frontiers of Literary Studies in China* 14, no. 1 (2020): 48–75.

———. Review of *Song qian yongshi shi shi* 宋前詠史詩史, by Wei Chunxi 韋春喜, *China Review International* 18, no. 1 (2011): 113–16.

———. "Self-Canonization in Zuo Si's Poems on History." *Journal of Chinese Humanities* 5, (2019): 215–44.

———. "Tao Yuanming's Perspectives on Life as Reflected in His Poems on History." *Journal of Chinese Humanities* 6 (2020): 235–58.

———. "Teaching Classical Chinese Poetry through Reception Studies." *ASIANetwork Exchange: A Journal for Asian Studies in the Liberal Arts* 26, no. 1 (2019): 75–95.

———. "Wanjin Beimei Hanxue yanjiu fangfa yu wenxueshi bianzhuan guankui" 晚近北美漢學研究方法與文學史編撰管窺. *Guoji Hanxue* 國際漢學 20, no. 3 (2019): 185–91.

———. "*Zuo Si ji*." In *Early Medieval Chinese Texts*, edited by Cynthia L. Chennault, Keith N. Knapp, Alan J. Berkowitz, and Albert E. Dien, 514–18. Berkeley: University of California Press, 2016.

Zhang, Yue, and Chen Yinchi 陳引馳, eds. *Zhonggu wenxue zhong de shi yu shi* 中古文學中的詩與史. Shanghai: Fudan daxue chubanshe, 2020.

Zhao Wangqin 趙望秦. *Tangdai yongshi shi zushi kaolun* 唐代詠史詩組詩考論. Xi'an: San Qin chubanshe, 2003.

Zhao Wangqin and Pan Xiaoling 潘曉玲. *Hu Zeng "Yongshi shi" yanjiu* 胡曾《詠史詩》研究. Beijing: Zhongguo shehui kexue chubanshe, 2008.

Zhao Wangqin and Zhang Huanling 張煥玲. *Gudai yongshi shi tonglun* 古代詠史詩通論. Beijing: Zhongguo shehui kexue chubanshe, 2010.

Zheng Zhenduo 鄭振鐸. *Zhongguo wenxue shi* 中國文學史. Beijing: Xinshijie chubanshe, 2012.
Zhong Shulin 鍾書林. *Tao Yuanming yanjiu xueshu dang'an* 陶淵明研究學術檔案. Wuhan: Wuhan daxue chubanshe, 2014.
———. *Yinshi de shendu: Tao Yuanming xintan* 隱士的深度: 陶淵明新探. Beijing: Zhongguo shehui kexue chubanshe, 2015.
Zhou Changmei 周昌梅 and Zhang Ying 張鶯. "Houjin・qiangsheng・shuaibai—Liuchao Chenjun Xieshi jiazu de lishi guiji" 後進・強盛・衰敗——六朝陳郡謝氏家族的歷史軌跡. *Shixue jikan* 史學集刊, no. 6 (2007): 3–8.
Zhou Ming 周明. *Wenxin diaolong jiaoshi yiping* 文心雕龍校釋譯評. Nanjing: Nanjing daxue chubanshe, 2007.

Index

"affective image" (*xing* 興), 36
Annals of Lü Buwei (*Lüshi chunqiu* 呂氏春秋), 186n16
Annals of Spring and Autumn (*Chunqiu* 春秋), 19, 21, 39
Annals of Wu and Yue States (*Wuyue Chunqiu* 吳越春秋), 21
Autobiography, 30, 31, 33, 155

Baili Xi 百里奚, 196n68
Ban Chao 班超, 32, 167n21
Ban Gu 班固, 19, 21–22, 25, 34, 45, 148, 165n43; "On History" ("Yongshi" 詠史), 21–22, 25. See also *Hanshu*
Bao Zhao 鮑照, 25, 55–56, 145, 147, 150; "Imitating Poems" ("Nigu" 擬古), 56, 175n23; "Yongshi" 詠史, 25, 55–56, 145–47
Biographies of the Former Worthies of Runan (*Runan xianxian zhuan* 汝南先賢傳), 75
Bo Yi 伯夷, 76
Book of Documents (*Shangshu* 尚書), 16, 30, 83, 185n10
Book of the Extinct State of Yue (*Yue jue ji* 越絕記), 21

Cangjie 倉頡, 189n57

Cao Cao 曹操, 25, 133; "Poems on Qiu Hu" ("Qiu Hu shi" 秋胡詩), 25
Cao Pi 曹丕 (Wei Wendi 魏文帝), 25, 30; "A Discourse on Literature" ("Lunwen" 論文), 30
Cao Zhi 曹植, 6, 24, 26, 131, 133–34, 137–38, 144, 153, 195n51, 196n73; "Poem on the Three Good Men" ("Sanliang shi" 三良詩), 131, 137
Chen Ping 陳平, 38–39, 169n55, 198n111
Chen Zuoming 陳祚明, 56
Chong'er 重耳, 189n57
Chongyang Festival (Chongyang jie 重陽節, the ninth day of the ninth month in the lunar calendar), 104, 115–16
Classic of Mountains and Seas (*Shanhai jing* 山海經), 19–21
Classic of Poetry (*Shijing* 詩經), 30, 36, 65–66, 83, 131–33, 136, 185n9, 195n52, 195n60, 195–96n61, 196n74; "Great Preface" ("Da xu" 大序), 30, 185n9; "Yellow Bird" ("Huangniao" 黃鳥), 24, 92, 131–34, 195n52, 196n74
Collection of Music Bureau Poetry (*Yuefu shiji* 樂府詩集), 25

communicative memory, 3, 99, 101, 109, 112, 119–20
Confucius, 13, 44, 52, 65–66, 78, 81–82, 85–86, 88, 143, 171n88, 182n48, 182n55, 185n12; *Analects*, 65, 81, 85, 88, 168n32, 171n88, 181n39; Confucian, 17, 76, 78, 80, 83, 87, 94, 116, 136, 145–46, 183n75, 198n99
cultural memory, 1–6, 8–11, 29, 73, 97–99, 106, 109, 113, 119, 121–22, 129, 144, 153–57

Dao de jing 道德經, 89–90, 183n78; *Laozi*, 16, 139, 146
"dark learning" (*xuanxue* 玄學), 73, 139, 179n2; Neo-Daoism, 73
Definite Record of the Three Adjuncts (*Sanfu juelu* 三輔決錄), 75
delighting in the Dao in poverty (*anpin ledao* 安貧樂道), 81–82, 84, 88–89, 94–95
Documents of Liang (*Liangdian* 梁典), 19
Dong Zhongshu 董仲舒, 76, 103; "Rhapsody on the Unappreciated Scholar" ("Shibuyu fu" 士不遇賦), 103
Du Fu 杜甫, 149; "Hanging White Hair" ("Chui bai" 垂白), also known as "White-headed" ("Bai shou" 白首), 149
Duan Pidi 段匹磾, 130–31, 194n38
Duangan Mu 段干木, 33, 167n27, 167n28, 197n91
Duanmu Ci 端木賜, 85, 182n55

early medieval China, 1–3, 5–11, 13, 15–18, 20–27, 29, 31, 55–58, 63–65, 70, 72–73, 82, 118, 120–21, 144, 146, 153–57, 159n2, 174n5, 197n92

Empress Jia (Jia hou 賈后), 43
Evaluations of Historical Personages (*Renwu zhi* 人物志), 17, 127

Fan Tai 范泰, 10, 24, 97–98, 107–8, 119–20, 156; "Poem on Passing the Temple of Emperor Gao of the Han" ("Jing Han Gao miao shi" 經漢高廟詩), 24, 107
Fan Wuqi 樊於期, 41
Fang Dongshu 方東樹, 98
Feng Tang 馮唐, 36–37, 51, 61, 70, 147–49, 168–69n46, 169n51
Finest Literary Writings of the Tang Dynasty (*Tang Wencui* 唐文粹), 15, 24, 165n48
Five Ministers (Wuchen 五臣), 166n12
Five Sacred Peaks (Wuyue 五岳), 107, 188n56
Four Old Men of Mount Shang (Shangshan sihao 商山四皓), 111, 186n20, 189n73

Gaixia 垓下, 100, 110, 186n17, 189n58
Gan Bao 干寶, 19–20, 164n31; *Annals of the Jin Dynasty* (*Jinji* 晉紀), 19–20, 75; *In Search of the Supernatural* (*Soushen ji* 搜神記), 19
Gao Jianli 高漸離, 40–42
Gui Youguang 歸有光, 89
Guo Maoqian 郭茂倩, 25
Guo Pu 郭璞, 55

Halbwachs, Maurice, 3
Han Fei 韓非, 78–79, 94
Han Kang 韓康, 58, 175n26
Han Xin 韓信, 104, 109
Hanshu 漢書, 19, 21–23, 43, 75, 122–25, 145–46, 148–49, 165n43, 168n45, 169n50, 169n54, 171n85, 171–72nn87–89, 175n27, 175n29,

183n77, 196n73, 197n97, 198n104; *Annotations of the Hanshu* (*Hanshu zhu* 漢書注), 19; *Continuation of the Hanshu* (*Xu Hanshu* 續漢書), 75; *Continuing Hermeneutics of the Hanshu* (*Hanshu xu xun* 漢書續訓), 19; *Pronunciation of the Hanshu* (*Hanshu yin* 漢書音), 19
He Xun 何遜, 24, 121, 165n45; "Passing by Sun Quan's Tomb" ("Xingjing Sunshi ling" 行經孫氏陵), 24
He Zhuo 何焯, 56, 98, 185n10
histories of hegemons (*ba shi* 霸史), 164n36
History of the Chen Dynasty (*Chenshu* 陳書), 18
History of the Jin Dynasty (*Jinshu* 晉書), 32, 35, 43, 50, 125, 141–42, 149, 179n1, 192n17, 194n38
History of the Northern Dynasties (*Beishi* 北史), 57, 68–69, 75
History of the Song Dynasty (*Songshu* 宋書), 75, 82, 101, 104–5, 107–8, 113, 115–16, 118, 139–40, 179n1
History of the Southern Dynasties (*Nanshi* 南史), 82, 101, 113–14, 116, 179n1, 187n32
History of the Sui Dynasty (*Suishu* 隋書), 6, 15, 18–21, 27, 29, 164n36
Hu Yinglin 胡應麟, 56
Hu Zeng 胡曾, 190n83; "Historical Poem on Bolangsha" ("Yongshi shi · Bolangsha" 詠史詩·博浪沙), 190n83
Huan Xuan 桓玄, 88–89, 104, 115
Huang Zilian 黃子廉, 156
Huangfu Mi 皇甫謐, 35, 64, 175n26; *Biographies of Lofty Figures* (*Gaoshi zhuan* 高士傳), 87, 145, 175n26
Huo Qubing 霍去病, 60, 175n28

individual collections (*ji* 集), 18

intertextuality, 4, 7, 10, 55–56, 59, 129–30, 150, 154–55

Ji 稷, 77, 93
Jia Chong 賈充, 116
Jia Mi 賈謐, 35, 37, 43, 50, 149
Jia Yi 賈誼, 32, 58, 60, 76–78, 94, 127, 166n15, 175n30, 180n18, 180n23; "Faults of Qin" ("Guo Qin lun" 過秦論), 166n15; "Rhapsody on Lamenting Qu Yuan" ("Diao Qu Yuan fu" 弔屈原賦), 76
Jian'an 建安, 25, 72, 121, 133, 195n51
Jiang Chong 江充, 176n33
Jiang Yan 江淹, 55–59, 62–63, 70–72, 175n24; "Poems of Various Forms" ("Zati shi" 雜體詩), 56, 58; "Preface to Poems of Various Forms" ("Zati shi xu" 雜體詩序), 57; "Rhapsody on Bitter Regret" ("Hen fu" 恨賦), 175n24; "Rhapsody on Parting" ("Bie fu" 別賦), 175n24
Jin Midi 金日磾, 168n45
Jing Ke 荊軻, 40–43, 74

Kong Jing 孔靖, 97, 104, 115–16, 120

Li Bai 李白, 147, 150, 190n83; "Ancient Air" ("Gu feng" 古風), 147; "Passing the Bridge at Xiapi, I Think of Zhang Zifang" ("Jing Xiapi yiqiao huai Zhang Zifang" 經下邳圯橋懷張子房), 190n83
Li Shimin 李世民 (Tang Taizong 唐太宗), 18
Li Si 李斯, 48–49, 60–61, 79, 173n108, 198n111
Lian Po 廉頗, 126–27, 130
Liezi 列子, 85
Lin Xiangru 藺相如, 23, 126–31, 192n19, 193n33

literary criticism, 7, 17, 57, 63, 68, 121, 155, 162n4
Liu Bang 劉邦 (Han Gaozu 漢高祖, the founding emperor of the Han dynasty), 9–10, 98–100, 102–3, 106–11, 119–20, 156, 185nn14–15, 186n16, 186nn18–21, 187–88nn37–40, 189nn57–59
Liu Can 劉粲, 130
Liu Che 劉徹 (Han Wudi 漢武帝), 37, 149, 168n45, 176n33
Liu Gong 劉龔, 86–88, 156
Liu Heng 劉恆 (Han Wendi 漢文帝), 22, 37, 148–49, 168–69n46
Liu Jiao 劉交 (Chu Yuanwang 楚元王), 107, 119
Liu Jing 劉敬, 80
Liu Jingxuan 劉敬宣, 89
Liu Kan 劉衎 (Han Pingdi 漢平帝), 168n45, 171n88
Liu Kui 劉逵, 35
Liu Kun 劉琨, 55, 72, 130–31, 192n17, 193n36, 194nn38–39
Liu Ling 劉伶, 140, 197n91
Liu Muzhi 劉穆之, 104–5, 113, 118
Liu Shi 劉奭 (Han Yuandi 漢元帝), 168n45
Liu Xiaochuo 劉孝綽, 121, 165n45
Liu Xie 劉勰, 57, 63–64, 70, 72, 177n56, 177n61; *Literary Mind and Carving of Dragons* (*Wenxin diaolong* 文心雕龍), 57, 63–64, 177n56, 177n61
Liu Xun 劉詢 (Han Xuandi 漢宣帝), 123, 168n45, 171n83, 176n49, 183n77
Liu Yi 劉毅, 187n32
Liu Yilong 劉義隆 (Song Wendi 宋文帝), 114
Liu Yu 劉裕, 9–10, 88–89, 97–109, 112–13, 115–16, 118–20, 156, 187n24, 187nn26–27, 187nn29–30, 187n32, 188n40, 190n78, 190n94
Lou Jing 婁敬, 61, 111, 176n32
Lu Chen 盧諶, 23, 126–31, 153, 192n17, 193n36, 194nn38–39; "Poem on Surveying the Ancient" ("Langu" 覽古), 126
Lu Ji 陸機, 71, 116, 175n23, 179n90
Lu Zhonglian 魯仲連, 33–34, 51–52, 114, 119, 167–68n29, 190n86, 197n91

Ma Chao 馬超, 133
Mandate of Heaven, 34, 101–2, 106, 108, 119, 187n35, 189n60
manuscript culture, 6, 8, 13, 26–27
Marquis Wen of Wei 魏文侯, 33, 167n28, 172n107
Master Dan of Yan (*Yan Danzi* 燕丹子), 40–41
master works (*zi* 子), 18
Mei Fu 梅福, 175n27
Meng Jia 孟嘉, 75, 180n19
Miao Xian 繆賢, 128
Miluo River (Miluo jiang 汨羅江), 180n18
mimetic memory, 3
miscellaneous biographies (*zazhuan* 雜傳), 21
miscellaneous histories (*zashi* 雜史), 21
Miscellaneous Records of the Western Capital (*Xijing zaji* 西京雜記), 17

nostalgia, 5, 15, 156

palace-style poetry (*gongti shi* 宮體詩), 157
Pan Yue 潘岳, 56, 71, 116, 179n90
poems meditating on the past (*huaigu shi* 懷古詩), 6, 10, 13–15, 24–26, 163n6

Index | 219

poems on things (*yongwu shi* 詠物詩), 16
poems on visits to famous sites (*denglin shi* 登臨詩), 6
prospective memory, 4, 7–8, 55, 70, 72–73, 101, 103–6, 109, 119, 154–55, 160n16
pure conversation (*qingtan* 清談), 6, 16–17, 26, 139
pure discussion (*qingyi* 清議), 16

Qu Yuan 屈原, 47, 76–78, 94, 143, 180n18, 180nn21–22; "Divination on Dwelling" ("Buju" 卜居), 180n22; "Encountering Sorrows" ("Lisao" 離騷), 76

reception studies, 2, 4–5, 7–8, 16, 35, 51, 53, 55–57, 62–63, 68, 71–72, 131, 138, 154–55
Records of the State of Wu (*Wu lu* 吳錄), 75
Records of the States South of Mount Hua (*Huayang guozhi* 華陽國志), 145
retrospective memory, 4, 6–8, 29, 51, 55, 73, 101–2, 109, 112, 119, 154–55, 160n16
Rong Qiqi 榮啟期, 84–85, 94
Ruan Ji 阮籍, 76, 139–43; "Songs of My Cares" ("Yonghuai" 詠懷), 76, 122, 141, 143, 163n6
Ruan Xian 阮咸, 139–40, 197n91
Ruan Yu 阮瑀, 6, 26, 133

Selections of Refined Literature (*Wen xuan* 文選), 6, 8, 10–11, 15, 21, 24–25, 27, 31, 33, 36, 38, 40, 44–48, 59–63, 65, 70–71, 78, 91, 98–99, 115, 117, 121–23, 126–27, 131, 133–34, 137–38, 140, 144–45, 147, 149–50, 156, 172n92, 185n12, 191–92n3, 192n17, 194n42, 195n49, 196n73, 197n91, 198n111

Seven Worthies of the Bamboo Grove (*Zhulin qixian* 竹林七賢), 17, 139
Shan Tao 山濤, 16, 139
Shen Deqian 沈德潛, 56, 150
Shen Yue 沈約, 75, 139–40, 177n60, 197n92
Shi Gao 史高, 44, 171n83
Shiji 史記, 18–19, 21–24, 34, 37, 39–42, 49, 74–78, 80, 86, 92, 94, 103, 109–11, 113, 126, 128–29, 131, 133, 135, 138, 148–49, 165n43, 167n18, 167n28, 167–68n29, 168–69n46, 169n53, 169n55, 169–70n57, 170n58, 172n98, 172–73n107, 173n108, 175n28, 175n30, 176nn32–33, 180n20, 185n11, 185nn14–21, 188n39, 189nn58–59, 190n85, 192n19, 193n33, 195n52, 196n68; *Pronunciation and Meaning of the Shiji* (*Shiji yinyi* 史記音義), 19; *Pronunciation of the Shiji* (*Shiji yin* 史記音), 19

Shu Qi 叔齊, 76
Shun 舜, 84, 93, 180n20, 182n54, 189n57
Shusun Tong 叔孫通, 80, 94
Sima Dewen 司馬德文 (Jin Gongdi 晉恭帝), 105
Sima Dezong 司馬德宗 (Jin Andi 晉安帝), 105
Sima Qian 司馬遷, 19, 39, 76–78, 80, 103, 113, 128–29, 143–44, 148, 165n43, 166n10, 169n57, 188n39; "Grieving the Lack of Appreciation for Scholars" ("Bei shi buyu fu" 悲士不遇賦), 76, 103; "The Letter to Ren Shaoqing" ("Bao Ren Shaoqing shu" 報任少卿書), 78, 166n10. See also *Shiji*

Sima Rangju 司馬穰苴, 31–32, 52, 167n18, 198n111; *Marshal Rangju's Arts of War* (*Sima Rangju bingfa* 司馬穰苴兵法), 167n18

Sima Rui 司馬睿 (Jin Yuandi 晉元帝), 20

Sima Xiangru 司馬相如, 32, 38, 44–45, 52, 166n16, 169–70n57, 170n58, 171–72n89, 193n33, 197n97, 198n111; "Rhapsody of Sir Vacuous" ("Zixu Fu" 子虛賦), 31, 166n16

Sima Yan 司馬炎 (Jin Wudi 晉武帝), 47, 70

Sima Zhong 司馬衷 (Jin Huidi 晉惠帝), 43, 125

Sishui 泗水, 102, 187n37, 188n39

social memory, 2

standard or official histories (*zhengshi* 正史), ix, 1, 18–22, 27, 32, 57, 68, 75, 77, 82, 122, 155, 179n1

Stories of Emperor Wu of the Han (*Han Wu gushi* 漢武故事), 19

Stories of the Ages and Recent Anecdotes (*Shishuo xinyu* 世說新語), 16, 19, 32, 35, 141–42

Strategies of the Warring States (*Zhanguo ce* 戰國策), 40–41

Su Qin 蘇秦, 48–49, 52, 60–61, 172n107, 198n111

Tao Kan 陶侃, 93, 184n87; Commandery Duke of Changsha (*Changsha jungong* 長沙郡公), 184n87

Tao Yuanming 陶淵明, 8–9, 24, 55–56, 61–64, 68, 73–95, 103, 153, 155–56, 161–62n26, 174n4, 174n5, 175n23, 179n1, 180n19, 181n24, 181n32, 181n38, 182n42, 182n44, 182n47, 183n68, 183n75, 184n86; "Biography of His Excellency Meng, Former Chief of Staff to the Jin Generalissimo for Subduing the West" ("Jin gu Zhengxi dajiangjun Zhangshi Meng fujun zhuan" 晉故征西大將軍長史孟府君傳), 75; "Biography of Mr. Five Willows" ("Wuliu xiansheng zhuan" 五柳先生傳), 75; "Command to My Son" ("Mingzi" 命子), 93; "In Praise of the Paintings on a Fan" ("Shanshang hua zan" 扇上畫贊), 75; "Meditating on the Past in a Farmhouse at the Beginning of Spring in the Guimao Year II" (Guimao sui shichun huaigu tianshe qier 癸卯歲始春懷古田舍 其二), 81; "Nine Poems after Reading the *Shiji*" ("Du *Shi* shu jiuzhang" 讀史述九章), 23–24, 75; "Poem on Jing Ke" ("Yong Jing Ke" 詠荊軻), 74; "Poem on the Three Good Men" ("Yong Sanliang" 詠三良), 74, 91; "Poem on the Two Shus" ("Yong Er Shu" 詠二疏), 74, 90–91; "Poems on Impoverished Scholars" ("Yong pinshi" 詠貧士), 55, 62, 82, 87; "Presented to My Cousin Jingyuan in the Twelfth Month of the Guimao Year" ("Guimao sui shier yue zhong zuo yu congdi Jingyuan" 癸卯歲十二月中作與從弟敬遠), 84; "Reading *The Classic of Mountains and Seas*" ("Du *Shanhai jing*" 讀山海經), 181n24; "Rhapsody on Being Stirred by the Lack of Appreciation for Scholars" ("Gan shi buyu fu" 感士不遇賦), 76, 81, 103; "Suffering a Fire in the Sixth Month of the Year Wuwu" ("Wuwu sui liuyue zhong yuhuo" 戊午歲六月中遇火), 182n47

Three Good Men (Sanliang 三良), 6, 24, 26, 74, 91–92, 94, 131–38, 194n45, 195n49, 195n52, 195n54, 195–96nn59–61, 196nn72–74

Tian Qianqiu 田千秋, 61, 176n33
timeliness (*shi* 時), 74, 77–79, 81, 93–95
Tiying 緹縈, 22
Two Shus (Er Shu 二疏), 23, 61, 74, 90–91, 94, 122–26, 183n77, 192n6

unofficial histories (*yeshi* 野史), 19, 27, 32

venting frustrations (*fafen* 發憤), 78, 144

Wang Bo 王勃, 149; "Preface to the Prince of Teng's Pavilion" ("Tengwang ge xu" 滕王閣序), 149
Wang Can 王粲, 6, 24–26, 76, 131, 133–35, 137–38, 144, 153, 195n51, 195–96n61; "Poem on History" ("Yongshi shi" 詠史詩), 6, 24–25, 131, 133–34, 195–96n61; "Rhapsody on Climbing the Tower" ("Denglou fu" 登樓賦), 76
Wang Feng 王鳳, 175n27
Wang Fu 王符, 148; *Comments of a Recluse* (*Qian fu lun* 潛夫論), 148
Wang Guowei 王國維, 18
Wang Jian 王儉, 97–98; *Seven Categories* (*Qizhi* 七志), 98
Wang Mang 王莽, 175n27
Wang Rong 王戎, 139
Wang Yan 王衍, 16
Wang Yin 王隱, 194n38
Warring States period, xi, 33, 39–40, 76, 79, 159n2, 180n18
Wei Qing 衛青, 60, 175n28
Wei Zheng 魏徵, 18
Wen Runeng 溫汝能, 89
withdraw after making contributions (*gongcheng shentui* 功成身退), 89–93

Xi [Ji] Kang 嵇康, 139, 197n91

Xiao He 蕭何, 100, 109–10, 186n18
Xiao Tong 蕭統, 24–25, 31, 62–63, 71, 73, 121, 165n45, 179n1, 183n79, 191–92n3. See also *Wen Xuan*
Xiao Ze 蕭賾, 57
Xie An 謝安, 191n104
Xie Hui 謝晦, 113, 116–18
Xie Huilian 謝惠連, 64
Xie Lingyun 謝靈運, 55–56, 97–98, 113–14, 116–19, 153; "Poems on Narrating Ancestor's Virtues" ("Shu zude shi" 述祖德詩), 56
Xie Tiao 謝朓, 9
Xie Zhan 謝瞻, 9–10, 97–99, 101–20, 153, 156, 187n23, 187n30, 190n94, 194n42; "A Valediction for Director Kong of the Imperial Secretariat Written at the Command of the Duke of Song on the Ninth Day at a Gathering at Xima Terrace" ("Jiuri cong Songgong Xima tai ji song Kongling shi" 九日從宋公戲馬臺集送孔令詩), 115; "Poem on Zhang Zifang" ("Zhang Zifang shi" 張子房詩), 97–99, 105–6, 113, 115, 119–20, 194n42; "Response to Lingyun at Ancheng" ("Yu Ancheng da Lingyun" 於安城答靈運), 117, 120
Xie Zhuang 謝莊, 9
Xu Guanghan 許廣漢, 171n83
Xu Shen 許慎, 18
Xu You 許由, 46–47, 51–53, 172n98, 198n111
Xue Cheng 薛瑩, 8, 68–72
Xun Yue 荀悅, 149; *Annals of the Former Han* (*Qian Han ji* 前漢紀), 149

Yan Junping 嚴君平, 56, 145–47, 174n12, 197n94, 198n99

Yan Yanzhi 顏延之, 17, 25, 64, 75, 89, 139–44, 153, 194n42, 197nn91–92; "Poem on Qiu Hu" ("Qiu Hu shi" 秋胡詩), 25, 194n42; "Poem on the Five Lords" ("Wujun yong" 五君詠), 17, 139, 197n91

Yang Xiong 揚雄, 44–47, 51, 53, 56, 62, 146, 148, 171–72nn86–89, 172n92, 174n12, 197n91, 197n97; *Exemplary Words* (*Fayan* 法言), 127, 148, 171n87; *Supreme Mystery* (*Taixuan* 太玄), 171n87

Yao 堯, 93, 172n98

Yao Hong 姚泓, 98, 107

Ying Qu 應璩, 68

Ying Shao 應劭, 128, 196n73

Ying Zheng 嬴政 (Qin Shihuang 秦始皇), 42, 49, 113

Yong Chi 雍齒, 110, 186n18

Yongshi 詠史, as poetic subgenre, 1–2, 4–11, 13–17, 21–27, 29, 51, 58, 61, 63–64, 67, 73–75, 87, 89, 93–95, 97, 121–22, 143–44, 149, 150–51, 153–57, 161–62n26, 163n6; section in the *Wen xuan*, 8, 21, 24, 121–22, 131, 133, 137–38, 144, 150, 156, 195n49, 197n91, 198n111

Yu Xi 虞羲, 24, 194n42; "Poem on General Huo's Northern Expedition" ("Yong Huo Jiangjun beifa shi" 詠霍將軍北伐詩), 24, 194n42

Yuan Hong 袁宏, 25, 55; *Annals of the Later Han Dynasty* (*Hou Hanji* 後漢紀), 75

Yuan Xian 原憲, 84–85, 94, 182n53

Zhang Fang 張方, 50

Zhang Hua 張華, 35, 43, 50, 64, 176n40; "Poem on Frivolous Behavior" ("Qingbo pian" 輕薄篇), 176n40; *Treatise on Manifold Subjects* (*Bowu zhi* 博物志), 145

Zhang Liang 張良, 9–10, 97–114, 118–20, 156, 185–87nn15–23, 187nn27–29, 187n38, 188n40, 190n83, 190n85

Zhang Tang 張湯, 168n45

Zhang Xie 張協, 23, 25, 55, 61–63, 91, 122–26, 153; "Yongshi," 23, 25, 55, 61, 122

Zhang Zai 張載, 35

Zhang Zhengjian 張正見, 46; "On [Zuo Si's] Poem on the Frustrated Scholar in the Poor Alleyways" ("Fu de luoluo qiongxiang shi shi" 賦得落落窮巷士詩), 46

Zhang Zhongwei 張仲蔚, 58, 60, 62, 86–88, 94, 156, 176n34

Zheng Xianzhi 鄭鮮之, 10, 24, 97–98, 101, 107–8, 119–20, 156, 187n32; "Poem on Passing by the Zhang Zifang Temple" ("Xingjing Zhang Zifang miao shi" 行經張子房廟詩), 24, 102

Zheng Zhanyin 鄭詹尹, 77, 180n22

Zhong Jun 終軍, 58, 60, 175n29

Zhong Rong 鍾嶸, 17, 21, 23, 55–57, 62–68, 71–72, 177n56, 177nn60–61; *Gradation of Poets* (*Shipin* 詩品), 17, 21, 23, 55–57, 62–67, 71, 177n56, 177nn60–61

Zhu Maichen 朱買臣, 38, 169n54, 198n111

Zhuangzi 莊子, 16, 50, 61, 139, 173n109, 181n28, 186n22, 192n17

Zhufu Yan 主父偃, 38–39, 169n53, 198n111

Zi Xia 子夏, 167n28

Zuo Fen 左棻, 47, 70

Zuo Si 左思, 6–8, 25, 29–53, 55–73, 76, 147–50, 153, 155, 167n20,

172n98, 172n100, 197n91, 198n111; "Poems on History" ("Yongshi" 詠史), 6–7, 29–31, 35–37, 40, 43–44, 46–47, 51–53, 55–65, 67–73, 147, 149–50, 178n88, 198n111; "Rhapsodies on the Three Capitals" ("Sandu fu" 三都賦), 29, 34–35, 45, 64

www.ingramcontent.com/pod-product-compliance
Lightning Source LLC
Chambersburg PA
CBHW030648230426
43665CB00011B/997